D1715691

SHATTERED DREAMS, BROKEN PROMISES

THE COST OF COMING TO AMERICA

SHATTERED DREAMS, BROKEN PROMISES

THE COST OF COMING TO AMERICA

MICHAEL VINER

ISBN: 1-59777-537-1
Library of Congress Cataloging-In-Publication Data Available

Book Design by: Sonia Fiore

Printed in the United States of America

Phoenix Books and Audio Inc.
9465 Wilshire Boulevard, Suite 315
Beverly Hills, CA 90212

10 9 8 7 6 5 4 3 2 1

TABLE OF CONTENTS

FOR TAYLOR ROSE
WITH ETERNAL LOVE.
DADDY

INTRODUCTION

Some of the most compelling and, so far, unanswered questions about the women of the former Soviet Union are: What makes them so unique? How have they managed to assimilate themselves into America with such lightning speed? Why have so many of them taken a sexual path way to accomplish their goals? For as far back as memory serves us, the former Soviet Union was our sworn enemy, and although, in theory, this is no longer so, we still know pitifully little about the women who left their country to come to our land, and we know very little about how they lived their lives or what their expectations are. They are, as a rule, mysterious to us still; they look so much like many Americans, though the majority of the women who arrive in our country are unusually attractive. In many ways, they are not only from another world, but are also from another planet.

Are the answers based on amorality or immorality, or just steadfast and understandable ambition to escape to a better life? There are no simple answers. The roads they have traveled are as diverse as the lands they came from. The Soviet Union in its heyday comprised one-eighth of the world's surface and spanned eleven time zones (as Russia still does today). Despite Russia's geographical size, its population is only 142 million and is shrinking at the rate of over 750,000 each year, before including the influx of immigrants from even poorer neighboring countries. Tens of thousands of its citizens make a yearly exodus in search of a better future elsewhere. Most of them do so in order to escape having their lives shortened by pollution, AIDS and many other diseases for which medical treatment is inadequate, unavailable or unaffordable.

This book is the culmination of three years of research, including frequent trips to Russia and the Ukraine. More than two hundred women from the former Soviet Union were initially interviewed. Preliminary outlines and copious notes were compiled about the lives of approximately one hundred of those women. From stories of love, romance, prostitution, strip dancing, and starvation, these stories reveal a gradation of emotions. I found myself sharing laughter, horror, and tears with many of these ladies. Their success stories were exhilarating. But their tragic failures were devastating. Many of them will forever be etched into my memory.

I narrowed my focus to twenty-three stories which, to me, were the most interesting and representative of an entire generation's forays out of the former USSR and to the United States, where they have, in the vast majority of cases, been able to assimilate and make new lives for themselves. Many have obtained their financial goals. These women have changed the complexion of America practically overnight. In many cases, the names have been changed as well as some of the corollary material to protect the identity of the woman.

There are no moral judgments made here. If judgments are to be made then I leave that task to each individual reader.

As someone who is Jewish, yet attended Catholic school, and who has lived in many parts of the United States, I have become quite familiar with ethnic humor, particularly humor based on exaggerated stereotypes that often bear only slight resemblance to a small portion of the targeted group. For example, there's a joke about how you can tell if your home was robbed by an Asian: your children's homework has been done and the dog is missing. If the same joke centered on Russian women or their Eastern European counterparts, the answer would invariably be that you could tell your house had been robbed by a Russian woman if your husband was missing and your son had married a beautiful woman to whom he was teaching English in exchange for an advanced course in sex education.

Do many women from these countries marry solely for visas, green cards, or citizenship? The answer is certainly yes. Why, we may ask ourselves, do such a high percentage of these women start by working in strip bars or becoming prostitutes?

Is there an equivalency here to the 1993 hit movie, *Indecent Proposal*, starring Robert Redford and Demi Moore? In that movie, a once affluent couple was having great financial difficulty. To regain their way of life, Demi Moore agrees to have sex with Robert Redford for one million dollars. Was this prostitution? According to the dictionary, the answer is, of course, yes.

But for one uncomfortable minute put yourself in the shoddy, well-worn shoes of a young girl from Siberia. She would have been lucky to find any job, much less one that pays more than ten dollars a week. Tell her that she can make $100,000 or more in the U.S. as a stripper or a prostitute. If Demi Moore succumbed, think what many of the poverty-stricken girls might say. They would seemingly have little to lose and would be able to support their mothers, sisters and, possibly, their children. Many of these women hope they'll be able to eventually bring their family to the U.S. so they also might benefit from a better way of life.

Even in the comparative financial affluence of Moscow and St. Petersburg, a very fortunate few young women such as the ones working in Ekaterina Akhuzina's exclusive fur salon, Ekaterina in Moscow, make five hundred dollars a month. They work ten hours per day, not including the brutal commuting time and perpetual bumper to bumper Moscow traffic. If they work for the government, they earn less. A university professor is paid only about two hundred and fifty dollars a month. If they are lucky enough to land employment at an international company like Dannon or the Swiss Hotel corporation, their salary could grow to $1,000 a month for managerial positions.

The cost of a one room apartment in Moscow is no less than $450 a month. For the few super rich like Ekaterina and her husband, Igor, the sky is the limit. Ekaterina explains that her husband, a serious soccer fan, and his friends bought a private soccer field near their palatial home, just three minutes outside of the Moscow city limits. She often dresses in elegant Italian leather, a mink and chinchilla wrap and carries Louis Vuitton everything.

The poor watch the rich, such as Ekaterina, on TV soap operas like *Santa Barbara* and *Baywatch* and think life would be like that if they could live in the U.S. Is Russia in a state of moral decay? Vycheslav Pushkarev, a Russian Orthodox priest, who presides over several small congregations, told a reporter from *The Moscow Times:* "We are left with this infection in us, this sickness of degradation in everything around us because we were all a part of it. We're living in a huge bowl here, and we're all getting boiled together."

AIDS has reached epidemic proportions and particularly threatens a population where twenty percent of its citizens earn less than $38 per month and prophylactics are considered a luxury item.

According to the Serbian National Research center for social and forensic psychiatry, more than half a million Russians committed suicide in the last ten years, indicative of just how miserable many of the people really are. Because of the pollution, life expectancy for the Russian man is sixteen years less than an American man.

With all due respect to Thomas Friedman, the world is not yet flat for Russian women and probably never will be. As women willing to fulfill the sexual fantasies of American males, Russian women remain an enigma wrapped in an ever changing rainbow of moods and desires.

I will never forget many of the ladies whom I have met. One in particular was a seventy-year-old woman who had been exiled to the island of whores and yet there was an indomitable spirit still simmering within her. Many of the stories I was told have not been included in this book, yet they contributed to my knowledge and my view of these ladies and their journeys.

One of my favorite ladies is the Russian ballerina from Saint Petersburg. Her life as a ballerina began at age six. All she knew was ballet. She proudly told me she was the prettiest and sexiest woman I had ever seen. When I told her she certainly possessed both those attributes, but her claims were somewhat overstated, she looked sincerely into my eyes and replied, "Those words do not fit into my ears." And she meant it. Once she took me to a Russian night club in Los Angeles to show me what night clubs in the Soviet Union were like twenty years ago. She asked me to dance, which I reluctantly and awkwardly did. The third time she asked me to dance, I explained that I didn't dance well and I looked foolish. She responded without hesitation, "Who will be looking at you?" With her beauty and dance ability, I knew she was right. She came to L.A. by marrying a prominent film company executive. She told me she went to bed on her wedding night with a forty-three-year-old millionaire and awakened the next morning to a man who was fifty-five years old and deeply in debt. She then learned that she was his fifth wife. I asked what happened to her marriage and she explained: she knew it was near an end because the diamond and jewelry he was giving her kept getting smaller.

Another of my favorite stories is about the Russian grandmother who, after much stress, got a visa to visit the U.S. for her daughter's wedding. Instead of going to the wedding, she found herself under arrest at Kennedy Airport in New York for drug smuggling! It seems she did not trust American laundry detergent so she brought a bag of her own filled with white powder. They let her go after the drug test came back negative, but many Russian immigrants are equally ill-prepared to face the realities of American life.

These stories are not unusual. They are a microcosm and, in some cases, a combination of many the hurdles faced by thousands of Russian women who come to the U.S. to pursue their fortunes. While writing these stories, I fell in love with more than one of these women and I think you will too.

KIEV, UKRAINE, AUGUST 14th, 2007

Chapter 1
A NICE PLACE
TO VISIT

There is no mention on the map of Russia of this place. But just for a few minutes imagine a port city called Astrakhan; a city that is rich with watermelons and fresh fish near the Volga River where a small island, a cursed land, is located. This island is about five hundred meters away by ferry from a fishing village called Ikryanoy. The island of sin is named Suchyi Viselki (Bitch Exile). But not all local neighboring residents know its history. It was the home for exiled prostitutes who were victims of the former Russian system of repression. Officially, it was named Ninovka.

The Soviet Union's authorities, beginning in 1919, exiled immoral women from all over the country and they forbade these women to live in their places of residence. The only document in those days for a person's identification was a birth certificate. The government even took that away and stamped "not suitable" on it. In the village most women didn't feel insulted or exiled. Why should they? They had all practiced the same trade. On this bit of land they all had equal rights. For them, there was no possible future. Here they lost touch with all normal Soviet life and its developing society.

In those days, women were arrested without warning. Faithful servants of the government and other gossipers tracked down their neighbors and acquaintances. Then they reported them to the people who were in power. The fate of that luckless person would be determined within an hour. It did not matter to the government who they got rid of. It could be married women with children, singles, or widows. If a woman found herself under suspicion, even without a reason, she had to be ready for retribution within an hour. Arrests took place everywhere: on the streets, at home, in the market, and other public places. The authorities cleaned the cities before visits of important people or on the eve of national celebrations. From major cities like Moscow and Leningrad, you could get to "Suchyi Viselki" village only by boat.

The entire village was composed of thirty similar little houses that were built in a single row along the Volga river bank. You could only distinguish one house from another by looking at the roof. Some of them had chimneys; others had lofts. Every house was surrounded by a broken fence and gooseberry bushes. On this one road, clumsy houses showed half-open windows, and wires spread across the fences that held dried Vobla fish.

Many of these small houses were run-down with peeling paint and broken windows. Sometimes it seemed like there were no people in the village.

When they first arrived, the women shut themselves off and didn't show up outdoors. Some almost went insane. It was scary enough to look at the houses, not to mention living in them. It seemed like a simple breeze could knock them down. Roofs leaked when it rained and, in order not to get water on the floor, the residents placed saucepans under the hole in the roof. Still, when it rained, the entire house was damp. In the winter, holes in the roof were covered with turf. All winter, the women stocked up huge rock stoves, covered with blankets, and slept on top of them. They were very warm. By the river, the women built a dock from a few planks that they fastened to a car tire. It moved from one side to another on the water. Such construction proved the skills of Russian people and their ability to adapt to any life conditions.

* * *

I was among the last ten prostitutes who were exiled to sin land, as we sometimes called it. As I said, everything started in the spring of 1919. Then at the end of 1934, a new type of residence appeared. They were impoverished peasants and with them came more prostitutes from the Astrakhan and Saratov regions. After that, life slowly improved. Families started to form. People didn't even think about the past. Many didn't even know that they lived in a neighborhood where everyone had once been prostitutes.

During the Second World War, it seemed like everybody forgot about this small village. People ate fish and the vegetables that they grew in their home gardens. Many of the oldest residents died. And in the early 1950s, cholera took the lives of even more. In their place, in 1955, the Soviet brought the last ten exiled prostitutes. I was one of them.

* * *

I was breast fed and I was baptized in the Orthodox Church, Spasnakrovi in Stalingrad. During the ceremony, I pooped on the priest. I am told that my grandmother said, "Kill her! She will be a prostitute." Those damn words were prophetic not only for me but also for my mother. Our family wasn't rich. No one was wealthy at the time among simple Russian people. My father worked in a weapons manufacturing factory. My mother had never worked. During the Bolshevik Revolution in 1919, she was accidentally wounded and lost her right hand. After that, she felt she was professionally useless. She sat at home and, with my grandmother's help, looked after the garden where we had potatoes, tomatoes, greens, etc.

I don't remember much about my childhood. My mother spent the whole day cleaning, cooking, tending to the garden or going to the food kiosk. I went to school and learned about Stalin. My father worked a lot. Every day he came home drunk, but he was always quiet. He sat outside of our house and smoked cigarettes from home-grown tobacco. Before my grandmother died, she sewed me a doll, which was the only one I had during my entire childhood.

When World War II was declared, my father went to the front line. One year later, we received a letter from the commander announcing his death. They said that my father was killed defending Moscow. It stated that Ivan Semenovich Troshkin perished as a hero by the hand of the Nazi enemy while fighting for the homeland.

My mother went crazy. She started to have sex for money. During the war, men were hungry for women's bodies and warmth. They found their way to my mother. As a result, she gave birth to my first little brother, Stepa. He was conceived by a stranger. I was young and afraid of those men. When they came, I hid under the table or under the curtain that divided one of our rooms. I was eleven when my mother gave birth to my second brother, Nikita.

When I became older, I used to take my little brothers and go outside. I did it to avoid my mother's men, who still make me shake from fear when I think about them. To my brothers, I was like a mother and a father. My mother was very loud with the men, but I didn't know what was happening. Later, smoke came out of the window along with a man's laugh mixed with my mother's.

I loved my mother very much. She had long dark hair, which I would comb almost every evening. I always felt sorry for her. Every day, when she had a man, she cried bitterly at night. I used to hug her and tell her that I loved her very much and would never leave her.

Good times never visited us for long. Before my father was killed and my mother began to see these men, we ate meagerly. Most of the time, our stomachs were swollen from hunger. The main food that we had was rotten potatoes that we picked from the neglected potato fields. I still remember the taste of them. Potatoes were always sweet because they were frozen and remained in the ground for years. In the mornings, I took a little spade and went to those fields. It was good luck just to find a potato equal to the size of a pea. We also would pick nettles and make soup out of them.

Then, times got better. It happened when my mother started to sleep with these lustful soldiers. Suddenly, in our house there appeared tea, black bread, and sometimes canned meat.

In 1949, I came back home with my brothers and found mother dead. She was killed by one of the men who visited her for sex. Nobody investigated it. The police said that it could happen to anyone in a fit of jealousy or during an alcohol-induced rage. The women in the neighborhood used to say that everybody got what they deserved. They said that instead of caring about three hungry children, she was busy spreading her legs for lustful men.

I was thirteen; I was absolutely alone with two little brothers on my hands. The youngest was two years old and the older one was three. They were always hungry and begged me for food. But how could I feed them?

At that time, as the saying goes, women delivered as many children as God would give them. Nobody knew about birth control and, actually, didn't care. Generally, women delivered a baby once every two years. Big families were the norm at that time. Seven to ten kids was frequent. Of course, half of them died from typhus, hunger, or were lost.

I quit school. I had greater responsibilities and needs. With difficulty, I found a job at a local shop. Mornings, I sold newspapers; evenings, I washed clothes for sailors and soldiers. Most of the time, they paid me with a can of army food, bread, or pieces of sugar. Sometimes they gave me food coupons, but that was the worst because there was no food in the shops. Still, my earnings weren't enough. Our food reserves were gone and we had no warm clothes to shield us from winter's fury.

Once, my next-door neighbor, Klava, offered to walk with me to the embankment where now the "Aurora" ship probably still stands. We talked about women who took money for love. Since I did not see any other choice, I decided to give this a try. I sewed up my mother's only white dress, and stitched some lace on it. I made a red plastic necklace and ironed a red ribbon for my hair. I worked that first night doing what I had to do.

In the morning, I was in pain. I felt disgusted. I felt like I was dirty. My dress was torn and my hair was all messed up. But I only felt such shame for a short time. You can't judge me for becoming a prostitute. I had no other choice. In any case, I had fifteen rubles in my pocket. From that day, I began to have some money in my purse. I was able to buy my brothers felt boots, pants, and warm jackets. They were so happy to have semolina cereal cooked with milk. I worked four days a week. It was enough. My clients were mostly soldiers. It happened fast and I did it everywhere: garages, haystacks, rooftops. I don't remember having any feelings. I was probably just satisfied by the fact that my brothers didn't swell up from hunger and that they had warm clothes.

Years passed. My brothers grew up. I taught them how to read and write. They started to help me with the garden. They dug the soil. They kept the house clean.

One day, I was sitting in a local bar. One of the soldiers there said that important international government dignitaries were supposed to visit Stalingard. He laughed and said that two days before their arrival, local officials would check all the streets to make sure there were no prostitutes. It was forbidden at that time to speak that word. No such word was supposed to be in a Soviet person's vocabulary.

Suddenly, the door opened. People dressed in ordinary clothes grabbed five of us. They put us in their car. At first, we didn't understand what was happening. The soldiers we were sitting with at the bar didn't defend us. Who were we to them? We were young women to hang out with and to have easy sex with. Nobody treated us with respect.

The police explained nothing to us. They brought us to a small room like a jail cell. They lined us up in a row. They read the charges. They made us sign some papers. At the sentencing, they read a line that called us "FBW." It translates to frivolous behaving women. It said that we were harmful elements who disgraced the entire Soviet society and had to be isolated. They instilled in people's minds that our country didn't have, and couldn't have, prostitution. The authorities couldn't put us in jail, according to the law. That is why they exiled us far from other people.

The officers told us later that we had to sit in that room until the morning when we would be exiled. We were not allowed to see our relatives even one last time. But, in exchange for giving sex to the officers, they agreed to accompany each of us to our homes. I remember my officer was very strict. As soon as a person with a small job receives a little power, he turns into a terrible man and a people-hater.

Once I was home, I saw my brothers sound asleep. I kissed them for the last time. I took with me a blanket, an old samovar, a packet of tea, and my birth certificate. I left thirty rubles on the kitchen table for my brothers. I departed with tears in my eyes. I knew that nothing good waited for them ahead. I was scared that they would die without me. I was nineteen. I never saw my brothers again.

They brought us to "Bitch Exile" village at night. First, we had taken the train. Then, they ferried us across the Volga River to what seemed a deserted island except for a few distant lights. We were surrounded by bushes, trees, and the dark. They threw us out on the river bank with all of our stuff. They left us with ten pieces of bread and some water. They promised to bring food later.

As it happened, those lights were from the windows of the little houses on the far end of the bank. Their dull lights came as if from the ground itself. I started to cry. It was scary to find myself in a Godforsaken place like this after life in the city. In those little houses lived the very first women who were exiled in 1919 from Petrograd and Moscow. Right after the revolution, the Soviet authorities did not persecute the prostitutes nor accept them as victims of poverty. But, within two years, they started to clean the city streets, getting rid of the degenerate elements as they called representatives of the most ancient profession.

The first residents on the island lived in sheds. They put up a wooden shell and then spread clay over it. To this very day, I am told people still live in those houses. Even if all the founders are dead, their children and grandchildren still live there. They probably can't even guess about their mothers' and grandmothers' past.

I was lucky. I didn't have to wait for a new house to be built. When we arrived at the village, people were mourning. A lonely witch named Makarovna had died. They asked us who was the bravest among us? She could go live in the witch's house. The other girls were afraid. But I volunteered. I didn't care that much. I didn't believe that in such a wretched place there could be anything for me in my life anyway.

I started to live deep in depression in this village. I imagined that if I went to hell, the living conditions might be an improvement. I lived in a house with almost collapsed walls. They hardly looked like part of a house, just something left over from a ruin. If I hadn't had little windows with curtains almost at ground level, I could have easily called my house a shed or a bomb shelter.

When I moved in, people started to gossip and talk even more. Some thought that a devil's spell made me choose that house. People said the witch had died in torment right before our arrival. There was a big new hole in the roof. It was made by local residents. They said the witch, Makarovna, couldn't be allowed to die slowly in a closed space. She agonized for nearly two weeks prior to her death. People said that all witches on their death bed have to pass their knowledge and secret skills on to one of their blood relatives; otherwise, they cannot leave their body. But if their knowledge was passed on to somebody then the soul could leave the body and the witch could easily die. Makarovna didn't have anybody. She lived alone her entire life. Local women said that Makarovna helped everybody. But they were all afraid of her.

In "Bitch Exile," men were deceitful. For available men, women would fight to the death. The women had come to Makarovna's house to alter their fate. I believed that was true. The road to her house, I was sure had been trampled by women's feet.

The witch helped them, she separated families and made men fall in love with certain women forever. She freed men from alcohol addiction and from the habit of sleeping with any women they could.

Macarovna's death was a big loss for the village residents. They thought it could mean failure in personal and family life and it was the end of their psychologist. On the other hand, some people were glad that there wouldn't be any more mystics and evil forces.

I cleaned the house. I threw away a lot of burned candles, dried herbs, and wax figures. I only kept a handwritten witches' conspiracies manual and her diary, just in case I would somehow need it one day.

Upon arriving at the village, she had written:

March 25, 1919: It's the eighth day and I am hungry. The trip was very difficult. The train was a trade goods train. There was no place to sit down. Impossible to breathe and no water to save yourself from thirst. Then for two round-the-clock days, we walked on foot. Vitta fainted and fell down. The escort man pulled her by the hair. He kicked her everywhere. We managed to get to a village across a frozen river. There was nothing to eat. They promised to bring rice but they didn't say when. They left us in a land pit that masqueraded as a house. It was the only construction on the island. It was a white desert and emptiness of the soul.

* * *

All the knives in the house were dull. I could barely slice a piece of bread. In Russia, it was said that if the knives were dull, there was no man in the house because he was the one who traditionally did the sharpening. This was certainly true in my house.

I kept all her dishes. I had brought only a samovar, two spoons, and plates. During long, lonely evenings, I boiled the samovar, drank tea with the local women, and listened to the gossip. When I first arrived on the island, my neighbor Vitta told me: "Evgeniya Ivanovna, you better live in peace with everybody, which means you don't flirt with other women's men. If you decide to lead somebody astray, you will be in trouble. The local women will beat you to death with rakes."

It was like a prison. We were newcomers. We had to pass all the village tests. We had to live according to unwritten and unspoken rules and the village laws. It was impossible for any residents of "Bitch Exile" to leave the village. The officials took our documents. Once a week, a local policeman came from the Astrakhan region. He checked to see if we all were in our appointed houses and lived in peace. We didn't have any security, watchmen or barbed wire. Everybody understood the reality of their situation.

It was impossible to run far from the island. People told stories about residents who tried to escape. There were three women who ran away one day with a fisherman to the outside world, which we called "Big Land." But they couldn't survive there more than a week. They had no chance to find a job. They had to hide from people because in the villages everyone knew everyone else. Besides, in order to even go to Astrakhan city, they needed money they didn't have.

Those three women were returned to the island. All the other residents were threatened that from that time on, they would be supervised twenty-four hours a day. If anyone decided to run away, they would be dealt with by the NKVD (National Committee Department of the Interior). People often called them Bolshevik executioners. They were workers of an oppressive machine. They exterminated everyone who might be a disgrace to the Soviet people; those who didn't serve the Soviet State and its beliefs and truths. They would arrest representatives of the professional class, Ukrainians, and Jews. They were violent with their victims. They tortured people, hammered nails in their heads, pulled the nails out, bound their hands and feet with barbed wire. People were afraid they'd end up in the executioners' hands. In addition, the residents were ashamed of their past life.

We were allowed to go to the city, but only to the bath house where the midwives helped deliver babies. We made do the best we could. The people across the river sometimes brought us food to the island. We also exchanged food with fishermen who very often came to our island for strawberries. Our strawberries were a sensuous pleasure.

Natasha was the first woman on the island who delivered a baby. She became pregnant with a stranger; a fisherman who visited only once. When the time came for her to deliver, we asked a local policeman to take Natasha to the city. He gave her a notice that said she had to return to the village in five days. But her delivery time was late. When a local policeman went to the hospital to pick her up, he arrived as she went into labor. Maybe he felt sorry for her, but he hid the fact that Natasha had to return on the appointed day. Later, he married her and took her to another region. She was a conspicuous woman; although she wasn't tall, she had curly brown hair and a baby face. Natasha was always clean and nicely dressed. She would sew different colored ribbons to her dress and it looked like a new one. So, until her due date, she dressed in the latest fashions she made herself.

When I was twenty-five, I fell deeply in love with a local sailor named Peter. He was forty and was an interesting man who courted me for a long time. He brought me fresh peaches and pike fish. Slowly, Peter repaired my entire house. Later, he started to sleep over at my house and one day, he stayed.

I loved him very much. He was so manly and had an extraordinary appearance. He was very tall and skinny, but wiry and strong. Sometimes I thought that a wind could blow him away when he walked. He was full of energy and couldn't sit in one place without being busy. He played an accordion which was very valuable in village life. Sometimes, we sat outside and he played as I sang an old song: "There are so many lights on the streets of Saratov city. There are so many single men. But I love one married."

Peter loved me, too. Once, he came back from a trip and rolled up his shirt sleeve. On his left shoulder was a tattoo: I love my Jenya. He said that his feelings were forever and he wanted everybody to know that he loved me. We lived together for a while, unmarried. The people started to condemn us for not having a wedding. In reality, all they wanted was a celebration and to have some fun. Peter wasn't against the celebration. He loved to drink samogonka. It was village-manufactured vodka. Almost every resident of the village knew how to cook samogonka and let it stand with herbs and berries for a long time. When Peter became drunk, he was very quiet, not even noticeable. But sometimes he talked about his childhood and difficult years. After that, he would fall asleep.

We didn't have money for jewelry and wedding rings. Peter made our rings from silver wires. He melded them, let them cool and put the ring on my finger. We got married. All thirty houses joined the celebration. We partied for a whole week as is the Russian tradition. We ate and drank. We danced, sang, and fought. Two years later, we finally had a honeymoon. We never fought. People always came to our house because it was warm and comfortable.

But our marriage didn't last. I couldn't have children. In the beginning, Peter said that we would live our life without kids because the most important thing was that we loved each other. But Peter couldn't live like that any longer.

One day, my sailor went to Saratov City and came back with a new wife. I cried and worried for a while. But mostly, I submitted to my fate. I could survive when I didn't see him. But sometimes when he would appear with his new wife, Katherina, I went crazy. I threw plates at the wall and couldn't eat, breathe, or live. I tried everything. I ended up in the hospital on the mainland with a heart attack. I was dying from lost love and decided on suicide by drowning myself in the river. I jumped in, but a fisherman saved my life.

Some time later, I found Makarovna's witch book with its spell for getting a man and getting rid of melancholy. I did the whole ritual. I went to the cemetery and found a tombstone with the name Peter on it. I lit a candle and read the spells. Then I put a mirror on a wooden crucifix and said something like, "God's slave named Peter has to come back to his loving slave, Jenya. I want him and he can't live without me, like a fish can't survive without water."

I waited. I don't know if it worked, but Peter began to come to my house. He stayed for a while but never slept over. He made love to me, drank samogonka, and went home to his wife. He used to say that I would love him forever and wouldn't disappear from his life. It hurt me very much. But I loved him like crazy.

Today, the only reminder I have of my first marriage is an old picture. I keep it carefully with the wire rings and shawl that Peter gave me. I have never been happy in my life since. In my memory, I am forever reminded of the day when I wore the only wedding dress we had in the village. It was an expensive rose colored dress which Marina, a resident in our village, had bought from her past life. Every woman on our island was married in that dress. You can't even count how many times that dress was taken in, embroidered, altered. Even now, somebody probably owns that dress, and is getting married in it.

Peter still came to hurt my feelings. I decided to prove to him that I could be happy without him. Again, I pulled out the witch's book and read a spell designed to find a loving man. A lonely winter passed. The snow and the ice on the river melted. Spring came. Peter still visited me, but he didn't stay. I suffered and was an object of gossip. You can't hide from the village people. You can't escape from their contemptuous eyes.

One day, a foreign man came to our island. He was fat and short. He was dressed differently and talked with a heavy accent. He seemed funny to me. I was walking back from the river and had a yolk on my shoulders with water baskets. I was a simple Russian woman with a braid down my back and bare feet in rubber boots.

He asked me in broken Russian if we had a hotel or a place to sleep over. I laughed. He looked in my eyes and paused. For a few minutes, he just stood as if rooted to the ground. I tried to explain to him that this was a simple village and we didn't even have hot water. I told him we washed in a banya, built from beams; a little house with two rooms. In one room, we were supposed to wash our body. In the other, was a steam room where we sat and warmed up. The steam room had a rock stove on which we poured from a scoop to create the steam. We washed our hair with a homemade soap that was infused with herbs.

The man introduced himself as David. He told me that he was writing a book about Soviet people and their methods of survival. He came from America. He had been in Moscow, Stalingrad, and Astrakhan. He had heard about this interesting village and decided to do some research. He asked my permission to live in my house for a week. He offered to pay a crazy amount of money. I agreed. In addition, he would be my company for a week so I wouldn't feel lonely.

I treated him with boiled potatoes, sliced onions, and corn oil. I sliced a herring which I had salted myself in a barrel. I gave him a shot a vodka. A shot of vodka is always offered to an acquaintance. Russian people are very hospitable. David drank that shot with great difficulty. Then he asked me to teach him how to be Russian. He said that he was fascinated by the Russian people who seemed to him unpredictable and very sensitive.

He asked me where I had a restroom. I showed him a little room divided from the kitchen by a curtain where there was an iron bucket instead of a toilet. The first few days, David was shocked. Then he began to bring me water from the river and chop firewood. He began to learn how to play an accordion. He always wrote things down in his notebook in a language unknown to me. We became friends.

I told him that I wanted to find my two brothers in Stalingrad. He wanted to come with me. In addition, he got permission from local policeman for me to leave the village for a couple of days. When we came to my old house in Stalingrad where I lived with my brothers, there was only a vacant lot covered with grass. Our house was destroyed.

Nobody from our neighborhood was alive, or else they had moved to other places. I knew I had lost my relatives forever. I felt so sorry for myself. It was painful to realize that I had nobody close and nobody needed me. I cried bitterly. David cried with me. He said that in my eyes, he could see so much pain and suffering that he couldn't keep his emotions to himself.

We went back to the village. In the evening, Peter came over. He saw David in my house. He became angry. He started to beat his fist on the table and screamed, "You prostitute, how could you? I visited you as a saintly woman; I wanted to come back to you."

I started to cry. David went up to Peter and said, "Don't scream at my fiancée or you won't be invited to the wedding in three days." I was shocked. Peter sat on the chair in order not to fall down from the unexpected news. I don't know if that spell I did earlier helped me and brought me David.

But David had appeared in my life. I wasn't lonely anymore. We started to prepare for a celebration. He didn't even propose to me. He decided everything by himself. I didn't mind. David was forty-eight years old; I was thirty-six. I was once again a fiancée. Women in the village were envious. But everybody wanted to have fun and eat well. That happened only during celebrations.

A local priest named us husband and wife. David was an atheist and this was his first marriage. That was a good thing because otherwise there would have been problems. He had spent his entire life before he met me doing research and traveling all over the world. He was a freelance writer.

The question came up of how a Soviet woman could go to America with her husband and keep everything secret. At the time, any allegiance other than to the Soviet was considered to be high treason. But David loved me very much and didn't want to lose me. He was amazed by my eyes. He would sit for hours straight and just look into my eyes. He always felt sorry for me because in my eyes was a lot of pain and loss.

At that time, one possible way for a Soviet citizen to leave the native country was to get an Israeli visa for a family reunion. David was Jewish and I was now his wife. He went to Israel to see what he could do. He had a lot of powerful contacts all over the world. In Israel, he created fake, but official-looking documents and certificates for me. He applied for a reunion permit. In reality, no more than one fourth of the Soviet Jews leaving Russia immigrated to Israel. All the rest preferred the staging post in Vienna and applied for political asylum in the United States, Canada, or other countries.

I almost had no contact with David while he was in Israel. He sent me two telegrams that said, "Be a little more patient my dear, be a strong Russian woman. We will soon be together."

Women in the village laughed at me. They gloated that I wouldn't live better or happier than they did. Furthermore, it seemed to me like my new husband had abandoned me. As the saying goes, he gambled with me for a while and then quit the game.

Then one night in 1975, two important looking men dressed in civilian clothes knocked on my door. They told me to pack all my goods quietly and very quickly before the sun came up. I was worried. I couldn't understand anything. I thought I was being arrested for communicating with a foreigner.

In the morning, the men came for me. They gave me a new passport. We left the village by the least traveled paths. I did not say goodbye to anyone. They drove to Sheremetyevo airport by minor roads. The men left me and David joined me. On the airplane, he sat close to me. He gave me a new birth certificate and the rest of the papers. I went from Jenya Troshkin to Sara Shtolts. David made me Jewish. I was scared during the entire flight. I had never been on a flight in my life. I was scared that we would fall down and perish.

All my future prospects seemed empty to me. I didn't know any other life than what I had. We landed in America.

Immediately, we applied for political asylum for me. We got married again. I started to learn Hebrew. We lived in Ridgefield, Connecticut. I was afraid of America, but it began to seem like I had found myself in heaven. It was a wonderland place, where there was food in stores with no lines and with smiling people who were happy. As soon as I came to America—that very moment—I was very thankful to fate for such a gift. I never missed my homeland, which deprived me of a normal childhood, youth, and which stamped a huge stigma on my whole life. I have adopted America as my native country. Jenya Troshkina died inside of me many years ago. I have only memories of her.

I remember how difficult it was for me to communicate with people for the first time. To learn a new language, without ever having a high school education, was very hard for me. But David understood me and tutored me everyday.

He saw that it was also psychologically hard for me. There weren't many Russians in America at that time. Not everybody knew about us. That is why I was taken as something novel and everyone came to look at me. In spite of that, even though David gave me comfort and a heavenly lifestyle, I was still the same Russian woman.

I had the character of a caring mother. Every morning I woke up and cooked breakfast for David. He loved thick Russian pancakes with sour cream and raspberry jam. He learned how to make borsht or rasolnic soup from cereal and chopped dilled pickles. But for dinner, he insisted we go out. He used to live one day at a time. He even took all of life as just one day. He always did what he felt like doing and even when he went to the store, he kissed me a thousand times and said, "I love you just in case I don't come back." He spent so much money on my clothes and for our pleasure. Sometimes, I think I loved him for all he did for me. But when we lived together, he was more like a friend to me than a husband. He used to tell me that he was very thankful to me for being around and for allowing him to love me.

I never once worked during all the years we lived together. He didn't want me to. David published eight books and that was enough income for us to live well. He died six years ago in his sleep. He fell asleep and never woke up. The doctor said that he had a heart attack. He was seventy-eight. Without David, I feel lonely and empty.

He held my hand in his all the time. Everyday, he bought me little presents like chocolate or flowers in pots. Today, if you visited my house, you would think it was a green house. But I don't know who will get all my treasures when I die.

I still had only one true love of my life: Peter. But that was in a past life, which I don't remember clearly. I know that respect is more valuable and that it means more. David idolized me until the day he died. I have even taken in a kitty and named him Dave. Every week, my schedule looks pretty simple and the same. I wake up and feed the kitty. I go to the cemetery and visit my husband's grave. I talk to him and tell him all the news in my life and about our neighbors and then I go back home. Sometimes, a few acquaintances come to visit me and we play cards or tell fortunes from the coffee grounds. It's not boring for me to live this life. I am writing my autobiography, which could be very interesting after I leave this world. I am happy. I am enjoying my freedom and every day God is giving me. I am seventy-two now. I think that I lived a fully emotional life that I have never felt ashamed of.

If Bitch Exile still exists, nobody is probably alive among our old residents. I heard from a friend there, who came to America and called me, that as soon as the old Soviet regime was withdrawn, and the residents got passports, many people went back home or were exiled to other cities like Astrakhan or Moscow. One girl suddenly disappeared even earlier. One day, two men dressed in military uniform came to the island. They asked young girls to volunteer for a very important job and sent them to Vasilisa.

One in particular was very beautiful. She had blonde hair and blue eyes. Some people said that she worked at Krushev's dacha, a country house which was on our neighboring island.

SHATTERED DREAMS BROKEN PROMISES

There were other people who were detained and couldn't leave the island. They didn't want to leave their small houses on that little sin island in the middle of Volga River. Too many things connected them with that place. Perhaps they lived to see the end of their century. Maybe they are alive today, engaged in village gossip, the continual struggle for survival, and their memories of the secrets of the past. And they would not be alone. A part of me lives there still.

Chapter 2
HEAD GAMES

I always wanted to live a beautiful life. I don't know where this longing came from because I grew up in a nightmare of poverty. My mother died when I was two years old. I don't remember her at all. I only have a couple of old pictures and my father's stories of her. My father loved her very much and he spoiled me as much as he could under the circumstances.

We lived in a kommunalka, a community shelter, in a town called Ivanovo in a remote part of Russia. I hated that the children's playground only had one swing that was made by an old alcoholic named Vasya. It was really only a cable tied around a stick. I always felt envious of the other children I saw on the streets, the ones who had more food on their table than they could possibly eat. As I grew up, pretend stepmothers appeared one after another at home as regularly as the changing of the seasons. I was sixteen when my father died. He was crushed to death by a machine at the fabric shop where he worked. After he died, I graduated from night school and worked part-time at the vegetable market as a stocker.

I met Mitya at one of the town's disco clubs. I was a bright and pretty young lady. I had bleached-blond hair and big brown eyes that I emphasized with heavy eyeliner. I used to have a wonderful voice, like a princess in a fairy tale. But now, I have smoked out my voice. When I talk over the phone, sometimes it's hard to know if I am a man or a woman. But when I was young and I sang, all the men fell at my feet. Mitya and I fell in love instantly. We married when I was seventeen years old. Mitya was the only single man I knew.

He was a plumber at the factory where my father had worked. According to the statistics, in Ivanovo there was one man for every two girls. That is why the other name for our town was "the city of fiancées." Mitya was a nice man; I was lucky. He was paid more than his co-workers and brought his entire salary home and gave it to me. He used to drink a lot, but not with the money he earned: others always supplied drinks for him. Everybody respected Mitya. That is why he was always welcomed with a shot of vodka.

Mitya beat me, as every Russian man is prone to do, but he did it rarely and only when I deserved it. He loved me very much, but he was also jealous. He argued with me and claimed that I spent all our money on lipstick and boots. He wasn't greedy, he just didn't understand why I wore makeup and dressed up. "For whom?" he asked. He used to tell me that I was a married woman who looked available, even like a prostitute. When he was angry, he put a blue shadow under my eye with his fist. But there would be no other punishments.

Eventually, because I was a flirty and interesting lady, Mitya began to punish me quite often. I knew there was nothing I could do about that. It was the nature of Russian men. I found a wonderful Soviet-brand foundation cream called "Ballet" and I hid my blue bruises with it. I still can't understand why they called it "Ballet." I thought it was perfect for making up dead people. One application and you would look alive and have baby-smooth skin.

But I still think that he was a nice man and that I was lucky to have him. Compared to other married women I knew, one of whose husband had cut her up in small pieces with an axe, my husband was a prince. He had only one shortcoming that irritated me very much. He loved sweets, especially "Sgushenka," sweet condensed milk. He used to come home from work, make a little hole in the can, and suck everything out of it. I took this as the worst sign of being uncultured. I lived happily with Mitya for three years. We had good and bad days, but I knew there are no perfect people or perfect relationships. Once in a while, I felt that with my beauty and dreams of living a life of wealth, I needed somebody else, someone richer and more intelligent. But I didn't want to cheat on my husband.

One day, I went to Mitya and asked him honestly to forgive me, because I didn't love him anymore. He was upset for a while, and then he moved in with another woman. As I said, available men were a rarity in our town. If one woman threw her man out, another woman was waiting to pick him up. It was like each was on a conveyer belt. To most men, it made little difference who the woman was. The most important thing was that a woman was always nearby for his pleasure and that food was on the table.

We started the divorce process. I felt like my happy star would knock on my door at any moment, although I was upset that at twenty-one years old I would already have a divorce stamp on my passport. To most men, as in old times, marrying a divorced woman was like marrying a woman who wasn't a virgin on her wedding night. I had no choice but to bribe the judge who helped me hide the traces of a bad marriage and thereby save my reputation.

I sold a room in the town of Kommunalka that had been left to me by my father as an inheritance, and rented an apartment close to downtown. I spent half the money shopping. I believed that a young single woman needed to always look perfect. It didn't matter whether I was going to the store for a loaf of bread or to throw out the garbage, I knew that a woman needed a certain image in order to find a happy future. I was doing my best to assist my destiny. You never know when your happiness will find you and that is why you always have to be ready for battle, like a soldier with his gun always by his side.

Unfortunately, money in a poor person's pocket doesn't last long. One day, I realized that I couldn't go to restaurants or stroll around looking for a man to make me happy. I knew that I had to do something to survive and keep what money I had in my wallet or even make it go further. I made a decision.

I answered an ad inviting young girls to work in the USA. When the man called, he asked if having sex for money would be fine with me. I quickly thought about it and answered yes. I had nothing to lose. I had nobody left and no one to embarrass. I didn't tell anybody about my plans. I was not proud of them. But I doubt if you could point a finger at one girl who didn't at least dream of escaping from the former Soviet Union? Show me just one who didn't want to become an American and be paid in dollars.

I had my passport ready. I went through the interview. I learned that I would be working as a striptease dancer and part-time prostitute. The rules were simple: be a good girl; don't talk too much; stay clean and use protection; don't use drugs; share your earnings with your boss; and be nice to the customers. If you did all that, you would earn your boss's loyalty, a flexible work schedule, and a permanent driver. You would be treated nicely by your local colleagues and, possibly, even be offered other opportunities. I agreed to all of the conditions.

I had to go through a period of non-paid training in the city of Krasnodar. My teachers seemed pleased with my progress and pleased is what they wanted to be. After a week, we were to receive our visas and plane tickets, all paid for by the company we were going to work for. It was not easy to train to become a prostitute. I had difficulties with learning how to strip dance. I didn't know how to move or jump on the pole. I fell down all the time and was soon covered with bruises and other minor injures. But I knew that if I could serve nasty, drunk Russian men, every client in America would be like a date. As the saying goes, if you keep trying hard enough, you'll get it.

I learned how to strip and passed the exam. I packed my suitcases and left for the airport. I had never taken a flight before. When the plane took off, I got scared. At the end of the flight, the poor fellow next to me was more frightened than I was. All through the turbulent zone, I would hang onto his neck and shout things like: "Oh mother, I'm afraid we will all die…we're all going to perish."

When we were getting close to America, he became nervous as well. He jumped with me at every bumpy moment. I laughed hysterically. I said: "My dear friend, calm down. We'll all be dead. We'll be nicely buried. People will remember us as heroes of the former Soviet Union." But he didn't like my sense of humor. He nodded his head and turned red. He pulled his hair and drank Stolichnaya vodka right from the bottle. When we landed, everybody crossed themselves.

Before passing through customs, we girls were all warned regarding questioning about our purpose for coming to America. We were told that we should answer that we were taking part in a seminar about trade-market relationships with foreign countries. I didn't speak English, and even if I had, I would never have been able to repeat that phrase. I understood that I had to play a role just like an actress. I braided my hair, put on glasses to look serious, put a bandage on my cheek and put a walnut I had with me in my mouth in order to look like I had a swelling due to an abscess. Everybody felt sorry for me and they let me go through the immigration process quickly.

My work started the day after I arrived. I was given one day to adapt and look around my new hometown of Las Vegas. I do not have the words to describe my amazement. It was as if I had entered a dream world. Day and night blended into each other like lovers in a passionate embrace. I made myself comfortable in a big tract house several miles from the large hotels. I had no trouble fitting into the large group of people who worked in my new trade.

My bosses ran a small empire and could do as they pleased as long as their girls stayed out of trouble. They explained all the rules. As a rule, they charged four hundred for sex for one hour and one hundred and fifty dollars for a half-hour private dance. I couldn't have even dreamed about such money a week earlier. I threw my old dresses in the garbage and bought new ones. My new life had started.

There were trips around Las Vegas in a limousine, cell phones, expensive clothes, and sometimes recreational sex with my driver. What more could a young woman, who never ate anything sweeter than a carrot, dream about? I adapted to my new country very quickly. In this type of work, a girl wants to have stability. You want a steady work schedule. You want to have a permanent driver who, if you're lucky, will become your bodyguard, friend, and psychiatrist.

Believe me, very few men understands that we are just normal women. Some of us are fluent in several languages and have a college degree. Some of us have children. A driver is like a safety net for us. He sees everything in our lives. He jokes, talks, and, most importantly, understands.

We worked outcalls only. It was a good thing because it made us feel at home. That is very important when you are far from your homeland. Clients were mostly good to us—at least better than a Russian husband. They were different but not bad. I had only a few bad cases in seven years. Some clients asked for sexual perversions. At first, they wanted sex in just a few different positions. Some wanted to be beaten or get peed on, which is called a golden shower.

Everything was supposed to be discussed before we started. Customers would explain what they wanted to get and how much they'd pay. Our phone girl knew what each girl did. She would decide whether or not a girl would take a job. Everything, even prostitution, is more civilized in America. The company had a website with our pictures and short made-up background stories about our lives.

After two weeks of working there, I understood that there was a difference between having sex with your husband for black eyes, and having sex with a stranger for money. But the feelings were almost the same. The process was a little different but it was easier to survive with the stranger. We had a choice: we could work as prostitutes only, as strip dancers only, or both.

First, I worked in both positions. I was so greedy for money. Of course, I'd never seen so much cash and I wanted only to earn more. But I also spent more. I needed to take care of myself to look desirable. But that was only for the first month, when every girl is trying to earn every possible dollar.

After that, you choose what is better and easier for you. I chose prostitution; others chose dancing. Our agency was one of the few very solid ones that didn't take advantage of its employees. Every girl signed an agreement that she agreed to work honestly for the agency for one year as discussed in the initial interview. The girls were supposed to work off the money the bosses paid for her visa and airplane ticket, and they took their percentage of her earnings. At the end of the year, she had to have paid back all the money, and then she could decide whether to go or stay.

After the first week of work, a girl would count all the money she earned and find it easy to live with herself and the work she did—at least in the beginning. At our agency, many of the girls came from the countries of the former Soviet Union. They rarely hired any local girls because our girls were mostly unique, reliable, and trustworthy. I worked for two years, first as a stripper, then as a prostitute and became a best friend of many of the girls.

Our boss asked for, and respected, my opinion. Our security guys cried on my shoulder about their difficulties. Everybody wanted my advice: to be or not to be? Or whose fault problems were and what should they do about them?

One day, Yurik, our boss, called me to his room and said: "Nastya, I see you're smart. You know everything and notice everything. I started to think recently about what was missing in our big and happy family. We have a private gynecologist and physician. The girls have vacations, good security, and money. They can call their homeland any time. But I noticed that our girls still go to you all the time and whisper.

"I trust you. Would you ever decide to do something against me and my business? If something bothers you, or you don't like something, it's better to say it to my face. I think I would understand. I care about all of you. You earn money for me and in return, I provide you with a job, and care. If you need something else, it's better to tell me. I will think about your request overnight and give you the answer in the morning. I am a man who tries to live according to the laws of humanity."

Between the girls, we nicknamed Yurik "Mr. Intelligence." He never raised his voice or spoke dirty. He treated everybody with respect, and he didn't take advantage of us even though he could have. I thought for a second and told him that what the girls needed was a real psychiatrist. They were young, lonely, and many of them were heartbroken.

Yurik looked at me and asked, "Don't you think you've been a prostitute long enough? You have brains and intelligence. You have to think, Nastya. I will too. Tomorrow, I will meet you in the morning and we'll decide your future."

That night was my last night as a prostitute. I had already earned and saved a lot of money. I woke up the next morning already thinking of myself as an amateur psychiatrist; a sort of local 911 for the hard-working girls. Yurik was waiting for me that morning with a professional psychiatrist. She began to train me and taught me how to council people with serious depression and suicidal tendencies. I knew plenty about all that just from personal experience, but not the scientific terminology. I had a great deal to learn.

The psychiatrist helped me enroll at a local university in the Department of Psychology where I took all the useful classes I could, including those at summer school. Until my graduation, I continued to work as a therapist for my former colleagues. My workday was 24/7. I was either at school or counseling the girls. For every hour of my time, Yurik charged the girls a hundred dollars.

I have now earned my degree. My best reward is the appreciation from my girls and their peace of mind. My income is even more now than when I worked as a prostitute. Girls stand in a line for an appointment. They all want to talk and share their problems. Everyone desires to be loved and to love. As I'd hoped for so long, I now have both, a career and the opportunity to help others like me. And now, my native language is sometimes even more important because of my patients. I want to help these girls because I am sure that as soon as they are able to stand on their own two feet, they will quit the business, find a husband, start families, and be happy.

Besides, since we can't stop this business, then at least we have to bring about better conditions and help others gain some understanding and respect for these women. But I am not judging any of them. I have found in America all that I wished for, and now I am able to give back a little. It is finally, after such an unusual journey, a beautiful life.

Chapter 3
LIFE GOES ON

I was born in the very heart of Siberia forty-five years ago. My mother was a bookkeeper and my father served in the Russian military. I was delivered by Caesarian section and, because men were not allowed into the surgery or delivery room, my father climbed a tree outside the hospital to peek into the operating room and see what was happening. When the doctors cut open my mother's stomach, he fainted and fell a long way to the hard frozen ground. He then had to be rushed into the hospital himself and treated for various broken ribs and bones.

That was the beginning of my story. My parents loved me very much and I was spoiled. We lived in an apartment until I was eleven years old, when my parents managed to get us into a two-bedroom house with a living room, kitchen and bathroom. We had central heating and hot and cold water. There was no air conditioning, but it didn't ever get very hot in Siberia. Summers were warm but brief, and the winters were brutal.

Even though it was Siberia, there was the change of seasons, gorgeous springtime and beautiful autumn, endlessly long wintertime and very bright summers. My parents had to work hard to provide for our home and buy and raise food. We had our own garden where we grew fruits and vegetables. It was hard labor to keep up our gardens, especially the potatoes. For the wintertime my mother stored all kinds of preserves made of fruit and vegetables, that we ate all through the long winter months. I think it was always a challenge, but Russians love to eat, and we never lacked food in the house. On Fridays, my mother baked bread and buns, and the whole family got together and ate them through the weekend. Meat was essential during the long Siberian winters, and I remember my mom and her sisters would gather on Sundays to make pelmeni: Russian ravioli with meat inside. My mother would freeze it outside—no need for a freezer in Siberia during winter. These raviolis were our fast food. We also ate a lot of cabbage and cole slaw. Soup, potatoes, and meatballs were the staples.

My school was very strict and I attended six days a week, with a half day on Saturday. The students were given a great deal of homework. Most parents in Russia sign their children up for all kinds of activities, so usually after school we took art classes or sang in the choir or took gymnastics. I loved folk dancing and was very good at it.

We had a local clinic that served our whole area; if someone got sick, you went to the clinic to see your doctor. Sometimes you had to wait in line for an hour or so, but usually there were enough doctors. After the visit, we went to the drugstore to get our meds. If you were really sick with a very high fever for example, you could call an ambulance. They would come to your home, check you out, write the prescription for you there and give you shots, if necessary. The health-care system was very good.

When I was thirteen years old, I developed a crush on a boy who lived in my neighborhood, but I never told him about it. He was much older, eighteen at the time, and one day he moved out and was gone. I never saw him again. I remember in eighth grade one of my classmates became pregnant, and it was a terrible shock to me. We were quite sheltered. I knew nothing about sex other than you should not have it until you were eighteen and married. My parents had raised me to be very modest.

Several years later, when I was in high school, I met a man. He was the first person I ever kissed. My boyfriend was seven years older than I was and worked in the entertainment field. I loved him very much. He was, we were told, killed in a car accident or at least that is what the police told us. You could never be sure about such happennings.

As soon as I finished high school, I danced in a professional folk dance company. There was an announcement in the newspaper one day that the circus was looking for a magician's assistant. I didn't tell my parents. I was afraid they would stop me. But I went to the audition, and the circus hired me. My parents were very surprised to hear that I was leaving with the circus. For two and a half years I traveled all over Russia with this circus. Every time my dance company went anywhere to perform, Japan, Yugoslavia, or anywhere else, for some reason I was never allowed to go. At the time, I had no idea that my family was being monitored by the KGB because my mother had been imprisoned in one of Stalin's concentration camps.

Back in the fifties there had been a witch hunt on Jewish people in Leningrad. Then there was a wave of arrests and killings through Russia. At that time, the KGB was arresting anyone who was Jewish or in any other way suspicious to them. As a child I never even knew that my mother was Jewish and spent several years in Stalin's camp. Before Stalin died, her family appealed to get her out, but it took five years to "rehabilitate" her. Her sister suffered too. She was arrested along with my mother and was also imprisoned. The family also appealed for her to be set free, of course. However, my aunt's paperwork was lost, so they had to start all over. It took ten years to free her.

"Rehabilitated" meant that my mother was free to go home. That was it. No one even apologized or said anything. They just told her she was free. For years the family went to court, appealing, and finally the officials decided my mother had been wrongly charged with all these criminal counts. It was all so wrong. But back then there were so many people in prison for no reason. All they wanted was to get out and go home and be free. No one expected any sort of apology. Even so, KGB continued to monitor my family for many years. Because my mother had been imprisoned, I was never allowed to go anywhere out of the country with the circus. I had learned that my family was under constant surveillance, at least until the nineties, when Gorbachev came into power and things changed. That is why this thing happened to me in the circus. The organizers were preparing to take the show abroad, and I was left behind. I quit, and returned to Siberia.

After high school, I attended fashion design college in Siberia. I was able to get a job doing costumes for some major theatrical productions in Moscow. Besides being a fashion designer, I was a very good seamstress and dressmaker.

I immediately met another man in Moscow who was strong and knew what he wanted. I was very submissive. Russia has a big deficit of men, and women suffer from it. When a man notices a woman and pays attention to her, it seems that a woman must go along with it. I started to live with him and soon became pregnant. He was not a very nice person to begin with, but after I became pregnant, he was actually cruel.

At one point, when my son was still very small, I knew I had to leave him. I was home packing my suitcases when he showed up suddenly and saw what I was doing. He flew into a rage and tore my clothes off and raped me, while our son was right there with us in the room. I was crying so hard, not so much because of the pain or the fear, but because he would do something like this in front of our own child, who was only one and a half years old and very frightened. I was too afraid to tell anyone. In fact, for many years I would never have dreamed of telling anyone. As women, we are all conditioned, in Russia, to try harder, improve ourselves more, and keep our man happy. But there was only so much I would tolerate.

I left him that day and went to live in a tiny one-room apartment in Moscow. I worked as a costume maker. I never had any contact with my son's father after I left him. He never helped us at all with money nor asked to spend time with his son. I don't believe you can make anyone act like a father or mother if they don't want to, so I didn't even try. If someone refuses to take on the responsibilities of being a parent, there is nothing I can do. I knew that I had to take care of this child myself.

I met an American woman in Moscow who was traveling all over Russia. She had been on a ship cruise. I couldn't speak much English, but I could tell she was lonely. She was happy to have my company. A girlfriend and I invited her to spend a couple of weeks with us in Moscow, trying our best to be nice hostesses. We showed her all around. Out of the blue, this woman invited both my friend and me to come to the United States.

"Miriam, I can't just go the United States, I have a child here," I told her. My son was living with my parents in Siberia at this time. But after I thought things over, I decided that I was lucky to get the chance. Everything was a mess in Russia at that time; I figured things couldn't be worse anywhere else. I accepted her invitation and came to the United States on a visitor's visa.

The timing was really quite fortunate. Six days after I came to America in February of 1992, my homeland literally disappeared. The Soviet Union did not exist anymore; it had become Russia. The people who lived in Russia, who I had left behind, had to change their passports, citizenship, everything. Since I had come here from the Soviet Union, which no longer existed, I think it made it easier to stay.

I had no idea what to expect, because we had all been very much brainwashed in Russia. We didn't have much real information about America before the nineties. It wasn't so much that I wanted to come to America, it was more that I had the chance to leave Russia. So I did. I landed in Flint, Michigan because the woman I had met in Moscow lived there and I was her guest. Life in Michigan was hard for me at first; I didn't speak English and had no friends. But I met a man who I liked very much. This man taught me how to drive and how to speak English better. We became good friends. I tried my best to show him affection, but he never seemed interested. Finally, I just said to him, "If you are gay, that is fine, we can still be friends."

Next thing I knew, we became lovers and I found I was pregnant. He was very upset. He accused me of trying to trap him with my pregnancy and of having his child so I could take all his money. It wasn't true, so I just told him he was free to go and I didn't need his money. He went.

I know some Russians here in this community, but most of the time I stay away from them. I heard from another Russian woman in Flint just today. She is planning to divorce her husband and is looking for a lawyer who will really stand up for her and help. It's funny: I tend to hear from other Russian women when they are in trouble. That's when they find me. I would say of the seven Russian girls I know who married Americans, five are happy and two, after five or so years of marriage, are not.

American men are very, very different from Russian men. They are not as spoiled. In Russia, men can get away with murder. There are so few men that most of them use the situation to their advantage. Men have wives and a couple of girlfriends too, and most women are afraid they will have nobody, so they put up with the situation and stay silent.

I had a good friend in Russia with two children who was married to a terrible alcoholic. But she just went with it. Americans make fun of Russians for being alcoholics, but it's really not a joke. Many times when Russian men drink, they become violent. There is a lot of physical abuse in Russia. The women suffer a great deal.

Eventually, I was granted political asylum in 1995, which involved a lot of paperwork, but I am now a legal resident. And I was able to bring my son back from my parents in Siberia. I receive public assistance from the state of Michigan, and I also have a job. I work in a rehabilitation home taking care of disabled people for ten dollars an hour. A girl, my younger son's friend, also lives with us. I found her sleeping in my living room a couple of mornings in a row and asked my son what was going on. He told me that her father had died when she was two and her mother was in jail. Her grandmother, who she lived with, had a boyfriend who didn't want her around. So I took her in and now basically I have three children.

I attend a Christian Orthodox church here, which I really enjoy. I sing in the choir; sometimes I think that's why I go to church.

I recently visited Russia and it was very sad. All those people telling me, you would not believe how Russia has changed! I didn't find it had changed. Yes, the exterior had changed. Everything looks better, they've built new houses, they have cleaned it up, there are more new cars, that kind of thing. But the people are still the same, they don't smile. I had a man approach me in the street and he said, "You're not from here." I said, "Why do you think that?" I was thinking he would say it was my clothing. I was wearing a bright yellow down jacket. But he said, "You smile." I said. "Yes, because I have reason to smile; I am happy with my life and who I am."

I was happy to visit there, but I was glad to return home. Michigan is now my home. I can't imagine living anywhere else. I can work, make money, live my life, and have my freedoms. I would not want to go anywhere else. Oh yes, I would like to go to Russia to visit again, because there are so many things there I miss seeing, like Saint Petersburg. I visited Saint Petersburg once, many years ago, when I still lived in Russia, but I would love to return now, as a tourist, and really enjoy it the way a tourist would. If you are in Russia and you have money, you can live very well.

But you're always very insecure. Your money can be taken away from you at any moment, and then you immediately become nothing and really struggle. In Russia, the ground is always shifting under your feet. But if you are just coming to visit, Russia is wonderful. You wander around the beautiful parks. I would love for my children to see it. In fact, I would love to see the world, not just Russia!

My joy in life comes from watching my children grow up into good people. My older son is very good with his hands and, although still in high school, he works in construction. He comes home very dirty and tired, but he enjoys work. My younger son is a real bookworm, and reads everything about animals. He enjoys Harry Potter, and he is just wonderful. I also love to read. I love to sing. I love to help people when I can, and I always do my best. I truly enjoy my work, taking care of people who need it. Every time I work with the disabled, I understand how lucky I am to be able to take care of myself. The people I take care of have no choices.

I keep myself busy, so I do not have to think about how lonely I am. Because I am still a Russian woman with the same Russian soul which tells me I have to belong to some man. And here I am running around the community and helping others when I am the one whose very simple needs have to be fulfilled.

I want to be loved and I want to be in love. Why should I see something beautiful if I have no one to share it with? Why should I have good looks and a brain if I can't find someone who would appreciate me? I would love to meet a good man, stronger and smarter than I am. I live for my kids and long for this wonderful dream to come true someday.

Chapter 4
ALL THAT GLITTERS

My name is Natalie. I took all the bricks that were thrown at me and built a bridge. Some Russian women wall themselves in; others try to take a shortcut and go down a self-destructive path. Whether real, enhanced, or imagined, their colorful and melodramatic stories are often utilized to garner sympathy, empty wallets, and sometimes alter the lives of the unsuspecting American men that they target. In these modern times, the trap is often times a website. An attractive place where willing, young Russian women lay the bait for fantasy-driven American men.

To be put through a test in life is to have a testimony. Some people find a purpose in their pain and do extraordinary things. Others become victim-predators that do unto others what someone else has done to them. And they do it with a vengeance, all the while smiling sweetly and making their victim feel like the love of their life.

But, as we all eventually learn, there are no shortcuts to success and happiness. However, there are sacrifices great and small as well as faith, a determined and unwavering spirit, perseverance, hard work and, above all, a vision. It is a vision of ourselves that is greater than our circumstances.

If I had a choice, I would have chosen a different set of circumstances for my life. However, I took the lemons and made lemonade, then a lemon pie, and then a lemon pie manufacturing factory. Not without many mistakes along the way, mind you. But, I learned from those mistakes, never sold out, and always looked ahead. I believe there are no coincidences in life, and that my life has not been a haphazard set of unrelated and irrelevant events. My personal set of circumstances provided me with a unique knowledge, and, thus, opportunities, to be the person that I am today, and to be a positive force for good in so many ways.

My mother came from a port city in Russia and my father is from Saint Petersburg. My maternal grandmother was a seamstress and my grandfather was the town's sheriff. On the surface, it was a legitimate and, some might say, powerful job. But there are no right jobs in a corrupt system and so, one day, he had enough.

Two wrongs may not make a right. Nevertheless, grandfather decided to use his authority for greater good and illegally helped transport many long-suffering oppressed people from Saint Petersburg to China. He did this successfully for two years before he was caught by the Bolsheviks and became an inmate in the prison he had once presided over.

A few years later, they killed him. My mother was three years old at the time. While he was in prison, there was only one way the family knew that he was alive: grandfather waved a white handkerchief from the tiny, barred cell window. One day, he didn't wave.

As a result of his demise, the family knew that they would be killed next. They paid a guide to get them over the unforgiving Amur River and into China. The guide took the money and robbed them of everything else they had. At last, in Harbin, China, they were all together but deathly ill. Mother was consumed by lice and welts. She barely survived the journey. Once in China, the family had an opportunity to build something out of nothing.

My paternal grandfather arrived in China under better circumstances. Grandfather was an officer for the Czar and got assigned to work in Harbin. However, once he got there, he decided never to return to Russia again. Thus, my father and uncles were born in China, oblivious to the oppression and struggles in their father's native land.

Father was an aloof character, yet a goofy guy who partied, and did not take life too seriously. Somehow, he did manage to get an education. My mother, on the other hand, was an intelligent and beautiful woman. This was not lost on my father the first time he laid eyes on her in a restaurant. She was gorgeous and also had her act together. And, she was in love with a Soviet soldier who worked on the railroad. Victor was the love of her life. She pined away for him as she listened to Shulzhenko's music and cried all the way to her old age. Mother returned to Russia at seventeen and searched for Victor until she found him. He promised mother that he would bring her back to Russia to be with him, but it never happened.

Mother's loss was my father's gain. She looked like Ingrid Bergman; innocent-appearing, but very strong willed. She was also the brains of the family—a family that hid their Jewish heritage in order to avoid persecution. Father reminded me of Tony Curtis: stunning in appearance, but a goofball who liked to joke around, gamble, spend money, and waste away his days.

On June 5, 1954, I was born in Harbin. My earliest childhood memory is of the Chinese government's campaign for population control. They had poster-sized photographs all over the streets that showed people how to put on condoms. There were children *everywhere* in China. I remember the diapers they all wore with the hole for going to the bathroom. One day, when I was three years old, I brought home a Chinese baby. I tried to remember where I had picked her up, but it wasn't easy.

China was largely nationalized by 1957, and we were asked to leave the country. My grandmother was the matriarch of the family, and she decided that we would all go to Chile. We ended up in Santiago as refugees and were taken in by Catholic nuns. They took care of us until my father got a job as an electrical engineer. He actually did rather well and we managed to survive. After some time, my uncles moved to America and got our family out of Chile.

I was twelve years old when I came to America and didn't speak a word of English. But I was already fluent in Spanish and

Russian. At first, I hated the United States. We lived in San Francisco and it was unbearably noisy. My Uncle Igor had done quite well for himself. He owned Lucina, a Russian restaurant on Clement Street. We were picked up at the airport and taken straight to the restaurant.

I missed my dogs terribly and didn't think I'd ever get used to living in America. My parrot had committed suicide by jumping out the window upon my family's departure from Chile. I felt like doing the same. We ate Russian food, but I had acquired quite a taste for Chilean cuisine. My mother made borsht, gefilte fish, and pelmeni (dumplings).

Eventually, Igor sold Lucina and bought a Best Western hotel in San José. Then he sold it and bought the Ramada Inn in Merced, California. My cousin just sold the Ramada for thirteen million, quite an accomplishment considering he came to this country with no money, no skills, no contacts, and no English.

Over time, San Francisco grew on me and I grew to like it. The Russian immigrant became a teenage American hippie. San Francisco was the center of the hippie era and I got into the full swing of things. My friends and I went to Santana and the Grateful Dead concerts. I loved my new life and began to fit right in. At first, English was a barrier, so I learned to completely wipe out my Russian accent and stayed away from the word immigrant—an insult to me.

I launched my first business at nineteen: a special events production. I learned the ropes at the Fairmont hotel in sales and public relations. Richard Swigg recognized my potential and put me in charge of the sales department. I was fortunate to learn from the best of the best. After a while, I started doing events for the clients I met at the Fairmont.

I visited Russia with my mother and met my first boyfriend. He was very French, and I was a thoroughly modern American hippie, and a spoiled brat to boot. I told my mother that I didn't identify with the communist bastards. Laurent, however, I fell madly in love with, even though we never made love. Today, all I have of him is pictures and my memories.

Upon returning to San Francisco, I informed my mother that I could not live without Laurent and planned to run away. But I was too involved with my work to pursue boyfriends, even though Laurent and I constantly corresponded. Meanwhile, my mother encouraged me to be patient and inspired me to listen to Edith Piaf and other French music.

I married a bum. I met him at San Francisco State University where he studied on the GI Bill. Alex was very good-looking indeed, but a complete moron. I brought him home one day and announced to my parents that I was in love with him and that we were going to live together. My parents pleaded with me to marry instead, and insisted that we live in their basement. Marriage of their only daughter to an utter buffoon was preferable to living in sin, which would surely bring shame to the family in the eyes of all fine Russians. Hence, my parents lavished us with a royal wedding for a marriage that lasted less than a year.

I left the Fairmont in 1980, and went to work for the Association of Independent Television Stations (INTV) as a consultant. Even though I was green, I was cool as a cucumber when the company sent me to a huge convention to pitch Herman Land in Washington, D.C. I may have been more than wet behind the ears, but I gave a clever enough spiel for Land to take a chance and warn me not to blow it.

The only thing that blew was the Eastern wind, because I ended up working for them for ten years. I did their events, as well as major events for Paramount, Warner Bros., and many others. I walked away from INTV when I met my second husband. I married the very handsome Shelton Merrill, had a beautiful daughter, Katja, and became a producer. This was a smart career move for me. Today, I produce television shows with my current husband, Rodion Nahapetov.

We met when he came to promote a film that Fox had bought. *At the Close of Night* was a World War II film that he had directed. It was a love story about a Russian solider and a German-Jewish passenger. I instantly fell in love with the film while watching it at a UCLA film festival and wanted to know who made it.

A friend of mine found out that Rodion was coming to America to promote the film and offered to introduce me. However, I was married.

I now realize that I kept marrying men who weren't on the same wavelength as me; I just couldn't get it right. My third husband, Alex Lavitsky, was a buddy of mine. When we divorced, I paid him $40,000 in compensation. What was I supposed to do? I had at last met my true love.

Rodion Nahapetov is an actor and director. I first fell in love with his film and, when I met him, I instantly knew that I would be with him for the rest of my life. I was in my early thirties and no longer a young silly girl. This was the real deal and I wasn't going to pass it up.

We have been married for sixteen years now. I still don't feel any different today than I did then; it is perpetual bliss. The only tragic thing was that we both had to end our previous marriages. He was married to a major Russian film star and they had children. They were the perfect movie star couple and Russia's sweethearts. Our situation made things very hard for us financially, professionally, and socially. I soon realized that I wasn't accepted in Russia, and wouldn't be for a very long time. I was the other woman who had come between their idolized couple. At public events, I was simply pushed aside and ignored. The Russian people's perception toward me started to thaw when Rodion and I began working with disadvantaged children. Still, they accepted me more as a humanitarian than as his wife.

At our lowest point, we started a foundation. Unexpectedly, one night my husband received a phone call from a stranger who said that his daughter was dying because of a heart problem. The desperate father pleaded for help because Rodion was a Russian in America and he was hoping against all odds that he might have some influence in the Los Angeles medical community.

I personally went to see Dr. Yokoyama and begged him to help the little girl. Within two weeks, seven-month-old Anya was flown to Los Angeles and he saved her life. At that point, we decided that we needed to do this for more children. Since 1995, we have saved more than two hundred children and continue to do so through our foundation. At times, we take teams from UCLA and Stanford to Russia where they perform surgeries and save the lives of these poor suffering children. This is the most meaningful part of our lives.

Today, I consider myself a full-fledged American. I am very patriotic and defend my country anywhere in the world. Russians hate America and all her ideals. This past Fourth of July, we were in Russia and wanted to attend a celebration at the U.S. embassy. However, we were told not to come as there was going to be a rally of skinheads and anti-American protestors. The embassy cancelled the celebration for fear of violence.

When Rodion and I married, both our careers came to a halt. The response to him was brutal. We ended up moving out of our house so that we could rent it, just to keep eating. We took up residence at my cousin's cabin. We struggled, but eventually started working again. We did a television series called, *Russians in the City of Angels* and a major movie.

Rodion wrote, directed, produced, and acted in the series. I played a role, as did Eric Roberts, Gary Busei, Sean Young, Karen Black, and others. The show dealt with all aspects of Russian life in the U.S.: mafia, drug dealers, and the like. Rodion wrote twelve episodes and the show was a huge hit in Russia, and got major air play all over the European Union.

So far, our life has been really great. My daughter is doing well. One of Rodion's daughters is a ballerina. She is engaged and expecting her first child. I wish to point out that Russian women are very practical when it comes to choosing men. Love is not at the top of their list of requirements. In America, I believe that very few women find what they are looking for and, as a result, there are a lot of shattered dreams and broken promises. The soul of a human being is very complex. But I do think that if you don't connect with someone on the soul level, it's never going to work. If I married someone for money as many Russian women opt to do, I would feel that I was ripping him off and cheating myself out of a rightful existence.

I am convinced that deep down inside, Russian women have good souls. But some have turned into money-hungry hyenas. They're brought up to believe that money is equated with being human. Their attitudes are completely twisted and perverted.

Most Russian women today are obsessed with designer labels and a luxury lifestyle that they see in American soap operas. They think that in America everyone is rich!

I speak with a lot of these young Russian women and I advise them not to come to America and think they will be the next Vivian Lee, because pretty faces are a dime a dozen here. I advise them to stay in Moscow and build a career and a life there. For instance, actors and directors in Russia are now making up to a million dollars per film. I'm taking Eric Roberts to Russia, not for a plum role, but because it's good money.

My message to young Russian women wanting to immigrate to America is: Don't do it. It doesn't work. What you are trying to do is wrong, and you will pay the ultimate price in the end. Gold-diggers end up doing a lot of digging and find very little gold.

Today, there are plenty of jobs in Russia. Many of you would be throwing away your lives and living in servitude if you came to America. You have become such drama queens and nauseatingly whiney with men. There's always some devastating drama in your lives and it's gotten old. You're annoying. As an American, I can't take it because you never look at the positive side of things. To Americans, you come across as professional victims. You are looking to be rescued and to live happily ever after. Only in fairytales.

Chapter 5
THE LIGHT AT RASPUTNAYA STREET

I knew from childhood how ugly life could be, but I have seen the good side as well. I was an ordinary girl who grew up on the streets of Minsk. I was raised in a dysfunctional family. My parents drank a lot and earned very little money; they earned so little that it would have been cheaper to kill us than to feed us.

My mother worked as a dispatcher on rotating shifts on a railroad. My father was a stockroom worker in a local grocery store. My mother was Russian. My father was a Muslim. I had three young brothers and a small dog named Max.

When I was thirteen years old, my father began to molest me. He came to my room at night while my mother worked. He raised my blanket and touched my breasts and buttocks with his shaking hands.

He came into the bathroom while I showered. He tried to make me please him orally. At times, I was able to reject his advances but I was not always able to do so. At least he did not penetrate my virginity. Still, he told me that no man would marry me and I believed him.

I didn't go to regular school a single day in my life. All day, everyday, he made me read the Koran. So, day in and day out, I sat at home, read the Koran and pleased him sexually. However, he allowed me to go on an excursion, to attend a religious school where I read and studied the Koran. At school, I could feel like a normal child.

I was afraid to tell my mother what my father was doing to me. I knew how much she loved him. She would run home from work ecstatic, with a bottle of vodka and pirogues, oval-shaped dumpling stuffed with boiled chopped eggs and onions. She ran home as fast as she could to kiss her lovely husband! We ate at a round table covered with old black and white newspapers. They drank vodka and hugged each other; they talked about their youthful adventures.

The evenings generally ended with a loud fight and many insults. Afterwards, the police would arrive. My poor little brothers hid under the table. They were scared to death by the whole scene. There's a saying in Russia that if a man beats you, it means that he loves you. Virtually every woman in my country lived with that belief.

By sheer luck, a pastor from America arrived at the religious school. As a result, there was an opportunity for three kids to go to America. Somehow, the pastor had gotten permission from the authorities of Belarus and America. I was one of the chosen. A visa wasn't a problem for a minor, we were told, and I could stay as long as the visa was valid.

When my mother learned of my intention to go to America, she was livid. She called me a traitor. She blamed me for deserting the family. She said I was running like a dog from reality and my native land. But her scorn meant nothing to me. I knew it was my only chance.

Before my departure, I finally told my mother about the sexual abuse. She responded by calling me an ungrateful viper. She said I was fabricating the whole story in order to ruin her poor life. My revelation was yet another occasion for my parents to get drunk. This is the last memory I have of my mother and father together.

I celebrated my fifteenth birthday in America. I was surrounded by good people and got lots of gifts and attention. I've never experienced so much encouragement. In America, I learned what it was like to eat tasty food. I learned how to dress nicely and to walk freely in the park. I learned about generosity. I felt this was the way a normal life should be and I loved it. The God-fearing family I lived with even offered to adopt me. As a result, I would never have to return to Belarus.

When I called home, the phone was always answered by a crying brother or drunk parents. Every time I called, I was reminded of the ugly life I used to live and just how much I never wanted to return.

A decision finally had to be made. I had to choose America or Belarus. I called my family in Belarus. My mother was drunk and barely able to speak. She informed me that my father had suffered a stroke. A week later, he died. Due to my mother's constant drinking, she lost her job. The family was left without a breadwinner. There was no money for them to live on.

My three brothers quit school. They gathered empty alcohol bottles wherever they could find them. They exchanged them for money and brought bread and milk. That was the most they could earn. I imagined the scene: my mother perpetually drunk and my brothers always hungry. They wouldn't be able to go to school. I wondered if they would die of hunger.

This meant only one thing. My brothers would disappear; they would become thieves and end their lives in jail. I had no choice but to return. I felt responsible for them. I was sure that in Belarus I would be able to find a position as a salesperson in a food store. I believed by working there I would be able to get free food and earn a little money as well.

I went back to Belarus after I had a taste of life in a caring family. I flew back home because I wanted to be supportive and useful to my mom. I wanted to help her to raise my brothers. My mother said that since I complained to her about my father's sexual abuse, I was already a little whore! *Why was I wasting my time?* I wondered. She said that if the female dog didn't want it, then the male dog wouldn't jump on her. She accused me of trying to cause problems between her and her husband. She blamed me and said that I would be just another mouth that she would have to feed. She advised me that instead of buying newspapers with the last of my money, I should just go and work as a prostitute. She wanted me to earn money and to help her. But I was so afraid, I didn't think I could do it.

For two weeks, I went through interviews to be a salesperson. All the store windows I passed were stacked with delicious food. I hardly could keep myself from stealing a chain of sausages. I could be hungry, but I couldn't bear to see my brothers go to bed and wake up with empty stomachs.

However, employers didn't want to hire me. They thought I was too young and not responsible enough to count money and sell food. Ten interviews and not one good result. My legs were swollen from walking all those miles. I had no money to spend on transportation. How unfair was this? I could have my passport at fourteen. I could have an abortion. But I couldn't have a common job? I hated this life.

One day, I walked down Rasputnaya Street. I noticed so many girls. They dressed in high heels and wore too much make-up. But there was no way they would be unnoticed. I walked up to one of them. I asked if she made a lot of money. She said she did and pointed her finger at a red Toyota Corolla as it drove up. The window was opened. A Georgian guy named Selim motioned for me.

He wore sun glasses and told me get in the car. I did. I had nothing to lose. I needed money badly. He asked if I wanted to work. When I said yes, we drove around for a few blocks. He asked if I had worked before. I was scared. I lied, I said I had. He told me that my spot would be at the third light on Rasputnaya Street and no one else would stand there. When he brought me a client, I would share the money I earned with him fifty/fifty. Anything extra would be mine. Prices are the same everywhere he told me. But I didn't know how much to ask for. He repeated that it cost twenty dollars for a fuck, ten dollars for a blow job, and twenty-five dollars for anal sex. I was sweating. He said I had to work six days without fail, and could have one day off. I needed to be dressed sexy and made-up dramatically.

I had to think about this. I had one more interview at the food store the next day. Dear God, I thought, please be good to me and give me this job. But I didn't get it. Couldn't they have seen that I desperately needed to work? It just wasn't fair. Life is not fair. My brothers had forgotten the smell of food. My mother devoured me with vulgar eyes. So I decided to become a prostitute.

Now I was so afraid. But I found a skirt I used to wear six years ago. It looked like a miniskirt. I borrowed my mother's high-heel boots. I put on makeup and curled my hair. I was ready to give this a try, but what if nobody wanted me?

I looked at myself in the mirror. Nothing special. Tiny lips, small brown eyes, freckles and thin hair. I didn't know what to do. God forgive me.

I forgot my purse. I'm superstitious. If you forget something when you leave your house, you can't come back. If you do, then you will have a bad day. I didn't want my first day to be bad so I decided to stay home. I would start tomorrow. I was scared.

Next day, I didn't think about anything. I will go, I decided, stand on my spot and, in the morning, I will bring home money. I am going to do this.

Selim placed me on my spot. I stood in my mother's boots. My legs were shaking; they looked like pencils in a cup. I was sure I needed to buy new boots or gain some weight. There was competition out there. All the girls were my age, sixteen to eighteen years old. They would hate me, because I was the newcomer.

People say newcomers are lucky. My luck arrived in an old Russian factory jeep. It stopped in front of me. Here he was: my first client. He asked me to move around and let him touch my butt. When he did, I wanted to spit in his old prune face and watery lustful eyes. Selim came up to us and got the money. This old guy brought me to a cheap hotel with a seven-foot-long room and dirty sheets. He didn't even ask my name which was a good thing since I hadn't made one up yet. I didn't ask nor care about his name. I was so frightened that I almost peed in my panties.

This first experience of what men call love was a baptism of fire. My client, oh my God, how terrible he was. And how scary. It was disgusting to see that something dangling between his legs. I never thought that a penis so terrible looking could become so dangerous when it's hard. It brought back the sick memory of what my father did to me.

The guy acted like he was crazy. He ripped off his clothes in just a few seconds. He pushed me down with his heavy, hairy body. He was consumed by lust. That idiot even damaged my new bra. As he did, I thought: What will I wear now?

All the while, he whispered to me: "Oh daughter, my little daughter." The bastard was a pedophile. I was sure. He thrust himself inside of me. I yelled and started to scream. I was told that losing your virginity was like a mosquito bite. But for me, it was like somebody was drilling a spike up to my stomach. My screaming turned him on. He probably thought that he was great in bed. I was dying from the pain.

He came. Thank God it was over.

I laid there straight as a stick and cold as steel. I felt crushed, destroyed. I felt that he took something of mine away, something special that I'd been saving for my future husband. I cried. He left without paying attention to me. I jumped from the cheap bed and ran to the shower. I scrubbed myself with soap for an hour. I felt that I would be dirty forever. I was afraid I would never be clean again. When I came out of the shower there was one hundred and fifty rubles, equal to ten dollars, on the table. That's all I was worth. It was enough to buy food for my little brothers. Theirs stomachs were swollen from hunger. Oh God, I thought, food or no food, I won't be able to do this again. It's too filthy.

Six months passed. One day, I fucked three idiots. One was worse than the other. The first one was a midget. I gave him a blow job because his penis wasn't big enough to wear a condom. The second was Greek. He paid me what I wanted but afterwards I could not sit on my butt. It was too painful. The third was a Russian and he was greedy. He haggled with me to save a few rubles on a blow job. Still at the end of the day, I was able to buy school uniforms for my brothers and new school books.

I finally bought my own high-heel boots and a new mini skirt. That day I thought, *I will beat my competitors*. My best friend became my red lipstick. My boyfriend was a pack of "Polet" cigarettes. Condoms to me were as essential as water.

Every time I had a new paying client, he became my love. But I knew really that only the money could fuck my body. It may be true that these men might recognize me during the day by looking in my empty and vacant eyes. But the night would come and my eyes would again become provocatively bright. Again and again, I sold myself as a fake. No doubt, I had become a cheap and used relation of my true self. Yet I was strong. I would survive this for my beloved brothers.

Four days before the New Year of 2005, I earned a hundred dollars. I decided to buy lots of gift for my brothers. I would buy tangerines and candy and a bottle of Stolichnaya vodka for my mother, so that she could get drunk and fall asleep. Oh! I would have to make sure I left enough money for condoms. During the holidays, the work load would be heavy.

At midnight of New Year's Eve, when the clock chimes twelve times and the honorable Vladimir Lukashenko wishes our families all the best, I will make a wish. I will wish that I can quit prostitution next year and attend night school. Also, I will wish for my brothers to always be healthy, and for my mother to stop drinking.

POSTSCRIPT

In mid-2006, the interpreter for this story returned to Belarus and sought Natasha. She could not be located. But a friend, Marina, told her that Natasha had been murdered on that same New Year's Eve. Her body was found in a forest on the outskirts of town. A police investigator said that Natasha, like so many others, was probably killed by one of her clients or by a pimp who had made an example of her for not bringing in enough money. Natasha's dream had been to return to the United States. She was eighteen when she died.

Her mother had dealt with the death by getting drunk and throwing herself under a train. Natasha's brothers were separated and sent to different boarding schools. The interpreter had given Marina one hundred and fifty dollars for Natasha's diary. Marina spent the one hundred and fifty dollars on a gravestone for Natasha.

Chapter 6
THEY CAN'T TAKE
AWAY YOUR DREAMS

Since the fifth grade, as soon as English lessons appeared on my school schedule, I knew without a doubt that when I grew up, I'd go to America and become a famous musician. At first, everybody only nodded, knowing that it was just the dream of a child. As an old Russian saying goes: "To dream is not forbidden, it is forbidden not to dream."

The chance that someone would notice my talents in this area seemed remote. Everybody must have thought that I would only get to see American movies and magazines. Realistically, the best I could hope for was to perform several times at the local conservatory. Then, for the rest of my life, I would teach music at a school, for pennies in Russia.

My name is Lika. I was born to a poor family in Voronezh, Russia. I am now twenty-three years old. I have a nice figure, although some call me skinny. This may sound ridiculous to you, but I am a musician in my soul and a strip dancer in real life. I am still a romantic person. I still believe in miracles. I forgot a long time ago what it is to live for my musical ambitions.

I spend all my waking hours in an inappropriately named "VIP Gentlemen's Club." I cannot afford to have a day off even for illness. I have so much to accomplish and so little time. For the near future, this will be my life's work unless a miracle happens and I meet my Prince Charming. He will take me away from this castle of topless witches, who fight each other for every dollar that a man might press into her G-string.

I don't need an alarm clock in the morning because I come back from the club around seven a.m. During the afternoon, the manager of the club wakes me up to make sure that I will work my shift that night. This is the most rude and hurtful call I could get. It puts me back into a state of sadness and melancholy. When I stop feeling sorrow for myself, I get ready, wash my dresses, choose the night's costume—deciding between the low cut dress of a mysterious vamp and an innocent school-girl costume.

I always think of the city where I was born. I was surrounded by familiar people and things: friends, classmates, my childhood home, and family. I miss Voronezh with its tree-lined streets and the poor half-ruined apartment houses of the Khrushchev era. We lived in such a tenement building with small rooms and a six-foot-long kitchen. We had hot water only in the winter and only for certain brief hours.

My reality today is very different and predictable: the same phone call every day from gossips who I work with; the same worn dresses and the same worn shoes. Even in America, I still pray for a better tomorrow.

I live in a one-bedroom apartment that I share with a colony of ants and assorted cockroaches. I don't want a better place. I am saving all my money for the future. Still, I am overwhelmed by the constant odor of smelly garbage containers in this ghetto of New York. The ability to survive as a night-club dancer in one of the cheapest clubs in New York, and to put away my savings, preserves my dream of being a musician. It is all that sustains me.

I was talented. I was told that I had a remarkable sense of humor and could grip in flight any note in every musical range. I could compose melodies with ease beautifully.

I played the violin and the piano and frequently performed at school. My classmates called me a musical genius. But now I use my talent to strip while twirling around a bar and hoping that men will give me money because I give them erections.

When I was young, as often happens with talented children who are born into poor families, my future was bleak. The amount of money my family had was barely enough to feed me and my three younger sisters. We dressed in old clothes handed down from sister to sister. I was lucky to be the eldest because I usually got new clothes, unless they were from my mom's old trunk.

My parents could not afford to pay for my education. I, with my talents, was forced to enter a professional school of cooking. But what is there for a cook to do when there is so little food in our country? I had to bring food from the house to school in order to learn how to cook. So, I learned every possible way to prepare meals from carrots, since that was the only food we had in our home.

After my eighteenth birthday, I planned to move to America. I dreamed about this moment almost from the time I was in diapers. I remember proudly telling my schoolmates, "You'll all hear about me! Just give me a little time and we will be famous." At other times I said. "I'll move to America and you'll send me greetings. You'll watch me on television. You'll show my school pictures and tell everyone that you played hide-and-seek with me when we were children. I'll achieve my goals no matter what. The United States is already stretching out her arms and waiting for me—the new talent on the horizon." I absolutely was certain that my low status would disappear and that everybody would be proud of me.

There was no doubt in my mind that newspapers and magazines would write stories about the improbable successes of the young Russian protégé who became a famous musician and an overnight millionaire. I remember my girlfriends telling me that I would end my days sitting on the trash containers of New York with a sign begging for money. They thought that, as they say in Russia, "It's better to have a titmouse in your hand than a crane in the sky." But I honestly believed that my star would shine. The main thing was to move from my hopeless situation in my homeland. Life's solutions seemed so certain when I was young.

In the movies, everything usually occurs predictably and ends beautifully. Your prince comes to you to rescue you in his snow-white Mercedes. His wallet is thick with one-hundred-dollar bills, ready to be at your disposal for the realization of all your dreams. Unfortunately, in real life, the prince turns out to be a frog with an old Honda and your dreams seldom come true. You find yourself in a strange country where you don't know anyone and where no one wants to know you. In the eyes of your potential employers, you are just an immigrant who must go through hell and overcome all kinds of difficulties before you are even considered an American.

As an immigrant, no one is interested in your dreams even if you are very talented. If you don't have any money to invest in yourself or an influential patron, usually a pensioner's age, and with whom it is necessary to play his game of love and live by his rules, then you are out of luck.

In Russia, I persistently attempted to learn English on my own. But I worked first as a waitress in an Armenian café at the market, then as a cleaning woman in different stores. It's easier to name the places I didn't work. All the money I saved, I carefully put into an empty chocolate box that was appropriately called "dream." I hid it under the mattress of my wooden bed.

My parents had no time to care for me. Each morning you could see them both near the subway with signs on their chests begging, "Give an invalid of the third degree" some money for medicine and food for our children. In Russia, there are three classes of disability. The third is the worst one.

Afterwards, you could see them near the beer stall with used shopping bags. They would be full of empty bottles. My parents exchanged the bottles for money. After receiving the money, they bought a new bottle of vodka. They drank vodka instead of buying food for us. This went on every day.

To me, it was shameful. My heart was torn up by the sight of my perpetually drunk parents. All of their evenings ended with fights. Often, the neighbors called the police. I knew that I would never become like them. To me, these were not my parents. These were only their remains.

Since childhood I have always hated two things: dentists and vodka. The dentists did not regularly have Novocain or other pain killers. The patients or their families had to obtain them, if they were even able to do so, through the black market or from a pharmacy, often with the help of some bribe money. In my case my mother would bring a bottle of medicine with me to the dentist's office and had me drink it before I went in to have my teeth drilled. I didn't know which was worse, the medicine or the drilling. I do not remember when I realized that the "Medicine" my mother had me drink was actually vodka! I said I would never drink vodka because of what it had done to my parents. I still associated the dentist and vodka in my mind as somehow related.

It was impossible for me to survive this way in Russia, to gather bottles and exchange them for a loaf of black bread or milk. I wanted to become successful. I didn't want people to point their fingers at me and cross the road quickly for fear of being contaminated by my presence. I didn't want to become like my parents.

One of my friends said that it was possible to find good work and earn money in Voronezh. She thought that I could marry a good husband, have children, and live a happy life like everyone else. She gave examples of people she knew in Voronezh who lived happy lives. They had jobs, families, and homes. It wasn't necessary to go anywhere else in order to attain this. In my friend's mind, it was possible to build your life in our own city.

But I didn't want to be like everybody else. I believed that every person is the creator of his own fate. The main thing, I thought, was to want something badly enough and to work towards that goal. Even then, I believed that my girlfriend was just envious.

Half a year later, I found an advertisement in a newspaper. It said that they were looking for young girls aged eighteen to twenty-five who were attractive and spoke English. To me, this did not appear suspicious. I saw on television how beautiful people walked down the streets of New York. I thought that the advertisement represented my opportunity and the solution to my problems.

Work as a waitress in a New York restaurant was offered in one of the ads. After seeing this help-wanted ad, my heart started to beat faster. I believed that my chance had finally come. I remember whispering to myself, "Thank you, dear Lord, for listening to my prayers and giving me this opportunity. This is my dream come true." I said to myself, "America, I'm coming! I'm already half way there!"

With these thoughts, I went to the office address mentioned in the ads. They greeted me politely. They said that this was one of the most elite restaurants in New York, and had been recently opened. They said the restaurant was quite successful but that there weren't enough Russian-speaking waitresses. They even showed me pictures of the restaurant. They described the customers and the custom of tipping, which I had never heard about before. In the evenings, I imagined that I would work at the restaurant and, in the daytime, I would audition my talents at various music studios. They told me that the company would supply me with a place to stay.

Without fully considering everything, I signed all the papers and agreed to take this job. It never occurred to me that this could be a trap. But then again, I probably didn't want to think about that possibility. All I thought about was that after several weeks, my American dream would become reality. I said goodbye to my family and friends and went to the airport on my long-awaited "voyage to happiness." After agonizing hours of awaiting the flight, it was finally announced that the passengers were welcomed by "Aeroflot" airlines.

"Here is happiness, the freedom of life, and the country of where my desires will be realized," I wrote in my diary. When I arrived in New York, people took me to the promised apartment.

It is the same apartment I live in now. Dmitriy, my future "manager," picked me up and said that we should go shopping and get an appropriate uniform for me. On the way to the mall, Dmitriy explained to me that the restaurant had changed management and been turned into a night-club. The waitresses were supposed to dance and entertain the customers. He told me that now my tips would be even better.

We got my first uniform at a Victoria's Secret store. At that moment, I was so amazed by the beauty of underwear that I didn't fully understand what was happening. The first day of work arrived. I had to work from 3 p.m. until 3 a.m. It was Christmas time and they dressed me in a Santa Claus hat, red boots, and a red bra with a white fur trim. They asked me if I could dance and, after my first glass of champagne, I proudly told them that I was a musician, that I can feel music, and that I had studied ballet.

Later that evening, two girls who were dressed like me, went up on the stage. They danced slowly. Then they took off their bras in front of all those men. I was bewildered. The girls were smiling and moved their panties to let the guys touch them with their hands and put dollar bills inside. When they announced that Lika would soon come on stage, I gave up. I realized that I couldn't take off my underwear and be almost like a porn actress. The other girls told me everything you do is just pretending. It's like in the theater, but the idea was to show men the sexy parts of your body and get tipped with higher denomination bills. I ran out of the club.

Dmitriy came after me. He gave me a cigarette. It was the first time I had ever tried one. He explained to me that I had signed a contract in Russia. They paid for my plane tickets and visa. They bought my costumes and gave me a place to live. He was very calm and didn't raise his voice. He simply explained that nobody would make me dance or take my passport away. Everything was under my control.

If I didn't want to work for them, I would have to pay off all the expenses they had advanced for me. I would have to pay seven thousand dollars and I would have no place to live. I had just one hundred dollars in my pocket and didn't know what to do. All my dreams were ruined in an instant. I sat on the stairs in front of the club and cried. I knew that I was trapped and that nobody would help me. I didn't know anybody. I knew that I couldn't go to Voronezh. I didn't want the poor life I left behind. I didn't want to sit with a sign on my chest begging for money. I didn't want to work as a housekeeper. I was ashamed to go back and live with no money. I didn't want alcohol to be my one and only source of entertainment. I didn't want any of my friends in Russia to tell me that I was a loser.

Lolita, another Russian stripper, came outside and sat with me. She gave me a hug and said to calm down. She told me that the club was managed by nice people. She said that if I don't dance, then I should bring the money I owed them and they wouldn't keep me here. Lolita told me a Russian proverb: "It's better to try and regret it later than not having tried." She said that I could easily play the role of a stripper. She said that she would teach me a few tricks and motions and that I would be ready. We went to the dressing room and she brought a bottle of champagne. She taught me while I drank and alternately I practiced while she drank. One bottle was not enough. When the DJ announced, "Lika, our star," we had already drunk three bottles of champagne.

I was warm and ready. I started to dance in the Latino style. I don't know where I learned it. Men looked at me with their mouths hanging open and it made me feel professional. I thought that maybe in another life, I was a dancer. However, when I waved my leg, suddenly my high-heeled shoe flew off and hit one of the men in the forehead. I easily took off my bra and got the first "shower" of my life. A "shower" is when a rich customer changes a one hundred dollar bill into singles and a waitress comes up on the stage and throws them at me. After another glass of champagne, the DJ couldn't get me off the stage. I earned three hundred dollars that first night and I didn't even talk to the customers. All the money came from dancing on the stage. From that moment, my life became banal and absolutely the opposite of my expectations.

The next day, I was supposed to work again. I was nervous. I went to the mall with my three hundred dollars and bought a long red dress with a high slit and low neck line, and a mask of the devil. That night at the bar, I went to up to a forty-year-old man with a long beard. He was a biker dressed in leather. I asked him if he wanted to have a lap dance. We went upstairs. I was trying so hard to be sexy, but I didn't know what to do. I imitated a horse fucking! He liked it. He kept on saying, "Yes baby!" and "You're a real devil." Somehow, it made me feel that I was in control and I liked it. It made me feel that all men could be managed with sex or a mere suggestion of it. No man could resist a woman who was sexually attractive and wild in bed. And I started to be wild. I was nasty with everybody and the men liked it. Since I was a devil, I had no problem with hitting on a guy, grabbing him by his tie, or silently walking up to him and asking him for a dance. I realized that the richer and more powerful the guy, the more he wanted to be controlled and helpless.

Lolita is my only girlfriend, but our friendship begins and ends at the club. I have a boyfriend from the club. He is a married fifty-year-old man named, believe it or not, Lenon. He has a wife who he loves very much. He has three kids and two grandchildren. He is a happy man. But, if I asked why he came to the club, he would tell me that he feels sorry for girls like me. He gave me two thousand dollars for three hours in the private room. We talked, kissed, and he left me a one-thousand-dollar tip. He thinks that he isn't cheating on his wife. It's just the normal process of getting old. His wife doesn't kiss him any more but that's not all he wants. Sometimes I think that I am wrong and shouldn't be having an affair with him. But he cares about me so much that I can't let myself lose him. Plus, I do have my brothers who need my support. Lenon gives me a lot of financial support.

My music career hasn't started yet. Once, I tried to get a job at a Russian restaurant that features live music. But they fired me the moment they found out that I don't have a green card. They also wanted modern pop music and I played just the great classical music.

I have already spent four years in America. I put those earned green notes into several boxes, each of them has a name: "New apartment in Voronezh," "Help my three sisters," "Back home," and "America." I guess that at the end of this year, I will open each of the money boxes and will determine my future. Will I stay in America or go back to Russia? I don't know the answer yet. Yes, it goes without saying that my life today is different from the life of my friends in Voronezh. I am definitely not like everybody else. But who am I right now? I am sorry that I moved to America. I grew up and, yet, I still believe that miracles will come.

Chapter 7
AT THE END
OF THE RAINBOW

My story started in one of those cities in Russia where it seemed like someone had pressed the pause button many years ago and time had stood frozen ever since. It is a city where alcoholism has become the way of life for many and where kids have to earn money from early childhood to survive. The present for most of us is so difficult that there is no time to worry about the future.

The name of that city is Lipetsk, located in the Moscow District. I was born into a poor family. I didn't know who my father was and he probably didn't know about me either. I have two brothers from different fathers. According to my mother, the men had married her.

One of my brothers was disabled from the moment he was born. Sasha has Down Syndrome. He can probably thank our always drunken, heavy smoking mother, and his biological father. They shared the same unhealthy lifestyle. But, after all, this was old Russia where men couldn't be bothered to waste their money on such luxury items as condoms. Sasha never saw his father. In fact, all the men who made my mother pregnant left her as soon as they found out about her condition. No one wanted to take on any additional responsibilities. They were hardly able to feed themselves.

What can you say about a pregnant woman, unable to work, and already with kids? My unhappy mother continually switched her men because they often beat her and us as well. She was rarely sober enough to notice. Men appeared suddenly and disappeared the same way a few months later. My mother seemed to be living with a perpetually broken heart. She would suffer over each break-up by drinking even more vodka, which for Russians is the mother's milk of sadness. From the age of ten to fourteen, I sold frozen and fresh fish in the local market. I tried to help my mother as much as I could. My mother worked as a tram driver. She never cared about my education and I had less than a consistent attendance record. I can't say that I studied much in school, but, still, I tried. Usually, when I showed up at my classes, I fell asleep. And I failed to do my homework. I had no time to prepare for school.

I needed to work and earn money to survive. I carried ten boxes, weighing thirty pounds each, every day to the marketplace. I didn't even realize how heavy they were. Almost a mile away from my house, depending on the direction of the wind, you could smell the fish. I washed my body a few times a day with soap and sprayed myself with the only perfume my mother owned; it was called "Red Moscow." But the results were not satisfactory.

To this day, I shower very often out of the force of habit. I was nicknamed "Scales" at the market I worked at. But it helped that everybody knew that I sold the best quality fish and never seemed to make a mistake in weight. In reality, I weighed it wrong, but I did it very carefully so nobody would know. I removed the measuring system on the screen of the scales and added new lines and points. The difference wasn't huge, maybe a few ounces. Anyway, nobody complained. On that little weight cheating I earned an extra ruble or two from each customer. At the end of the day it could be enough to buy a pound of oranges.

I always bought something for my little brothers. My mother had lots of reprimanding notes for talking dirty and for drunkenness in her personal book of work. A personal book of work is what we call in Russia an employment log. The first employer starts it for an employee and keeps a record. Necessary details include the place of work, the position, and the salary. It also states past experience and the reason for being fired, if that occurs. In addition, he—for the boss it was always a man—noted praise or complaints such as: "excellent worker," "always late," "thief," "alcoholic," "drug addict," etc. My mother was fired because of alcohol abuse and inappropriate behavior.

My mother's big binges could last for eleven days without stopping for a break. She would sit at the kitchen with eleven two-liter bottles of vodka called "Russkaya," and a length of bologna sausage known as Doctorskaya. When I was a child, I called vodka bitter water.

My mother justified her addiction to alcohol by saying, "I feel bitter in my heart, that is why I drink this bitter vodka."

We always had a fish on our table because I was selling it and could mange to bring pieces home without being noticed. We ate it in every possible variation: fried, boiled, and stroganina. Stroganina is a fresh frozen fish which can be thinly sliced while frozen. For that dish, you need to dip it in a sauce. There are two types of sauces for this. The first one is a mixture of ketchup and grated garlic. The second is a mixture of plain salt and pepper. You have to dip the frozen pieces of fish in either of these sauces. It's a delicious dish which originated in the northern part of Russia.

When I turned fifteen, I started to live with Sergey, my twenty-two-year-old boyfriend. We rented an apartment. I moved in with him not because I loved him or was in love. I just couldn't live with my continually drunk and unhappy mother any more. She even stole the money I earned and was saving for medicine, for my little brother and for healthy food.

When I was eighteen, I started to work as a waitress in a restaurant called "Nadejda." It was the only restaurant in Lipetsk where there were celebrations and edible food. Edible food for us was any food without cockroaches, dead flies, and mice tails. They hired me without any problems. I was thin and pretty enough to serve the food. Once an American delegation came to our city. It was for the reopening of the only fabric factory in town. They were investors and came to celebrate in our restaurant.

Our managers were nervous because foreign people were rarely guests in our God-forsaken town. The banquet started. I was serving dishes with red caviar, stuffed pancakes, and cold-cooked and seasoned pork. My knees were shaking from seeing such delicacies. I had never tried or even seen such lavish dishes. I was afraid that I would drop a plate on the head of one of the guests and get my salary deducted. I served another round.

Richard, an interpreter for one of the Americans asked me if I would like to work as a waitress in America. I had no answer, I never dreamed about that. I told him that I was afraid of lying and didn't know how to speak English. He said that it was nothing to worry about. He explained that girls like me have big opportunities in America. When my work day was over, I told Sergey about the offer I got at the banquet. He said that it was my big chance to run away from poverty and from barely surviving. It was like I was being given the opportunity to glimpse a rainbow where there had been only cloudy skies. But I stupidly missed the lucky opportunity by saying nothing.

However, fate gave me a second chance. The next day, Richard came back to our restaurant. He told me that he would be happy if I would work in his restaurant in America during the summer month. He promised me a free place to live, good tips, and a nice atmosphere. He said he would let me think it over for three days. This time, I agreed on the spot.

We started to make arrangements for my visa. I began to learn English. The day of departure came. I cried very much over leaving my little brothers and even my mother. Two thoughts made me feel better though: I knew that I would come back after three months of working in America, and that I would have earned a lot of money. I wouldn't be able to earn even close to such an amount by working five years in any restaurant in Lipetsk. It was hard to leave Sergey. We had lived together for three years and had become used to each other.

Richard met me at the airport. Even as we drove into the city, I saw New York was a city of lights, skyscrapers and surprising smells. He brought me to his two-story house, which reminded me of the country house in Russia. The walls were thin and painted.

The windows were wide and opened. Richard introduced me to his young Russian wife, Liza. She was in her thirties and a little bit overweight. I remember thinking that she probably gained weight because she was able to eat as much as, and whatever, she wanted in Richard's restaurant.

She was a housewife. They wanted to have kids. Liza was nice but not very communicative. Later, I realized that Russian immigrants are not always really friendly with newcomers. You couldn't do anything about that. Everybody somehow wanted to forget their past life. It's like new country, new life with some other girls. It was a two-bedroom apartment where two friendly Russian girls named Sveta and Luba lived. They had also arrived like I had. Unfortunately, we didn't become close friends because we were working on different shifts and met each other only at the restaurant. I worked longer hours than they did. They wanted money just for fun and shopping. I needed money to support my family in Russia.

We agreed with Richard that I would have more hours to work without days off. It was part of the deal we made in Russia. I explained to him that I had two brothers, that one of them was disabled, and that my mother didn't work.

Richard's pizza restaurant was located on thirty-fourth street in Manhattan. It was light, cozy, and with many varieties of pizza. I tried pizza for the first time in my life and became addicted to it. Every day I had a few slices and, over time, I gained several pounds. I stopped eating so much, but wasn't surprised anymore as to why Richard's wife looked like a doughnut.

From the first day, I worked twelve hours a day. After a week, I sent Sergey three hundred dollars and asked him to buy food and necessary things for my mother and my brothers. I didn't send money to my mother because I knew she would drink it up. Living in America, after a while, I was surprised by the fact that everybody smiled with or without reason. At first, it made me feel different from the others. I thought that they smiled at my beautiful appearance and did that for me only! Later, I realized that all the smiles were for everybody. Richard said, "There are no perfect people." He taught us that if you do something wrong, do it with a smile. I smiled at everybody so much that at the end of every day it felt as if my jaw was paralyzed.

I liked New York very much. It was still amazing to me to hear conversations in foreign languages everywhere. At first I couldn't understand at all what was being said. But, sometimes I found it a big plus being a foreigner. If you didn't want somebody to understand you, then you could speak your native language. When you wanted to be involved in a conversation, you could use English. The plus is that you could not be understood by other people but, at the same time, you would understand them somewhat.

My family in Russia liked the money I sent them every couple of weeks. I wanted to remain in America. It happens sometimes that, from the first minute you see or try something, you have a sixth sense that you knew it before. When I came to America, I knew that I had been here before, probably in one of my other lives. I never had any trouble finding any street in Manhattan. I knew where east and west were, even while surrounded by skyscrapers and with my eyes closed. I felt this was my fate.

Meeting Richard proved it perfectly. Everything was fate: if there hadn't been a dinner celebration and our chance meeting, I would not be in America now. There was no other chance for me to be here. I was from too poor a family to be able to afford the trip. I had no education and couldn't be enrolled in any student exchange program.

But the clock was ticking and my visa was close to expiring. I decided I must remain in America and earn more for my brothers. My roommates told me that if I got married, I would get a green card. This would give me a chance to be in this country legally and to be able to go to Lipetsk and to come back. I had no time for building a serious relationship.

Furthermore, I didn't want to. I knew that Sergey, the man I realized now that I loved, was patiently waiting for me back in

Lipetsk. To tell the truth, there wasn't even anyone who was interested in being my boyfriend. I didn't notice anybody around, but then again, I was too concerned about money. I worked days and evenings. Nights, I cried in a pillow and thought about Sergey.

I decided after talking to other Russian girls that the only choice for me was to make a fake marriage with a citizen and pay him off every month. Through an advertisement in a newspaper, I found a thirty-year-old American who asked for only ten thousand dollars for a marriage. Most wanted more. It was possible to pay him one thousand dollars every month for ten months. That was fine with me because I made seven hundred on tips each week.

My fake husband's name was Steve. We arranged a meeting. When I asked how I would recognize him, he told me that it was almost impossible not to. Steve said he was a strange looking guy. I didn't like that answer, but I decided to meet him anyway. I thought that he might be afraid that the police or INS was checking on him.

I went to the Sheepshead Bay subway platform in Brooklyn. I recognized him from the first minute. He was medium height and a thin guy. He wore glasses and had a backpack. I could see that he needed money badly and I sensed he wouldn't fail me. We went to a coffee shop. I bought him a cup of French vanilla. We discussed everything that same day. We set the day of our wedding ceremony and how we would assemble correct proof of our real-fake relationship and prepare for the interview.

We decided to meet once a week and get some pictures of us together. I said that I would cover all the expenses during these meetings. After a week, we got married at City Hall with the help of an attorney from Brighton Beach. My green card application process started.

When we were getting married, I thought about how wonderful it would be if, instead of Steve, it was with my Sergey. It's funny, but with Steve I matched perfectly as a couple. We were both thin and always smiling. I continued to work and met Steve once a week. I was surprised by his dress style. He was a thirty-year-old man who dressed like a poor student. Steve wore sports pants or cheap jeans, and a rewashed t-shirt in black or yellow. I couldn't understand how you could be born and raised in a rich country and be so poor.

But I liked to talk to him. He was different and that was why he was very interesting and charming. There was something about him that was very naïve. The most important thing I saw in his eyes was a big wish to help me. I remember how shy he was about taking my money from me every month.

I couldn't understand what made him feel so uncomfortable about it. He did his job. Steve played the role of my husband and I paid him for that. He never stopped feeling guilty about taking my hard-earned money. I didn't understand his sympathy, but it made me feel good about him.

Winter came. I started to call Sergey less and less and then stopped altogether. I had come to feel like I was on a different level than he was. He was still a man from Lipetsk who counted dimes and didn't want to look forward. He lived in his own world and took his poor life as fate. He used to say to me that you can't run away from your fate. God has scheduled everything for everybody. Those words always had reduced my dreams and wishes for my life to change.

I already knew a lot about Steve's life and he knew about mine. We became good friends. From the beginning, we agreed to say only the truth to each other. It was easy for us to be believed at the interview. Also it is easier to get lost in lies. The truth is always the same and never changes.

I knew that Steve's parents died in a car accident when he was eighteen years old. He was a student at Boston College where he studied computer programming. He worked part-time in college. He wrote programs in code. The money he got from his parents was hardly enough to pay for his tuition and living expenses. He succeeded at his part-time job and, after graduation, he got an offer to stay on full time.

But he wanted to go back to New York and didn't accept the offer. Since he came to New York, he moved from one company to another. He tried to find intelligent co-workers and a better salary. When I asked him why he didn't have a real girlfriend whom he could marry, he answered that in America all women were very independent and career-minded. Steve said that women don't like losers like him, and if someone did like him, he never liked her. He was sure that he wasn't able to give stability to his potential family and that is why he had no right to have a real one.

He agreed to a fake marriage in order to earn some extra money. Every day I felt more connected with him. He was very well-educated and kind. He understood the Russian mentality. He always tried to help me. But Russian women usually don't ask for help even if it's urgent. Steve couldn't understand that attitude and was always there for me.

We decided to celebrate Christmas together. We took a lot of new family pictures that day. That was the best Christmas and New Year of my life. Steve invited me to his modest apartment and cooked dinner. We talked and laughed a lot. We danced. In January, when I tried to give him the thousand dollars, he wouldn't take it. He asked me if I liked him. I said that I had never met such an amazing person in my life.

Suddenly, Steve kissed me. He said that he fell in love with me the first moment we met. He reminded me how I came with an important look to talk about a fake marriage. I explained to him that he could only count on the money each month, but no sex. I didn't know what to say about his declaration of love. I took a cab and went home. I couldn't understand how he could have lived in America whole life and yet the atmosphere in his apartment wasn't alive and comfortable.

The next day, I went to work. At the end of my shift, he came to see me. I waited for him. I missed him. That day, he came with flowers and said that he couldn't live without me. My heart started to beat fast. I felt that I loved him. And I was so lonely. I always tried to rely on myself. We went for a walk and he asked me to move into his apartment.

Steve explained to me that if I agreed to be with him, although he didn't have much to offer, he would love me forever even if he couldn't offer me financial security. He also said that if I decided not to be his girlfriend, we would remain good friends. He still wanted me to move in with him until the interview was final. He told me that at the interview, an officer would even ask about my menstrual cycle and where we kept the extra toilet paper. I knew we had to be ready.

Steve was my best friend. I also didn't like to live alone. I agreed and said that I would let him know what I thought our relationship should be in a few days. We set the date for my move. He said he would come with a big van and help me.

That day, I realized that I loved him very much. I knew that together we would be able to achieve the goals we had. We had to be one team and support each other. Steve came. I told him about my thoughts and feelings. He gave me a hug and thanked me for giving him a chance. We loaded all my things in the van. I looked at him driving and liked everything. I had gotten used to his style of clothes, his glasses at the end of his nose, and the way he talked. I loved him just the way he was. Later, I noticed that we were driving to Manhattan. We stopped in front of an expensive, attractive building with a doorman and security cameras all around. I got lost in my thoughts.

We went to the seventh floor. I remember when he pressed the button in the elevator; I thought that it was a lucky number. I thought that maybe we had stopped to visit one of his friends because we didn't take my suitcases. Steve asked me to wait outside of the apartment. A few minutes later, he opened the door. I went in.

The whole apartment was decorated with fresh flowers and lit candles. Steve got on his knees in front of me and held a jewelry box in his hand. I was shocked; I felt like I was in a fairy tale. I looked at him. I didn't recognize him. In front of me was an elegantly dressed man in an expensive business suit. His apartment was expensively furnished. I didn't care about his money. I looked at him and smiled. I wanted to jump on top of him, to hug and kiss him. But I couldn't move.

Steve was crying. He told me that he came up with the whole ten-thousand-dollar fake marriage scheme because all the girls he dated only cared about his money. He saw it as a test to find a girl who really cared for him and it worked. He asked me to forgive him for the lies, but he said it was lies that saved his life.

It's been one year now since we have been married for real. I am in the last trimester of my pregnancy. I am crazy about this man. I know that no matter what happens, I will always be close to him.

I'll always be here for Steve. Steve, from a poor computer code writer, miraculously turned into a successful businessman. Before our meeting, he had lost any hope of finding a wife who really loved him and of creating a family. All women, it seemed, only wanted money and gifts from him. No one wanted friendship and understanding as the basis of the relationship.

Steve has given me the happiest times of my life. He is everything to me. He is a brother, a lover, a friend, and the father of our future baby. I don't work anymore. I am taking care of my husband and decorating our baby's room. Two times a week, we go to Lamaze.

Steve is learning how to care for our baby. He practised on a baby doll. My family, of course, is still in Lipetsk. I help them a lot. Steve arranged, and paid for, medical treatment for my mother. She has quit drinking. And she has now read so much about the connection between smoking and cancer that she also gave up smoking. My mother, along with my brothers, will come to visit us this summer.

We will take my little disabled brother to the best doctors in America. I am the happiest woman in the world. I know that when you do everything in your life with an open heart and good thoughts, everything will go in the right direction. You have to be honest with yourself, and then you may find true happiness at the end of the rainbow.

Chapter 8
FOR LOVE
AND MONEY

I arrived from Kiev in the Ukraine, on July 4, 1999. It was a very special day for my new country and for me. I was supposed to come with my husband Victor. I loved him very much and devoted myself to him. He was forty years old; I was twenty-three. I knew that I would love, and be loved by him, from the moment we met. We met on my eighteenth birthday. We got married when I was nineteen. We lived happily; our souls intertwined. We always had money. Nothing bad ever happened to us. The only sad thing was that we never had kids. We were trying very hard to conceive, but it didn't happen. We visited lots of doctors and each of them had their own theories. Some doctors said that Victor was infertile; others said that we were not compatible. They had all sorts of medical explanations, but, in the end, it was very sad. Victor believed that there was a treatment abroad for couples like us. He said that we would go through the course or would undergo artificial insemination as soon as we had a chance to travel abroad.

I was born in Kiev to a modest hardworking family. I was an only child. I can't say they loved me very much. Our daily family life, like those of most of the people in our city, centered on the question of where to get money and how to survive. My mother worked as a kindergarten teacher. My father worked as a painter and a plumber. My parents were never happy about the life we lived. They envied the families who lived better lives than we did. Often, we couldn't afford anything.

That is why my childhood wasn't a happy one. I had one doll and wooden cubes with the Ukrainian alphabet to help me learn how to write. In school, I studied less than I should have and had average grades. At that time, nobody studied really hard. After all, it made little difference unless you were able to go to a university, and very few were so privileged after graduating from high school. I enrolled in a trade school to become a seamstress. It was the only prospect I had for my future. I could work doing alterations in a store for very little money. I wasn't happy about that. I knew I wouldn't be able to have a good future. I had a problem with drawing a straight line with a ruler since childhood. I had no idea how to sew. At that time, on Russian store counters, there were only four kinds of fabric: cotton, calico, flax, and some wool, so there wasn't that much to sew.

I didn't graduate from the seamstress school. My parents always said that an education wasn't a big deal. The key to a good life was a successful marriage. They meant a marriage to a wealthy man, who would be the happy ticket for their daughter's life and help them, so they too would live a less stressful and more comfortable existence.

We always had soup on the table from a frozen chicken that had turned blue. It stayed in the freezer for a while. Then that unlucky chicken would be kept in a refrigerator for a very long time. After the freezing and defrosting process, the chicken looked marketable. Smart saleswomen of the former Soviet Union then would apply an apricot color on the poor birds. After that, it would be purchased. Before it was put in a pot of boiling water, my mother washed the dye off the chicken, revealing a dark blue corpse. There wasn't even a drop of fat on the malnourished bird. Chickens were raised on a strict diet; the bouillon made from them was pure as water, but still it had the flavor of the meat. We ate soup with homemade noodles. For dessert, we had a homemade pie from rotten apples that my mother bought at a discount. If we didn't eat the pie within a few hours, then it became inedible and attracted many flies.

When I was a little girl, I was told that my family kept some farm animals: sheep, chickens and ducks, so we often had fresh meat on our table. Sometimes my father traded with our next-door neighbor who made homemade vodka. Many people made their own liquor, even though it was illegal, because there was no tax on this brew. It was said that it was stronger than store-bought liquor and without the morning after aches and pains.

Our neighbors also had a compost heap were they put all their waste and other garbage to turn into fertilizer. One day mama's duck escaped from our yard and went to graze on the compost heap next door. That evening my mother returned home to find her prized ducks dead in our neighbor's yard. She cried for her prized birds and for the many meals they would not be served at. Since they obviously had been poisoned they could not be eaten, but my mother did not hesitate to pluck all their feathers off for pillow and comforter stuffing before throwing their sad carcasses out in the trash.

The next morning she awoke to the most unusual sight she had ever seen. The dead ducks had all come back to life! And they were not happy. It turns out that they were not dead, just drunk from our neighbor's vodka waste! And they were not any happier about walking around nude. For months people would walk by our house and laugh at the home with the nude ducks.

At that time of my life, all of this seemed quite the norm. There were no joys and few troubles. Everything seemed monotone. During the second year of my life at the seamstress school, I met Victor. We fell in love and got married. Victor was an orphan. He never knew his parents. That was one of the reasons why we got married so quickly. He desperately wanted to have a family. He was a servant for his Mafioso boss. He carried out his orders. Such people were always considered at the very bottom of the criminal world. But to me, he was a hero. I was always proud of him. My girlfriends always envied me. By comparison with their boyfriends, Victor was very powerful. At that time, to have a new model like his first Toyota, was the height of anyone's dreams. Not to have a set work schedule represented a life of freedom that bordered on fantasy. It was great to have a carefree life and to know that at the end of the month, money appeared in your wallet. The most important thing was not to lose control and appear better off than everyone else. That was the law of the land. He who had money was the winner.

When I was twenty-two, Victor got an American green card. He was very happy. He piously believed that a miracle would happen and we would have our first baby. He was sure that American doctors could deal with all the health problems we had.

We got visas to go to America. At the interview, a representative of an American consulate was surprised that we would go to an unknown country without any English skills. When he asked what would happen if we couldn't get accustomed to life in America, Victor replied that we would return to the Ukraine and would start all over again. The administrator couldn't understand how it was possible to leave a settled life and go into a state of complete helplessness and unemployment.

The plan was set. Our apartment was sold. The suitcases were packed. There were three weeks left before we were to leave for America, our second native land. People say that trouble never comes just once, that it's always followed by more. And so it did. First, my father fell from the tenth floor of the building he was painting. It killed him. Then, during his funeral, my mother had a heart attack and died while embracing his dead body. In the course of three days, I too became an orphan, just like my husband.

That day I dreamt that I was losing my teeth. If you believe in dream interpretations, it means that someone close to you will die. I was sure that it would be my parents. But in my next dream when I dreamt that all my teeth fell out, I began to worry about Victor. Two weeks before our departure, Victor disappeared. He told me that he was going to a pointer and never came back. In the Russian criminal world, a pointer means an arranged meeting of two Mafiosos and their people somewhere out of town. There they would agree upon relations, settle debts, divide territories, etc. He didn't return. I never got to tell him how much I loved him.

Three days later, for the first time in my life, I met Victor's boss, nicknamed "Fly." He looked like an ex-con and had a constant cough, probably from his previous lifestyle. His body was covered with tattoos. He even had a tattoo that read: "Don't wake me up," on his eye lids. On the little finger of his right hand, he wore a huge gold ring with a large diamond. He handed me an envelope with a gold cross on a chain that had belonged to Victor. He said that he was sorry and advised me to leave the Ukraine as soon as possible. Fly explained to me that Victor did something very bad with their competitors and paid for it with his life. He said that these people would demand money from me because I was Victor's wife. He told me to go to America. As the saying goes: where there is no man, there are no problems.

I had the tickets in my hands. I felt a raging fear, pain, and complete hopelessness. Six days remained until my departure. The first three days, I drank Russian vodka like a fish. I placed a smiling picture of Victor in front of me. I cried. I kept the Russian tradition of placing a shot of vodka covered with a salted piece of dark bread in front of his picture. We believe that when a person dies, the soul comes back to say goodbye, to grieve together with those he or she left behind, and to drink a final shot of vodka. After several days, the vodka disappeared from the glass; the piece of bread became smaller as it absorbed all the vodka. We simply choose to believe and don't want to accept the real nature of the process. We don't want to accept the fact that evaporation had occurred. We do this because everyone always did it before us and will probably continue to do so after us.

After four days, I began to eat a little. I had a piece of bread with buttered red-salmon caviar. On the fifth day, I picked up the phone and got a threatening call demanding debts I knew nothing about. I was scared. I called my acquaintance and arranged a meeting with her. When I left the apartment, I noticed that somebody followed me. I began to run and hurt my knee; it bled. I kept telling myself that I would remain in the country for the sake of being near my husband's grave. Later that night, through the window of my already sold apartment, came a big stone. It changed my mind; I called Fly and asked him to give me a safe ride to the airport the next day. On departure day, an armored, metallic Mercedes jeep arrived to pick me up. Fly came himself with two tall bodyguards who surrounded me and my suitcases in the car. It looked like a tank. On the way to the airport, Victor's boss told me that I better stay abroad at least five years until all is forgotten.

I took a seat on the plane and cried during the entire flight. I didn't know what I would do in America without Victor and with only one word of English. I had $10,000 in my pocket when I arrived in America. That was nothing for a newcomer according to the Russian cab driver who took me from JFK to Brooklyn for $200.

He drove me to a strange woman named Clara. She was so overweight that no one could touch every part of her body in one night. She constantly chewed on cabbage leaves, explaining that it helped to grow bigger breasts. I didn't know why on earth she wanted bigger breasts. They looked like sacks of potatoes in their homemade bra. Clara was famous for helping people find a job and a place to live. She said she charged little money for her big help. For instance, she charged $500 to find you a housekeeping job where you lived with the family. You also had to give her your first three salary checks, which equaled $1,000.

I decided that I would find a job myself. I rented a basement for $150 per night. The basement was very small with a big mattress on the floor, a toilet, a little stove and a refrigerator. I stayed for a while, but every day I tried to find a place to work and a decent place to live. At the end of the month, I had $1500 left.

One day, I came back from the city and saw a woman sitting and crying on the mattress. That was the day I got a roommate. Her name was Natasha, or so she said. She seemed to be a good woman and I was sincerely happy that I had somebody to talk with. During the night, we told each other the stories of our lives and felt sympathy towards each other. We decided to do everything together.

The next morning, when we woke up and went outside, we were shocked. We looked identical, like two drops of water. The only difference was that Natasha's hair was a little longer and not as curly. It was amazing because we even had birthmarks on the same part of the face. It was very strange. I was from the Ukraine; she was from Krasnodar.

One day, it was my turn to do the shopping. I came back eight hours later. Natasha wasn't at home. I noticed that all of my documents were stolen. I didn't know what to do. I cried and waited for Natasha to return so I could tell her the bad news. I didn't go and complain to Clara because she was in Miami for the weekend. Natasha didn't show up for two days. I started to worry. I told Clara that Natasha must have been kidnapped. But Clara explained to me that Natasha left three days ago and said that she had solved her problems with the help of a new acquaintance.

I understood everything. Clara advised me not to call the police unless I wanted to spend the rest of my life in an immigration prison. I didn't understand the law. I didn't have proof of my identity. It would not be safe for me to return home. I didn't know what to do. Clara told me that I looked like an intelligent woman and that she would find me a job for free. She also invited me to live with her for $600 a month; she had a private room upstairs. I had the money to pay for the first month's rent and to feed myself. I imagined that Natasha had cut her hair, made it curly, and turned herself into the new me with my passport and documents for a green card.

One day, Clara said that she had arranged a job interview at a Dunkin' Donuts coffee shop. I was supposed to meet a Georgian man named Goga. Clara said that I would recognize him by his long nose and that he would be dressed in sport pants, hat and classic shoes.

I couldn't believe my good fortune. I quickly applied make up, put on a business suit that Victor had brought me from Turkey, and rushed to the meeting. I looked nice. I had curly, shoulder-length chestnut hair, large blue eyes, and full pink lips. I lost a few pounds during the two months of living in America; I looked even better. I was still a 32D bra size, had a small waist, and a firm butt.

Twenty feet away from the coffee shop, I already recognized Goga. To say that he had a big long nose was quite the understatement. Like the old saying goes: the nose grew for seven people, but only one got it. As soon as I arrived, he said that I looked like a doll and had the shape of a sex bomb. He said that girls like me never lie on a shelf and get covered with dust.

I asked him what position I was being offered. Goga looked at me, smiled, and said that they would hire me as an assistant to the minister of sexual relations in the corrupted community of America. I didn't understand, but it sounded like a solid job. I was curious and asked how he could give me that job if I didn't know the language. He said that if I didn't ask, I would live longer. All I needed was to have a working body, and Goga said I had that.

He said that the earnings would be a stable $2,000 a week and that I'd be working sixteen hours a day, five days a week, servicing clients from 5 p.m. to 9 a.m. daily. He said that it could lead to a great career and a bright future if I could go from a simple escort girl to a VIP girl for major customers with big money. I knew I couldn't exist in any other manner. I didn't need to think; I agreed. My working days began. The first three years, I worked more than all the other girls. Clients were contrary and rude most of the time. My first client was a thirty-five-year-old Mexican. He fucked me so hard that for a week I couldn't urinate without pain. There were Russian clients also. They would take me for several hours and would humiliate me for disgracing the Russian nation. Afterwards, they offered to help me with my life. Then they had sex with me and, at the end of the session, they would declare their love and ask me for my cell phone number so they could meet me outside of work, of course, free of charge.

I had a regular Chinese boyfriend. He took me out in the evenings. We had candlelit dinners and then went to his bedroom.

There, he would open up a Karma Sutra book and would try new positions with me as shown on the page he selected. He wasn't that interested in intercourse as much as he was in successfully duplicating all the positions in the book. I am sure that the people who invented Karma Sutra would pay big money just to see people try so hard to duplicate all of their fantasies in bed. We stopped all the experimentation one day when he injured his penis.

For three years I worked like a nonstop sex machine. Eventually, I got sick. I went to the gynecologist and, after I went through all the examinations, I was told that I had a lowering womb, and a malignant tumor. I had only one choice. After the surgery, I knew that I would never be able to have children or experience an orgasm. I had a wonderful doctor. He was a thirty-year-old blond effeminant seeming man named Misha. He knew about my job and lifestyle. He didn't judge me and used to say that at first you work for money and then money works for you.

Two weeks after the surgery, I was supposed to stay at home. I didn't work. One day I decided to see how much money I had earned during the three years. It was $300,000 in cash. I didn't know what to do with the money. Somehow, I became friends with Misha. We would go for coffee at Starbucks. I decided to open my own escort agency. I needed someone to help me. Misha agreed. We invested $100,000. We rented a five-room apartment, furniture and hired the girls. Misha offered that, since we worked together, it would be nice to live together. He saw fear and anger in my eyes. He told me that I had nothing to worry about because he was unhappy and he just did not want to be lonely. So, we lived together. Business went perfectly. It brought in a big income and everybody was happy.

But not our competitors. One day, there was a police raid and most of the girls were arrested. The worst thing was that Misha was there during the raid and went to jail with the girls. I found a lawyer who handled such problems. I paid $45,000 and a few days later everybody was free. Misha was smart enough to make up a story that he was a client who went there after seeing an advertisement in a newspaper. He didn't get a record.

That day I didn't know what to do next. I walked the streets and felt sorry for myself and for Victor. I found myself in front of a school for disabled children and orphans. Some of them cried, others talked or laughed. At that moment, I realized that I wasn't the one who had anything to feel sorry about. Those kids looked at me and every one of them hoped that I would adopt him or her. I went back another day. They remembered me. I went often and looked at them. A little black boy named Jayson was in a wheelchair. Every time I arrived, he was dressed in different t-shirts. He followed me on his wheelchair. He just looked at me and smiled.

I understood at that moment, that it was them and not me that had a bad life. I thought how they must suffer and hate their fates. I knew I had no right to complain. I could no longer visit those children empty handed. I realized that it wasn't a zoo or a circus, but that these kids needed somebody's care and warmth and that I could give it to them. I began to bring them gifts and medicine. I hired clowns to perform for them and to make them laugh. Once, I talked with Misha about these kids. We decided that we would adopt two of them, but would also provide as much as we could for all of them.

We adopted little Jayson and a five-year-old Japanese girl named Vanessa. I reopened the escort agency, but without Misha. If he got into trouble, then we would lose our kids and a chance to adopt more.

Yes, lots of young girls work for me. Money is the number one objective to them. Nothing else matters. But I can't say anything and I can't judge them because I was one of them. I do not spend the money I am earning on expensive things and a luxurious lifestyle. Almost everything I earn I give to the children so they can have better lives.

Misha and I recently got married. He offered to help me with my papers. I don't need a man in my bed. The one I need, I have. Misha is my best friend, a perfect father for our kids and a strong shoulder for me to lean on. I hope that I am the same for him. I am not jealous of Misha's boyfriends, but he doesn't go out with them a lot.

Now I am a happy woman. I have somebody and something to live for, my kids and their future which I will ensure. You can condemn me and wonder how such an immoral woman madam can lead such a contradictory life. I will tell you the truth: I don't.

Chapter 9
IMMIGRANTS
FROM ODESSA

I was born with a golden spoon in my mouth and I choked on it. My parents were immigrants from Israel. My mother was in her sixth month of pregnancy when she traveled the USA. America became my native land three months later. My parents lived well. My mother and my father were respected eye doctors.

When they came in the USA, they worked in governmental hospitals. They were very popular with their patients and had the reputation as being two of the best eye specialists at the hospital. They opened their own office and soon were considered exceptional plastic surgeons for the entire eye area.

English quickly became my first language. I was also fluent in Yiddish and Russian. I spent most of my childhood with baby-sitters. I played with my parents in the evenings for an hour, even though they were always tired. I never heard the word "No" from them. By the time I was five, I had already taken classes in swimming, ballet, painting, and figure skating. They enrolled me in every possible activity so I would not feel so lonely. I was spoiled, but I remained lonely.

We lived in a three-bedroom luxury apartment in the downtown Chicago. My mother never cooked for us. We went to restaurants every day or called out for delivery. There were no good restaurants in Chicago that we had not visited.

I wanted to become a professional figure skater. After my high school graduation, I took part in a competition in Minnesota.

I didn't win. I fell on the ice and broke my leg so badly that it took almost a year of therapy before I could walk normally. I was what Americans called a "basketcase" for a long time. My whole life before the accident was the dream of becoming a skating professional. I couldn't lose. To phrase it better, I didn't know how to lose because I always used to win. That was the first time I had ever had lost. For a few years, I didn't do anything.

I didn't know at that time how to communicate with men and I didn't flirt or even pay attention to guys. I knew they found me attractive, but for me they were all just young slackers.

I graduated from high school when I was seventeen. My parents decided to send me to Israel to study at business school for two years. It was a nice chance to see the land where I was conceived by my parents. The two years flew by very quickly. Twice, I came home for vacation to America and my parents visited me in Israel once.

I was never bored. From the early childhood I loved to be on my own. I always had something to keep myself busy. For me, Israel was a wonderful country with a deep, holy history. I walked down its streets and explored new things and people. I liked my school very much. It helped me gain accurate knowledge with numbers and the theories of mathematical possibilities. I found it interesting to meet presidents of different international companies and to learn about their strategy for success. I became a person who was communicative with others, but I never found a real girlfriend. It was a pattern from my childhood when I was too busy with all my activities. I had no free minute.

In Israel, I lived with a family. They were a wonderful husband and wife and treated me very warmly. His name was Zulya and she was Sara. They worked together in a bakery store which they owned. Sara took me shopping two times a week. They arranged a lot of excursions to historical places in Israel. They weren't religious, so I can say I was lucky. My family wasn't either. I didn't like to go for prayers in the Synagogue.

SHATTERED DREAMS BROKEN PROMISES

I graduated from the business school and went back to America. Even my looks had changed. I had become feminine, but I had still never dated a man before.

At nineteen, I enrolled in the University of Chicago. I took marketing and got excellent grades. My parents would never let me work while I studied in a school or university. They bought me expensive clothes and gave me money for all my personal expenses. But I felt I was really just an ordinary girl. I had my personal opinions and lots of attitude.

On my third year of the university, I was invited by my classmates to a party. About ten guys and ten girls were there with lots of beer, music and fun. A young man named George asked me to dance. He looked in my eyes and told me how beautiful I was. He said that the less I showed any availability, the more the guys were going to be crazy about me. It was nice to hear that I was attractive and to get his advice.

That night he offered to be my boyfriend. I was very drunk. I agreed. That was my last day of virginity. I lost it that night with George on the bed of one of his friends who slept in another room. I have no regrets but I didn't experience any real sense of pleasure about the process. It meant nothing to me. It just seemed the right time to become absolutely adult. After that party I dated George two more years. For me, it was just a new kind of relationship, not much more. He probably loved me otherwise he wouldn't have dated me that long. He made plans for our future. But I had my own plans without him in the picture.

I graduated high in my class and applied for a few marketing positions. An invitation came for an interview with a company in New York City. I had to be single so I broke up with George and turned the new page. My parents were never happy with George anyway. They thought that we didn't match as a couple. My mother used to say that I had big potential and was too well-educated for George. He needed somebody less beautiful and simpler, she said. Modesty is in short supply in my family, including me. My girlfriends say I am beautiful. I have bright-green eyes and a charming smile. I have long red hair and a slim shape.

In New York, I found a job as a market researcher in a successful company which produced and sold alcoholic beverages. It was a large association and my bosses were very strict and demanding about our work discipline. I had a girlfriend there, named Nicole. She worked in the company for a long time and knew everything about everybody. She knew who would get fired, sent on a business trip or receive a raise.

I worked in the company for six months when I started to pay attention to a man named Frank. He was attractive, thirty, and seemed to be interested in me too. After a while, he came up to me and said he had fallen in love with me at first sight. He asked me if I would mind if he started to care about me. I laughed and said nothing was forbidden. The most difficult thing, I said, would be to make me fall in love with him. I warned him that Russians are tough. I regarded myself as Russian.

At that moment, I was pretty sure that he was joking about everything. But later at a coffee break, Nicole told me that Frank was serious. In a month, we were inseparable. Everything happened so quickly between us. Everybody in the company was gossiping about us. Nicole talked the most. She seemed to be happy for us, asking me questions and advising me. She wanted to know everything. I was in the seventh heaven from happiness. I was crazy about Frank and he was very much in love with me.

This was the first time in my life when I believed that the kind of love that was written about in books really existed. It was wonderful! We couldn't live without each other for a minute. We were waiting for the end of the work day with impatience. In the mornings we didn't want to get out of bed. People say that when you are in love you can create miracles. Frank and I increased the quality of our work so dramatically that we were praised by our bosses.

It was Christmastime. I couldn't wait to celebrate that holiday with Frank. In the middle of December, Frank went on a business trip for a week. That was the first time we had been separated for more than two hours. I counted the days until his return.

The day of Frank's return came. My boss left for a meeting. I asked Nicole to cover me in case the boss asked where I was. It was three hours before Frank's arrival, I decided to prepare a candlelit dinner. Everything was ready in an hour.

Nicole called me and said that I had to return to the office before our boss came back early. She had told him that I left to the drugstore. I lived ten minutes from the office and I took a cab. I was very upset that my plans had been torn apart. I hated the whole world, my job and America. My only thought was that when Frank came back, I would be gone.

When I came in to the office I was surprised that Nicole wasn't there. The light in the boss's room was on. I knew he was there. I tried to dial him to ask permission to leave the office early. His line was busy. I was sat at my desk and looked through my work papers. Once in a while, I tried to reach my boss again but he was still busy. I called him several more times and somehow was connected. But by accident I overheard his voice talking on the phone with someone else.

At that moment, I was scared that he would run out from his office and fire me for eavesdropping. I heard him say he would come somewhere soon and I pressed the button to disconnect. I dialed him again and the line was again busy. I calmed down; he hadn't noticed anything.

My cell phone rang. It was Frank. He told me that he would be late and would come home at midnight. I was even more upset. When you wait to meet somebody you adore and it's delayed even for ten minutes—it's a terrible experience. That meant I had to wait for Frank for five more hours. It was agonizing. My last coworker left at 6:20 p.m. The working day was over twenty minutes ago. I cleaned up my desk, picked up my handbag and was ready to leave. I decided to stop at the boss's office and let him know that the next day I would be two hours late. I planned to say that I had an appointment with the doctor. I knew for sure that after a week without me, Frank would want to stay in bed a little longer, even if I had prolonged our pleasure with lies.

Sometimes I regret that I didn't go home immediately. Everything might have happened another way. I came into the boss' office and couldn't believe what I saw! My boss was kissing another man. The first thought I had was that I'd seen something I had no right to see. The second thing I realized was that the man was my Frank. I didn't move. I stood in shock. I couldn't understand. My Frank was kissing a man, our boss. I ran away. Frank heard me and broke the kiss. He called to me. He asked me to wait for his explanation, I don't remember how long I ran on the streets.

It was late when I found myself on the Madison Avenue. It was raining. I was all wet, and in despair. I hailed a cab and gave the address without thinking. I didn't know how to control my tears. I let myself into Frank's house as I always did.

He sat on the coach, gripping his head with his hands. In front of him were my two suitcases with my clothes packed inside. He looked up but didn't ask me to stay. He didn't ask my forgiveness. His eyes were terribly empty.

I moved back with my parents in Chicago. Frank called and tried to explain everything but I didn't want to hear. What could he say? A few days later Nicole flew in to Chicago to visit me. I told her everything. I had nobody else to cry with. It wasn't my parents' business. I couldn't tell them the truth. They were too old and wouldn't understand. Nicole confirmed with me that Frank was bisexual. She had dated him a long time ago but they had broken up because he couldn't stop his relationship with the boss. She thought that I knew everything but was hoping he would change. It was strange to me that Nicole, who used to know and gossip about everything, never uttered a word about this.

Frank called me a few more times but I wasn't willing to talk to him. In two months I found a job at a Chicago marketing company. I started to forget everything. But I didn't date anyone. Every man seemed to me as bad as Frank. One day I met another ex-coworker near the coffee shop. I was happy to meet somebody from my past life in New York. She told me that Frank and Nicole recently got married. I was badly hurt. In some weird way, I still loved Frank for the dreams we had once had about our future, yet I hated him at the same moment because he had destroyed everything. I couldn't decide what was worse: if the man was cheating with a woman or with a bixesual person like himself.

In two years, when the awfulness was almost forgotten, I got a letter from Nicole. I read the letter and began shaking. I thought I would die on the spot.

Here is the letter without changes:

My dear Masha,

I don't know if you will be able to forgive me. I have nothing to lose anymore. I know that my clock is ticking and I have almost no time to live. But above all I want your forgiveness. Everything that happened in my life was my fault. When I broke up with Frank I didn't know how to live without him. I tried not to show him. I loved and always was ready to forgive almost everything but I couldn't forgive a third person in our relationship.

Then you appeared in our office and became a successful worker. Your relationship with Frank started and he loved you as much as he probably ever loved anyone. I was waiting, hoping that you would make him give up his obsession. I was sure that if you did change him then I would find a way to get rid of you later. I am sorry. I waited quietly for my hour. I believed that because of that strong love for you he would break up with our boss. I thought of how to pry him away from you.

That day when you left early Frank called the office and asked me if I had seen our boss. I told him that he had left for a meeting a long time ago and said that he wouldn't come back. Then fifteen minutes later he showed up and I understood that he and Frank had arranged a meeting. Something happened in me. I still felt jealous about Frank and our boss. I called you and made you come back. Forgive me please.

I thought that a conflict would make Frank break up with our boss. But it happened just the other way. You decided not to fight for your love and left him. You have no idea how Frank suffered. I think that he always loved only you. I don't even know why he married me. But I didn't care at that time. For me it meant that Frank would be mine forever. I thought so but it was a mistake.

Later they found HIV in our boss's blood. Frank also was infected. Then they found it in me. A month ago, Frank died from AIDS. I have not got long to live. I'm not asking you to come and visit me. I just want you to forgive me. We will never see each other again but I will be calmer if you forgive me. Nicole.

I read the last lines through my tears, which choked me up so I couldn't breathe. I hated my ex-boss. I pitied Frank. I felt sorry for Nicole and for myself. I thought that everything that had happened a long time ago was already fading into the past. But I still love Frank even as I feel betrayed, and remember the smell of his hair. I remember the feel of his jackets, his hot hands. I remember his bottomless eyes. I remember the truth. I know it will be scary. I have nothing in my future, and probably never will have. I don't believe men anymore. They can leave you not only because of other women, but for other men. They can crush your life into little pieces. They can give you a disease and make you feel that the next day can be the last.

I don't want to know the truth. I don't want to put somebody down the way Frank did with me. But for now I just live and work. Everyday is just the same. I am lonely now and fear for me it will always be so. I have had my last kiss.

Chapter 10
I DIED YESTERDAY

My name is Marina. I am thirty-one years old. It will soon be eighteen years since I've arrived in America. I came from Saint Petersburg with my parents when I was thirteen years old. My father was a professor of philosophy and international relations. My mother was not just his wife, but his support system. My father's professional work as a Ph.D. required a healthy lifestyle, good food and comfortable atmosphere at home. This was my mother's main purpose and responsibility.

My father's entire life was consumed by his work. My mother dreamed about having a child. There was no reason not to have one. My father had a stable job, financial security, and was a solid member of the academic community. But my mother was not able to carry a baby full term. The first time she was pregnant, she lost her unborn child in the first trimester at the age of twenty-six. The second time, she was six months along when the doctors discovered abnormalities and induced a stillbirth at that time. Mother was thirty-eight years old.

After that ordeal, my parents played it safe and made no further attempts to conceive. However, when my mother was forty-two and my father was fifty-six, the doctors informed them that she was again pregnant. My parents didn't dare believe that their dream would come true after all. They also realized that they were past their prime and that this time it could end badly as well. But I came into the world a completely healthy baby.

My parents were overjoyed. I was born into a family where there was always plenty of love. I was a late child and as always seems to happen in such cases, my parents loved me more than it's possible to imagine. They gave me the world and fulfilled my every whim and desire. I was an excellent student. I was keen on sports. I took piano lessons. My parents imagined a secure and carefree future for me.

When I turned thirteen, my country became the former Soviet Union and many of the scientists who worked for the government found themselves unemployed and unemployable overnight. Fortunately, my father was well recognized in his field and as thus was invited to teach at New York University.

As there was nobody at school to say goodbye to, I wasn't liked there. Everyone envied my successes and accused me of being spoiled by my parents. Nor did my mother have friends after she became pregnant. The women of our society criticized her. A woman who decided to have her first baby in her forty-second year didn't fit into their systematic community and way of thinking. My mother realized that she didn't have any real friends. She knew that she only had her future baby and a dear husband. My father had often looked into the possibility of moving to America. It was a chance for a better career, an opportunity to financially support his family and be able to give me a good education.

I had never flown on an airplane before. It wasn't easy in the former Soviet Union to travel abroad. That is why it was such a great adventure for me. My parents bought me a pink rucksack with a doll picture. I helped them pack my clothes.

Before we left Saint Petersburg, my mother read in a newspaper that there were a lot of thieves on the streets of New York who would steal your money without being detected. So the question arose as to where we would hide all our hard-earned money from the sale of our country house and Soviet car. My mother was a perfect housewife. She divided the money in half. She sewed a pocket inside my father's underwear that he would wear on the plane. So if anyone tried to steal our money, they would have to steal my parents' underwear as well.

We sat in this airplane crafted from metals, soaring as an iron bird with its plumes reflecting the sun's light. We arrived in New York. All of us had a strange feeling of helplessness. We instantly forgot all the English we had learned. My father called the people who had arranged our trip. We took a taxi from the airport to the university. We came to our destination and the cab driver told us the amount due. In order to pay him, my parents had to get into my father's underwear or my mother's bra. First they checked their pockets trying to find a hundred dollars in cash.

The cab driver curiously observed their odd behavior. My parents didn't give up, but it seemed like they didn't have enough money. My father gave him the first fifty dollars, but the driver worried that he wouldn't get fully paid. My father told him no to worry as he put his hand in his underwear and looked at the driver. The driver got scared and shook his head and said, "No, money only."

But Russians never give up without a fight. My father scolded my mother for her bright idea of sewing the money inside the pocket and not leaving a hole to get it out. The cab driver began to sweat.

My father took his hand out of his underwear and said to the cab driver, "One moment, sir, my wife will pay you." My mother put her hands in the bra of her ample breasts. She was smiling and turned red. She was looking at the cab driver because my father told her to. He said that in America, if you want people to communicate with you and not judge you, you should always smile. The poor cab driver covered his eyes with his hands, sat in his car and, finally, just pulled out. We stood and waved at him until he disappeared from view. My father came to the conclusion that American people are kind and they can forgive your debts. In reality, I now believe the Arabian cab driver was afraid of being accused of sexual harassment.

We began life in America in a two-bedroom apartment in Brooklyn with a view of the ocean. We liked it very much. We felt like we had never left Saint Petersburg, because Russians were everywhere eating Russian food and speaking our native language. The area we lived in was called Brighton Beach.

We adapted. I enrolled in school, my father began to teach, and my mother studied English, but remained a housewife. It wasn't easy for me at school because I had the language barrier and thus wasn't up to speed with the rest of the kids. But, since I was athletically gifted, my parents sent me to a boarding school that emphasized sports. I decided from the first moment that I would become just like all the other girls there. I quickly learned how to smoke and drink. I became one of them quickly. I made a lot of friends. We went to house parties and cafes together. It seemed like nothing terrible ever happened. All teenagers lived like this. It seemed like a normal life to me. Every person always wants something new to try and to have new experiences.

I was fifteen when I met some hippies at one of the parties. They were quite extraordinary and seemed very exotic to me. They were long-haired and wore old torn jeans. They were different from anybody I had ever met. Talking to them, you could feel that they were always carefree and loved life. I looked at them and wondered why they were so happy. How could they be so happy without money, expensive clothes, and the creature comforts of life? I was curious. I wanted to be in their company. We smoked weed, laughed and danced. They played rock music and I listened to it. Everything was cool to me. I didn't know how scary it all was in reality. At that time, we didn't have drug users in the former Soviet Union. At least I wasn't told about such things. Nobody warned me how it could all end up if you messed with narcotics.

Eventually, my new friends offered me something more powerful and I agreed to try it. That was my first heroine experience. I liked it. I liked it because I didn't know what would happen to me later. The entire summer, I gave myself heroine injections and I was happy. Come September, it was time to return to school. One morning, I woke up and decided that I would not do anymore injections. I decided to get on with sports and study. However, I was surprised when I realized that I couldn't go to school. I didn't feel well. In fact, I felt awful. I thought that I had come down with a cold. My mother offered to call the doctor. A few hours later, I got a phone call from friends who asked why I hadn't come to school. I said that I was sick and didn't feel well.

They told me that I wasn't sick, that I felt like my body was a wreck because I needed a dose of the narcotic. I naively told them that I would come right away. They said that narcotics cost money and they would give it to me, but they had financial difficulties. I had to pay for it this time. But I had no money. Where can a fifteen-year-old girl get money? Nowhere. I knew how the girls I befriended earned money but I didn't know it could ever happen to me. I couldn't imagine that my life could come to this. I was brought up morally right. I couldn't possibly feel that kind of pain.

I went to Eighth Avenue in Manhattan to sell my body in order to get money for a dose. I came to a stopped car and offered the guy a blow job for fifty dollars and intercourse for eighty dollars. The longer I did this, the more drugs I took. I took more drugs to avoid the reality of feeling humiliated, offended, and used as an object. When I was twelve, like every other girl, I had dreamed about great love and the prince on a white horse. I had thought that my Prince Charming was somewhere waiting for me and that, one day, I would give him all my love and care. Instead, I was selling my body to anyone. I understood now that romantic love was a fairy tale, a thing that's written about in fiction. But there was no longer any room for thoughts of a real love in my mind. I remained on drugs another year. My parents didn't notice any major changes in me because five days a week, I wasn't at home. On weekends, I tried to behave normally by taking a dose in advance.

I was seventeen when I told my mother that I was a drug user. She was shocked. She started calling all the hospitals and tried to find somebody who was able to help me. We didn't tell my father because he was at a crucial point in his career. My mother was certain that he wouldn't be able to handle it anyway and would die from such news. My mother regretted their choice of school. She regretted that she had let me live on my own terms since I was fourteen.

After just two weeks of treatment, I ran away from the hospital. My entire body needed the drug. I resumed my self-destructive habit, I teamed up with my friend Alisha and the two of us worked as prostitutes. At one point, we got tired of it. We were mad at all men, the whole world and everything that had happened in our lives. We decided not to earn money this way any more.

So we began a new scheme. We stopped cars and offered men our services at home. When we came to their homes, we slipped sleeping pills in their drinks. Then we beat them up. We beat them to express our anger and disgust with them. We stole everything we could and sold it later. That was the money we lived on. I understood that only friendship could be real in life. I knew I could depend on a friend, who would never leave me in a time of trouble. I lived with this belief. One day after we robbed some unsuspecting clients, we earned a large amount of money. Alisha disappeared and left me without money or my dose of the drug. I was disappointed and finally realized that drug addicts couldn't have friends.

I was twenty-one when I decided that only a child could stop me from taking drugs. I decided to have a baby and devote my whole life to him instead of drugs. I found a guy from the hippies I knew and got pregnant. I gave birth to a boy. My father was a wreck. He couldn't deal with all that was happening. He had a heart attack and died in the maternity ward. He never saw his grandson. My baby was a drug addict too. He was born with heroin in his blood. The doctors detoxed him by regularly reducing his dosage.

When I returned home, I was happy for the first two weeks. I had a son I could love. But three months later, I understood that a child couldn't help me. My son was following my path to a world of drugs and dissatisfaction. The hole and pain I had in my soul still needed drugs and my child couldn't replace it.

Soon, I became a mother who lived independently of her child. I bought him expensive toys just to feel less guilty. Every year I asked for treatment in different New York hospitals and the best of them tried to cure me. As soon as I got up from the bed and my broken body was back to normal, I would decide that I wouldn't use drugs as much and often any more. I would take them only in cases of emergency. Of course, I lied to myself and a few weeks later I would realize that I was right back where I had started. I didn't see any exits from that dark tunnel.

Once, I overdosed. It was a miracle that I survived. My mother and my two-year-old son, Dima, coached by her, were praying at home. They stayed on their knees and asked God to save my life. He did. I had a clinical death at the hospital. I fell deep into a dark tunnel and saw a light. It showed me that my life was a big mistake and that I could change it. I was trying to find my usual easy escape and die. But I couldn't. Instead of death, I encountered unbearable fear.

After that experience, I realized that life continues after death. I understood that there is no death and that the life I faced after death was far worse than the life I had on Earth. I became afraid of death. After fifteen days in the hospital, I came home and was diagnosed with cancer in the blood. As gently as they could the doctors said that it was impossible to cure and the only thing I could do was to stay at home and wait to die. The fear of dying kept me drug-free but not for long. I concluded that I couldn't live without my fix. It was a vicious cycle.

One day, I had unexpected visitors. They didn't look like any of the people from my regular social club. My mother sought them out and they came. They told me that Jesus died for me, that he loved me just the way I am, and that he wanted to change my life. I didn't believe them. I didn't understand what use God had for a prostitute, a drug addict, and a thief like me.

My body began to rot from the blood cancer. I couldn't sell myself any more. My body became useless. My veins were shattered, I had injection roads and ugly ulcers.

But visitors said that God could forgive me and change my life forever. Still, I didn't believe them. In the past, somebody always wanted something from me. I finally saw that these people wanted to help me and didn't ask for anything in return. At the same time, the moment came when I knew that I didn't have much time left. I had nothing to lose and so I decided to go to a church and ask God to forgive me for everything I'd done on this Earth. On that very day my mother called a cab and took me to a church in Brooklyn. I told God that, if He existed, to please give me another chance and to help me change my life. On the way home, I felt a little easier in my soul; I didn't have the terrible pain. I took the stairs to my apartment and not the elevator. I didn't know what happened, but something surely did.

I am thirty-one years old and for sixteen of those years, I was a drug addict with a horrible past and a soul full of sin. I was sure that nobody was able to help me. But in the two months I visited the church, I gained twenty-seven pounds. I no longer had the desire for drugs. I have since never taken a drug and never had a thought about them. I haven't had a cigarette or a drink since that day. I have replaced that painful emptiness in my soul with God.

Now I am a happy woman. I wake up each day and thank God for saving me and for giving me a new life. I don't have dark moods anymore. My son Dima is completely healthy. He is eleven years old now and has many friends. He goes to school. God even gave me a husband.

Andrew used to be a drug addict as well. That world seems unreal to me now and to him. People used to see me on the streets and wouldn't know how to avoid me. They feared getting some disease or frightening their children.

Now, Andrew and I work together at a facility that helps people like we used to be. It's God helping people through us. Just remember that when you feel lonely, depressed, and you just don't want to live any longer, God is life. And he loves everybody because we are all His children. He will help you if you'll just believe.

I died yesterday. The former me is dead. That me was in a nightmare life where I was the living dead. I am reborn today. I will never kill myself again. There is nothing impossible in this life. I did the impossible. To those who are like I was back then, I say: "You can, too!"

Chapter 11
A NEW BEGINNING

Everyone tells me I am beautiful. They say I look like a model from one of the top fashion magazines. I have large green eyes, long chestnut hair that flows almost down to my sexy thighs when I perform sexy dances on the stage of a strip club in Long Island, New York.

Yes, I am a strip dancer with an unfinished university education and poor English skills. But answer me this? Why do I need an education? My job is to bat my long eyelashes, twirl my thighs, smile, and smell of expensive perfume.

I arrived in America from Nijniy Novgorod one year ago when I was twenty-one years old. I think it's almost impossible to overestimate the talent and mind of a strip dancer. I am not even talking about beauty.

My friend Marina came to America before me. She was my friend for almost eighteen years. Unlike me, she came with everything prepared for her life here. Her father and stepmother were already here, they rented a basement apartment for her. She didn't need to work to survive.

Marina called me excited about her life in America. She told me that I could live the life we had fantasized about back in Russia. We had been dreaming about living a wealthy life with expensive cars and fancy clothes. I remember how we imagined a typical day's schedule in our future life: we would wake up around 10 a.m., then go to work out at a gym; we would have a massage and facial followed by lunch in a cozy restaurant. We would shop in famous boutiques, eat a healthy dinner, and then go out with rich and handsome men who would eagerly pay for our expensive lifestyle. And, of course the night always ended with exciting sex.

Marina was from a poor family, raised by her mother. Her father left them when she was three years old. He sent money once a month and called once a year. Marina was very upset about this fact because her relationship with her mother seemed like one long fight. She told me she became closer to her father after she was raped by a stranger at the beach when she was seventeen years old.

She was scared and hid this fact from her mother. She didn't get her period. Marina called her dad. She explained that she was in trouble and asked him for money for an abortion. She was sure that he wouldn't be against it because he didn't really care and would not want to have to pay to help to support a grandchild.

She was right. Her father agreed. After the problem was solved they began to communicate for the first time in her life. Her father's new wife won the American government lottery and they added Marina's information to the application.

When Marina called me from the USA she told me that everything would be easy. America is the country which makes everything available to you. My life in Novgrod was absolutely hopeless in all spheres.

After conversations with Marina I dreamed of a different life in a different world, the world of a young, beautiful and rich Russian lady in New York. Marina promised to find a nice well-paying job for me. I visualized how I would arrive. I saw myself working in a major corporation, dressed in a fashionable business suite, with a laptop under my arm. I wrote in my diary my strategy of how I would succeed in America.

Everything was in order. I intended to get my papers by marrying a man who would truly fall in love with me. I was sure that someone as pretty as I would quickly and easily find a nice guy, fall in love, get married and create a family. In addition to all this, I dreamed about owning the most fashionable model of car, with a small dog on the front seat and at least a thousand dollars in cash in my wallet for small personal expenses.

When I sat down in the plane I placed on myself ridiculous time limitations. I was sure that one or, at most, two years would be enough to make all these dreams come true. There was nothing to lose by leaving Russia. My best friend was in the USA and she certainly didn't complain about her life.

All my friends in Russia suddenly became less interesting to me because they didn't share the same goals: In fact they didn't have any goals at all. I didn't plan to give up my parents. I was sure that they would always be around for me for my whole life. I knew that my absence would not be a long time for them. I have an older sister and I was sure that my parents wouldn't miss me a lot.

In Russia, I tried to save money, purchasing only necessities. I was tired of the same boring entertainments. I would sit in somebody's apartment and drink beer, smoke, and play cards. Or we would go to a disco club and once again drink and smoke. We hoped to meet the right guy; one with more money than our families had.

My family wasn't poor. My mother worked as a physician and her salary was forty-five dollars per month. My father was a cab driver and earned a hundred dollars a month. It wasn't easy for my parents to pay for everything we needed but we had clothes, food, and an education for us children. Summer usually wasn't boring. We spent it in our country dacha and had lots of fresh fruits, vegetables, fresh air and a lake near by.

I quit my two courses at my university, dreaming that such a Novgorodsky beauty as I was would be accepted at Harvard University. I didn't want to stop studying. I just wanted to study in that prestigious school, the only university in America I'd ever heard about.

I dated a twenty-three-year-old guy named Vadim. We dated almost four years. I always thought that we would get married, have kids and all the things that usually happen. He was my first lover. All my girlfriends thought I was lucky to be with

Vadim. In comparison to others, he had money. He brought me flowers, jewelry and took me to nice restaurants. His lifestyle never seemed unusual to me. I was studying till the late afternoon in the university and evenings we spent together. Once in a while he would disappear for a week. He explained that he needed to go to see his parents or go on a business trip.

But a tragedy was on the horizon. The love of my life was put into prison for a string of robberies. The moment I first found out about this, I thought about suicide. I cried for almost a year. Marina had already left for America.

My parents never understood me. They never liked Vadim. I was dying from the pain of love. I sat at home and wrote him letters every day. During his first year in prison I was able to visit him just twice. He would try to break up with me and say that he had never loved me. He told me he had just used me. But afterwards he would send me text messages with love and request me to be faithful and wait for him.

I was devastated and felt Marina's offer was my only chance to survive. Before my departure to the USA I went to visit Vadim in prison. I wanted to say goodbye, to inhale the smell of his body, to make love for the last time with the man I loved. This is allowed in Russian prisons if you stayed overnight. I wanted to make a picture in my memory of him to keep forever. I knew that the new door wouldn't open, if the old wasn't shut.

I dressed up in a new impossibly tight pair of stretch jeans, a white jacket with a deep décolletage and high heels. I blow-dried my hair and applied lots of mascara, all on purpose. I looked in the mirror at my melancholy face and liked what I saw. Everything I did was by my exactly designed scenario.

You may well ask why I went to the prison dressed as if I was going to a celebration. There is more than one answer. First, I wanted him to picture me in his memory as being beautiful to further punish him. The second reason you'll never understand, no matter how hard you try, unless you are a Russian woman. Russian women always want to look attractive a hundred percent of the time. For example if we need to make a choice of whether to spend our last thousand rubles on food or on a new dress, without a second thought, we will select the new dress. This should not be condemned. This is the blood of Russian women.

That day the densely greased eyelashes and my audacious look was all a game, a dream produced and directed by me. It was an attempt to impose the memory of me in him as brightly as possible, to hurt Vadim as deeply as I could and in turn to hurt myself. All this was so I could cry. It's like I had a need to have a reserve of emotions. I wanted to treasure my tears from the suffering that he brought on me. I wanted the mascara to run and drip onto my white blouse. I knew that I would always keep it and remember its smell because Vadim hugged me when I wore it. I wanted to remember the love we had.

Marina, as I said, had promised to find me a good job and told me not to worry about a place to live. She said that I wouldn't go hungry. The main thing was that we would be together. She met me in the JFK airport. We went to live in Brooklyn. A few days later she told me that she had found a good job for me. I would not need to speak English well or have work papers. All that was needed was a pretty appearance that I already had. The job was simply to dance. I wasn't afraid. I always liked to dance. I didn't realize that it was a strip club. When we first came for my interview I said no to the job.

Later on, Marina, who was supposed to be my friend, demanded payment for my housing and food. She started fights and conflict. She betrayed me. I found out that the entire time she lived in the apartment she had never paid rent and that she had put the lease in my name. The landlord demanded the rent from me. The whole thing cost me four thousand dollars. I started to dance at the club since there was no other choice. Later, I discovered that she got a commission for bringing me in on this job.

Then Marina disappeared. I was alone in the apartment. Once in a while she would call and promise that she would come back and pay her half, but finally she disappeared forever. Our friendship had already been broken as a cup shatters on the sidewalk.

When I first decided to try dancing it was not as simple as you might think. I had to undress down to my underwear and let dirty sweaty-handed men put dollar bills in my panties. They did so with excited expressions on their faces as if they were giving me one-hundred-dollar bills. The first time, I was the only one on the stage. I was as thin as a stick, and unable to move right. I was paralyzed with fear.

Later, I learned how to move and become a bitch. I learned the key phrases for making conversation with customers. A few weeks after I started, I knew not only the words "yes" and "no." I learned the key phrases to reject advances: "No suck, no fuck." This was very useful for my safety and well being. It also made clear that I had certain standards that the customers and other girls must be aware of. As a rule none of the girls would let anyone know that they did "extras" because if they did they could lose their jobs.

Slowly, I started to send money home. On questions from my parents about my work and schedule, I answered that I was working in a restaurant sometimes during the day, sometimes in the evening. It was very hard for me to lie because I had never lied to my parents before. But no one who works, even as a waitress at a strip club, would tell her parents or friends what she was doing. Indeed, all you want is to make them think that you are in America, the country of miracles, and that you've been noticed. You can't judge anybody in America. Everybody survives as best as they can. But how he or she does it depends only on one's individual moral principles.

When I first decided to remain in America, I said to my parents that I had been invited to work in a bank. That was one reason my parents agreed. I could feel when I talked to them over the phone how proud they were of their daughter's success, even as a restaurant worker. They certainly were not against my desire to remain there, because it seemed like the best prospects for my future.

I was dancing, but I couldn't save money. When every night ended, I left with a bag stuffed with money and a headache from the immeasurable quantity of cheap champagne drinks. I had only two cures for that: sleep and shopping. But when your body gets accustomed to this style of life, then you can't sleep longer then five or six hours. It seemed like it's necessary to go out and spend money on salon treatments, cosmetics, expensive toys and a pile of unnecessary things. You spend your money simply without thinking, making sure that the ever-present shadow of despair does not suck you in. This is how you prove to yourself why you work in this business and why you shake every part of your body in front of strangers' faces.

Working as a strip dancer, you can't build a serious relation-ship with a man. Indeed no man wants to learn that his dear girl shows her body in front of hundreds of salivating men. The men who work as the owners of the clubs, the drivers of the girls, the managers and guards have nothing against us. They know that we are normal. But it's not a good idea to have an affair with someone from the work place. For a woman, it is emotionally hard to hide the work she's doing from the man she loves. She lies because she is afraid to lose him. She works because she needs to survive. And she is always afraid to be alone.

Because she is far away from home and barely able to speak English she wants somebody to be there for her, someone who truly cares about her. When you are strip dancing you try to find an excuse for yourself and justify what you do. You blame your boyfriend. You tell yourself that if he helped you more financially and tried to understand you, you would never work in such a place. But all these excuses are just bullshit.

In my home country they say that "Russians invented love in order not to pay." But now I think that such beliefs were born in America. Russian men, at least here, understand that if they don't spend money on their girlfriends, they will leave them and meet somebody more generous. But many Americans will promise you the stars from the sky. Then they soon forget those promises. Of course, there are exceptions.

My boyfriend, Chris, who is of South African descent, was very generous to me. He was thirty years old, a cutie; he cherished me and never said "no." We loved each other and were going to get married. He trusted me and never forbid me to work. He was originally from Shanghai and in fact was a very famous pimp with the nick name of "Cry" in New York City.

But our relationship didn't work. He would disappear for weeks at a time and would never be with me for holidays, making the excuse that he had to take care of business. I was almost always alone. After one of our fights, he asked me to marry him and to move into his house where many of his prostitutes also lived. I agreed to this because I loved him very much. A few weeks later he asked me kindly if I would work for him and assured me that our relationship wouldn't change.

I was devastated. I changed my phone number, moved to a different apartment, and stopped dancing for that club. I realized that our Russian men are better, or better at least for Russian women. Later I learned that Chris, my hero-lover, would regularly find beautiful girls, make them fall in love with him, and then would ask them to work for him as a prostitute. A woman in love believes almost anything. He would make money from each of his conquests. And after he had made all the money he could from her, he would treat her like mud and call her a whore. He would do this over and over again.

These girls would usually grieve for some time but they would not leave this work. They would even work longer hours to be close to him. They would try to prove to him how much he needed them. But they also would become addicted to the money. I became disappointed in all men.

One day, my sister called me with tragic news. My parents had died in a car accident two months ago. She hadn't called before because she was afraid that I would come back to Russia and ruin my successful future in the USA. I began to support my sister and grandmother and to work even more. I frequently saw my parents in my dreams. I felt guilty and I regretted that I lied to them, and didn't call them as often as I should have.

After a while, I began to earn lots of money in the night club and began to speak English better. I earned thirty dollars for a five-minute lap dance and remained fully dressed when I did. For the first dance I took half of the money and the other half I gave to the manager. The money for additional dances I kept for myself.

The longer I lap danced, the more money I made.

One night after a short conversation with a gentleman in a Gucci suit, I offered him a lap dance for thirty dollars. This man looked at me contemptuously. He asked if I had a college education? Citizenship? Work experience? Could I speak English fluently? To all these questions I clearly answered. Then my rich potential client told me that not every American who had a college education, work experience and spoke perfect English could earn thirty dollars per hour. Why, he asked, should he pay this much for five minutes as well as buy me expensive drinks?

A Russian woman does not think long before she speaks. She never checks her Russian-English dictionary to find the right words, and take time to think about an answer. I stood up, fixed my dress and looked in his eyes and said that he has to pay that because he came in the club to look at such a beautiful girl as me. After all, I said, this is not a free movie theater.

As time passed, I realized how much I earned compared to others. I stopped feeling sorry for myself. I came to the conclusion that once you put money in your pocket, it doesn't know how it got there. Money has no smell.

I began to save even more money. When I count all my money now, I feel even less sorry for myself. I will work until I save two hundred thousand dollars and I will go back to Nijni Novgorod to live with my older sister and grandma.

The next thing I will do is try to buy Vadim's freedom by making payoffs to the right officials through a "connected" attorney. I now realize how much I loved him.

I know that with money you can live happily anywhere. In Novgorod no one will find out about my past. Everybody will view me as a bank worker. I don't want to make myself legal here and get my papers. I don't want to live here. Nothing gives me happiness here: not the people, not the skyscrapers, not the culture. Money here is the only God. I know when I go back to Russia, I will go to my parents' grave and take care of my sister and grandmother. I will start a beauty-salon business; buy an apartment downtown and a new Mercedes. I will erase the years of topless work from my memory. At the end of the day, I will have what I wanted. My life will start anew.

CALIFORNIA DREAMING
Chapter 12

I was born in the city of Vladivostok thirty years ago. My parents were religious Baptists. From childhood my parents raised me according to God's commandments and taught me kindness, love and respect for our neighbors. That upbringing made me absolutely confident of what I was doing and how I should socialize with my peers.

However, my excessive kindness and caring for people significantly distinguished me among my companions. To the question of why I was different from the other kids, my parents answered that I was a girl with broad intellect and spiritual values and everyone else should strive to have such qualities.

At that age, I was satisfied with their explanation. My mother and father often came home late after work because they attended secret meetings that were conducted in the places of brothers and sisters of our faith. Sometimes my parents took me with them to those meetings, but they saw that I was not interested in them so they took me with them less and less often. This did give me an opportunity to perceive the things on my own and to understand my own mind.

For the first time in my life, I felt an extreme estrangement from my classmates and the unreasonableness of my childish opinion. It happened this way: one day, in the fall, I heard on my way home from school, someone shout, "Throw stones at her. She is a goddamned Baptist. She's an enemy." A big stone hit my leg, hurting me severely. There were tears in my eyes. I ran attempting to save myself. Later, there was a question in my mind: Why had this happened? Could part of it have been that as an ugly duckling, at times, I felt deprived of love.

Then one day I accidentally overheard my parents talking in the kitchen. My father told mother that they fired him from his job and there was nothing he could do about it. Then things grew even worse. Arrests began.

I remember, I was eight years old when, in December, our entire family was attacked by huge guys with shaven heads and unreadable armbands. I don't remember exactly, but I think there were three of them and they attacked us when we were leaving a theater. Everything happened suddenly and very quickly.

My father attempted to protect my mother and I was screaming that we should run away. Then I saw my parents lying on the pavement panting, covered with blood. I seized the legs of the thugs, wept and begged him not to kill my parents. Another one of them looked at me, spat in my face, kicked me in the knee and shouted: "If you anti-Christians complain, we'll bury you alive and nobody will ever find you!" My parents suffered numerous bruises and fractures.

Then they decided to move us to a different city to hide from violence. We moved to Saratov. Our new neighbors didn't know anything about us. To continue my education, I enrolled in a new school. There they read the reference letter that I received from the school in Vladivostok and the teachers and principal started to look at me askance. My classmates ignored me on purpose. I asked my mother why this kept happening to me even in this new place. Mother replied: "Forgive me, my daughter. This is our life, our soul, our value!"

Then I understood that many people everywhere hated me because of my parents' Faith. At that time, I didn't understand the meaning of Baptist at all, and the word Baptist began to be associated in my mind with fear. Once Father came home bloody, beaten, and with his nose fractured. In his hands, he firmly held brochures with the Ten Commandments and with invitations to our house of prayer. My mother instantly began to pray. I sat next to her, frightened by the bloody scene. My father, injured as he was, told us that our creed was holy and that we had to be patient. He said that two men in uniform with swastika armbands somehow traced him, ran up to him and commenced to beat him with chains when he was taking out a new pack of brochures.

We called the police. But upon listening to the story, the policeman said that he would have beaten my father to death if he had been one of those who attacked him. Then he laughed and added seriously that it didn't make sense to rot a good society, and make zombies out of growing generations who were building the future of the country but hadn't yet formed their outlook on life.

At school, I suffered numerous humiliations as a daughter of Baptists. The teachers gave me grades lower than I deserved. During classes in history and social studies they directed the student's attention to the "inconsistent demagogy of lackeys of the rotten West." After classes, my schoolmates often traced me down and beat me. When my parents came to school to complain, our classroom teacher and school principal tauntingly said that in a normal, healthy society there couldn't be any other reaction to crazy people who impudently imposed their nonsense on intelligent folks.

Later, we started to receive threatening phone calls. Also people put notes on our door and in the mailbox saying: "Die, you beasts, there's no room for you heathens in the Orthodox world, get out of here." The situation was getting worse and life was getting more dangerous. Despite that, my parents were devoted to their faith and, together with other believers, they organized a house of prayer. They rented an auditorium in a movie theater. My mother told me that people came to their house of prayer to feel the warmth of hearts and comfort and to be filled with high spiritual feelings derived from the realization of the beauty of the world created by God. I always felt more like an outlaw as an adolescent girl.

When I turned fourteen years old, I fell in love with Igor. He was a very nice looking guy and was the dream of every girl in my school. But he chose me. I spent all my spare time with him, trying to show my classmates that I didn't belong to the Baptists, that I was like my peers and that I could be a good friend. I was so much in love that I hardly saw anything around. He didn't know that I was from a family of believers.

Later, I lived through another stress. One Sunday morning, my parents asked me to help prepare the house of prayer for a meeting. It was around noon when the people had gathered bottles containing some burning mixture and had thrown them through the windows. The hall was filled with smoke. There was instant chaos, screams and panic. With difficulty, I got into the street through the crowd of people and a police cordon. My parents were taken to the hospital with severe burns and traumas.

It was clear that the police, with the support of the local government, organized the action. Long before that, the police had insisted on the closing of the worship home, but they couldn't do it peacefully or legally. Arson was their final decision to solve the problem. So, the house of prayer only existed for a year and a half. At the site of the burned house of worship, a night club was constructed.

Before the tragedy, my father had talked to me in an effort to instill and strengthen faith and love in me. During those conversations I felt lightness and a mystery that was new to me. But the fears in me were stronger than the lightness. I told Father that I didn't want to be like him and my mother, and suffer for my beliefs.

The very next day, when I came back from school and my mother came back from work, we discovered a nightmarish scene that is still in my memory and that I see in my dreams at night. My father lay on the floor cruelly strangled, blood coming from his mouth and there was a note in his hand: "Die, you anti-Christian." Everything in the apartment was ruined. On the walls there was written in red paint: "Death to Baptist degenerates." Swastikas were drawn all over the walls.

When the police arrived, they twisted all the facts saying that my father died from a heart attack. They intimidated Mother warning that if she insisted on opening a criminal case, she and I would go the same way as Father. Mother said that we should take this tragedy as God's trial.

I developed severe depression and my mind lost its hinges. After learning what had happened, my friend Igor turned his back on me and so I simultaneously lost two people who were dear to me: my father and my dearest, only friend.

I was given a course of treatment in the neurological center for teenagers. Ever day my pain had been growing stronger and the desire to live in this cruel world was disappearing. After the course of treatment, my mother sent me on a tour around Europe so that I could leave behind my worries. During the entire trip I thought, "What was all this tragedy for? My father suffered and died for his beliefs. What good did it do?"

Over all those years my mother secretly attended the Baptist meetings and received threatening calls. The people around us treated her with contempt. I enrolled in Saratov State University when I was sixteen years old. I made new friends and acquaintances. Suddenly Igor reappeared and told some fellows that I belonged to a family of Baptists. At that time I didn't feel shame. I felt pain and sadness because my father had died for his Baptist faith. By then I wasn't religious and I still am not. If God exists, why did all this happen to me. And why does my anguish inside still continue.

One day, my fellow students saw my mother distributing leaflets about The Ten Commandments near the subway station and informed the dean's office about it. They had a talk with me, reminding me of my father's Baptist activities and insisted that we stop rotting people's minds with sectarian nonsense. I didn't try to prove anything. I just stood with my head down.

Just before the New Year, my mom was giving invitations to the church of Christ to a passerby and distributing evangelic literature. I came up to her just to say that I would be home late. A police patrol was going past us. The vehicle stopped and a policeman asked what we were doing. The policemen asked us to show the documents. My mother showed her passport to them and I didn't have mine with me. So the policeman said that I had to go to the precinct to establish my identity. They pushed me roughly into the van, poking at me with a club to make me hurry. The policemen gave me a ride around the city, and then stopped at a deserted place resembling a dump where all of them did bad things to me. They urinated on me and then started to beat and reprimand me. It was late when they brought me to the police department and explained to their colleagues that they found me beaten and dirty when I was offering my body for a bottle of vodka.

For two days, they kept me in a cell there. Then one of my mother's co-religionists found me and picked me up, and wanted to file a case in court against the policemen for beating me and keeping me in the cell for no reason. But the police said that there were no witnesses and this case would only aggravate my situation. For days, I was given medical treatment in the hospital.

One day, I was walking down a main street of our city when I was seventeen years old. I remember I was rushing to an exam at the university. A wolf pack of unknown hoodlums forced me into a car and four of them raped me. This was the way it worked in our lawless city at this time. A gang of three of four would leap on a young woman who would be too frightened to resist. Many friends of mine have told me the same thing happened to them. The police did nothing. How could we prove what had been done to us?

Worst of all, I got pregnant and had to get an abortion. When this stuff happens to you, you blame yourself. Society doesn't do anything to help you—that was our reality.

Men never paid attention to me anyway and I thought I would never be happy and loved. It was a feeling that there were no potential husbands or boyfriends for me. Most men at that time were alcoholics, drug users, and unemployed losers. When I was eighteen, I met Maxim, a nice twenty-five-year-old Russian man. We met in a public library. I was preparing for my final graduation examination. Maxim was an historian and was writing a research report about The Ice Age. He asked me for a pen and we started to talk. I liked him. He seemed to me very intelligent and, from the first minute around him, I felt protected. We started to date and everything was good between us. He introduced me to his family and I introduced him to mine. I didn't tell him that my mother was a Baptist. She was a normal kind of human being in her own world. My life story for Maxim was that my dad was killed by accident and I was raped by cruel people. He knew nothing else. I was smart and, now, pretty. I graduated from the university and, by that time, I liked Maxim a lot.

But when we made love he would try to hurt me by calling me different bad names like "bitch," "fool," and "dirty thing." But nothing else he did bothered me. I hoped that when we married he would stop calling me names and sometimes stop treating me roughly during our sex life. When I was twenty, we decided to get married. The only one thing I feared was I would never be able to have children. Maxim wanted them very much. We got married, started to live together, and soon I became pregnant. He was very happy from this news.

But after the baby was born, he decided he did not like the idea of fatherhood. He beat me time after time, paying no attention to the wild crying of our child. Finally, when the baby was a year and a half old, I decided I could not take it any longer.

Even as I was getting my clothes ready to move, he sexually assaulted me in front of the baby who screamed hysterically. When he left, I fled to my mother's. I tried to find a job and applied to every job agency in town for any position. The money which my mother received as welfare after my father's death wasn't enough. When Maxim and I divorced, he left us without any financial help. But I didn't want anything from him anyway. I wanted him out of our life.

One day an international job agency offered me a position in the USA as a housekeeper for a widowed rich man. They promised me $500 a week plus free lodging. I couldn't believe my luck. I agreed. I knew I would have to leave my little son with my mother for a while, but I knew I would come back. Here was the chance for me to earn money and to stop living this impoverished life. My mother could give my son a good upbringing and I could send them money. So I signed up for the job in Minnesota.

Bella, a Russian woman, met me in the airport in Minneapolis. On our way to the supposed place of work, to my astonishment, Bella said that she was a Madam. Before I could express my outrage, she said that I had better work for her, because I would earn much more money. She told me that this man I had to work for was freaked out all the time. She said he hadn't paid the last girls on time and fired her for a minor mistake. I said that I didn't believe her and at last she admitted the elderly widower did not exist. It was just her way of getting attractive Russian girls to the US where, without her, they would be stranded. She persuasively offered me work as a prostitute and I could live in her house. The money she promised I couldn't even dream about in Russia. I only half believed her, but I was exhausted. There was my poor mother with my little son. It did not matter to me what I had to do to earn money. I surrendered, weeping as I did.

So it was that a Russian madam handled my career as a prostitute here in America. She charged $3000 per date and took half. I could see four or five clients a day. In a shorter time than I expected, I had become used to it. Lots of people in Minnesota had money and for the most part my clients were very happy to help a poor little Russian girl. It was just a job to me. My first customer was a Greek man. He wanted to have sex three times per hour. The first time was the hardest for me because I couldn't stop thinking about my son, my mother, and all the kindness she taught me in my childhood. The only one kind thing I did with this man was to open my legs. But this Greek left me a $500 tip.

I was working for Bella two days a week. She had a lot of girls and each had special days and a scheduler. My days were Tuesday and Sunday from 10 a.m. to the last client. I needed money desperately when I arrived in America speaking no English. I slowly started to get girlfriends. One of them, Grishkin, worked in a go-go bar and helped me to get a job there too for the nights Bella did not need me. It meant dancing on stage. It was quick money that I could immediately send home to support my mother and to help her to raise my son. I was able to send her $300 a month, which was very good money in Russia. Most people with full-time jobs there earned something like $150 a month. I called Mother every two days. When I spoke to my little son I sometimes cried hysterically. I understood that it was not his fault that I was away. I couldn't even say when I would come back. Would he be in primary school or would he be a high school graduate?

After a while, I decided not to waste my time thinking about Russia and to try to get my papers. I dreamed that I had earned enough money to bring my mother and son to America. I believed that he would go to an American college and we would forget that poor miserable life in Russia. Here my mom would be able to be a free believer and attend Russian-speaking Baptist church. I decided to arrange a fake marriage. I found a man, Alex. I had a heavy debt to the marriage broker hanging over my head. What he was doing could put him in prison. I owed him $25,000 for this new life in America, and I paid him off every week in cash, $1000 each month. For this, he pretended to the authorities that we were truly married. I would eventually be granted my green card.

My first six or seven years in America were a grind; it was nothing but work, and much of it was degrading. I finally wanted to stop working for Bella. She was a smart woman and she dealt with escort services and with strip clubs too. So she offered me a job in a strip club in downtown Minneapolis. I agreed because I still needed money and a place to live. I saw a lot of women succumb to drug addiction and prostitution in the dancing business. I stayed away from all that. Certain bars had set schedules, others did not, but there were many days I worked fourteen-hour shifts every day.

For the first few years I worked seven days a week. For each shift I worked, I had to pay the house for the opportunity to dance—usually $50 a day. The tips I made were mine to keep. Also, since it was with Bella's help, I needed to pay her $100 a day. But living in her house, food was included.

We dancers were supposed to encourage the customers to drink, though we made no money on what they bought. All these places had separate back rooms for private lap dances at $20 a dance. Management looked the other way at what went on in the backrooms. I absolutely refused to have intercourse for money, but a massage was not out of the question. I could get a two- or three-hundred-dollar tip for giving a hand job. The money was too good to pass up.

Now I work as a dancer in a strip club. I give hand jobs to the thankful men. Soon I will be able to go home and see my nine-year-old son and my old mother. I am not planning to stay in Russia. I hate Russia and every year of my life there. I do have a lot of savings—almost $50,000. I want to bring my family to the USA. I want to buy an apartment. In six months I will have my citizenship. For now I am still working. But after I come back from Russia, I want to live in California where nobody knows me. I want to live in a place where I can build a new life, a new job, and build a new me.

Chapter 13
JOURNEY TO HAPPINESS

My name is Katya and I am twenty-three years old. Three years ago, I came to America. I was born in Tomsk, a small Siberian city located, as they used to say, on the edge of nowhere. I was an only child. My parents were wealthy business people. By local standards, we were rich. My parents earned $1,500-$2,000 per month. We took vacations abroad, had quality clothes, and ate delicacies at a time and place when just to have a closet of your own was considered a great luxury.

My parents owned two food stores located on the two opposite banks of our city. They sold bread, butter, milk, sausages, and all the necessary food. We sold almost everything that people wanted to buy and have on their shelves and in their refrigerators.

I was a happy child and was loved by my parents. My best friends were girls and boys whose parents had a similar socio-economic standing as my family. Together, we went to disco bars and on vacations to Turkey and Greece. Everything in my life went well, but, at the same time, I felt as if I lived my life in monotone; shades of gray were everywhere.

I graduated from high school with a gold medal for achieving top grades. I enrolled at the prestigious Tomsk State University Law School. I also started my own little business. I was eighteen years old when I rented a little kiosk in my parents' store. I bought lots of different pirated video tapes and opened a movie rental service. I started making a little money of my own. Soon many other stores started selling the same pirated videos. My profits went down, but I was still making a little extra money. I had a good-looking boyfriend named Alex. We used to share a school desk, and fell in love after the ninth grade. My parents weren't happy about him because the income of his parents was less than ours. My parents saw a future for their daughter only with a reliable and wealthy man. But as the saying goes: first love has no eyes. I remember truly believing for a fact that I would marry Alex and be the mother of his children.

I went to Egypt for a two-week vacation with my girlfriends. During this time, he found a new girl. Her parents were even richer than mine. His parents believed that he had to marry a rich girl in order to secure a carefree future. He was very handsome so the girls always had a crush on him. When he found the new girl, he quickly forgot about me. I returned home heartbroken, but wiser in the ways of the world. I suffered from unrequited love. I remember I couldn't eat, drink, or do anything. I went to bed with his picture and cried. But my parents were glad that it happened. They celebrated my break-up by toasting it with our store's most expensive champagne. That hurt my feelings even more. But as the saying goes, "Time is the best doctor and one of the few who makes house calls."

A few months, after I started going out and trying to smile again, I forgave him and released him from my heart. Slowly, everything began to seem better again, but I still felt that something was missing. I wanted to have a different life; not the one my parents wanted for me. I wanted to do something on my own. After my junior year at the university, I got an opportunity to go to America to finish my college education on a partial scholarship. My parents approved of my decision. I passed my exams and waited for my student visa. I happily said goodbye to everybody and celebrated my departure at a night club with my friends the night before.

The nearest airport was in Novosibirsk. From Novosibirsk, I needed to fly to Moscow and from there to New York. All my friends and my parents came to the airport to send me off. They knew I wouldn't be coming back any time soon. They kissed and hugged me and told me that there would be a huge party when I returned. I told myself that the party would be great, but not soon. I had an early morning flight. I didn't wear any makeup and was dressed casually. I looked like a teenager with a CD player and headphones on my ears. I took my seat on the plane, closed my eyes, and listened to the music.

Suddenly, a well-dressed man asked my pardon and took his seat next to me. I let him pass without saying a word and went back to listening to my music. He tried to strike up a conversation by saying, "Good morning," and "How are you?" I wasn't in a talking mood that morning. I wanted to plan my future during the flight. I knew it would seem impolite to ignore him. I analyzed him from top to bottom. He looked like a twenty-five-year-old solid man dressed in an Armani suit and shinny Gucci shoes.

Andrey was from Moscow. He was in Novosibirsk to meet with his business partners and do a deal. He told me his whole life story. After an hour, I knew that he was divorced and saw a picture of his five-year-old daughter. Andrey told me that he was the owner of a fabric manufacturing business in Turkey. He said that he was rather amused that so many of my friends came to see me off. He also added that I, such a wonderful young lady with sparkling brown eyes, couldn't stay unnoticed for a long time.

Andrey was standing behind me at the luggage check-in line, but I didn't remember seeing him. I never pay attention to people around me. When he found out my seat number, he asked a flight attendant to help him to change his first-class seat to economy to be near me. I guess the guy who was supposed to sit next to me couldn't believe his luck and made the switch. The first hour of our conversation, he seemed to me just an interesting person to talk to. But then I thought that I loved his blue bottomless eyes. Andrey asked if I'd sit off in another part of the plane with him so not to disturb other people with our conversation. We decided to drink some wine and toasted to my future life in America. He toasted to meeting me. He asked me why I was headed to America and I told him that I wanted to learn about the travel business; that it was offered through my university. I couldn't tell him the truth. I was a student who was going to work at McDonald's for $7 an hour and wanted to remain there.

After the first bottle of wine, we badly wanted to smoke. As people say, the forbidden fruit is sweet. We decided to smoke in the tiny restroom. It was so small that we had to be face to face, but that was okay as we both liked each other. Somehow, within a few minutes, we started to kiss and hug. I didn't understand anything at that moment; I just knew that I didn't want it to stop. After we left the restroom, we got a reprimand from a flight attendant about holding up people in line for a smoke in a no-smoke area. We took our seats. I got tired and fell asleep on his shoulder. Andrey covered me with his jacket. He touched my hair and whispered that he was looking for me his whole life and would never let me go. I heard every word, but I pretended that I didn't.

The plane landed in Moscow. When we left off of the plane, it seemed like we were a married couple. Andrey followed me and carried my suitcases like I was his pregnant wife. His driver met us there with his BMW. They gave me a ride to my relatives' home where I stayed overnight. I had a plane to America the next afternoon. Andrey said that he wanted to say goodbye to me the next day. We exchanged our e-mail addresses and he gave me his phone number. I didn't call him. I don't know why. I just was sure that we had no future. I was leaving and he stayed behind.

When I arrived in America, I sent him an e-mail. He answered me back with apologies because he took the wrong road and got stuck in traffic. When he got to the airport, it was too late, my plane had taken off.

My life in America began. When I arrived at JFK, I took a cab to Manhattan and didn't know what to do after that. Everywhere, there were yellow cabs and black drivers. That was scary. I didn't speak English fluently. All the students were gathering near Columbia University for orientation. It is there that

I met Rita and Zina, who were from Krasnodar. The agencies which helped us arrange the trip to America deceived us because the jobs they offered us didn't exist. We had no job, no scholarship, no place to live, or nowhere to go.

One of my goals in coming to America was to get my diploma in a shorter amount of time. How could I accomplish this in America? The answer is simple. I paid five hundred dollars for an "Official" college degree from any university of my choice. Through a secure internet site the diploma is sent along with completed transcripts with your desired grades to your selected university. The transferred credits are actually entered into the university database and then sent to an American university for further studies. This is why I don't just look at the degrees on the wall when I go to the doctor or dentist, I seek personal references.

We decided to stick together. Difficulties bring people closer. Zina spoke English, Rita and I only knew how to say, "How do you do?" It was late and we couldn't find a place to sleep. We couldn't afford to rent a hotel room in Manhattan for hundreds of dollars. Our first night we spent at a hot subway platform on 58th Street with black homeless neighbors.

We were afraid to fall asleep so each girl took turns and told the story of her life. The second night we spent at the Union Square platform. Third, at Canal Street. We spent a week sleeping on subway platforms. It was really extreme and we almost gave up and decided to go back to Russia and sue the education agencies.

One day, we met Russian students downtown who offered to help us. They found us an apartment in Brooklyn and showed us Russian language newspapers with help-wanted ads. My new friends started to work in Brooklyn restaurants. I found an ad in a newspaper for a job in Manhattan. I decided that it would be mine no matter what it was. I always wanted to work in Manhattan. I called. A Russian man said that they needed an art selling manager. I was excited. I left him my phone number and waited for an interview. I was sure they would hire me. Since my childhood, I drew nicely and was interested in artists of different epochs.

I knew a lot and could join any conversation. The interview day came. I dressed in high heels, a white shirt and a skirt. I met with my future boss at a Starbucks. He said that there were temporary repairs being done on the office. Conversation showed that my skills weren't necessary. I needed to have the skills of a seller and money counter.

I had to wake up early and work very late. He explained everything. The job did not seem to be too hard. The only thing that upset me was that I needed to be at Times Square at 6 a.m. every morning. I liked to sleep long hours.

I had to go to a storage room every day and pack a box of pictures and take a table and chair and put it all on a trolley. It weighed about one hundred pounds and I had to carry it down the streets of Manhattan and try to find a free spot to set my table and sell. I didn't feel comfortable selling the pictures to tourists who walked by. I remember how I went to the storage room in the mornings to get my stuff and the men looked at me and tried to get acquainted. I ignored them because thirty minutes later, I went back with the heavy trolley, my legs shaking and a sweaty forehead. I looked like Hercules because that trolley weighed more than I did.

Every day started at 4 a.m. I woke up, had a cup of coffee, a Newport cigarette, and got dressed. I walked fifteen minutes to the subway and it took me an hour and a half to get to Manhattan. At 6:30 a.m. I was already carrying the trolley and tried to find a free space to set up my stuff. There was competition between Russian and Chinese sellers for a better place and better business.

As a rule, whoever claimed the best location—by being the first one present—was sure to have the most business. My working day lasted usually from 6 a.m. to 1 a.m. the next day. Sometimes other vendors wouldn't leave their work locations and slept over on the boxes with pictures in order not to lose a place. Sometimes they would have fights, but, thank God, I didn't take part in them.

The first working week brought me no money, but only shame. The first day, I put copies on the table and hid myself aside.

I was too shy to do this job. This was because, in the mind of Russian people, to sell means to deceive somebody. I was an attractive young lady with three years of studying at the prestigious university of Tomsk, who had turned into a street seller in America. So I pretended that I didn't sell. How much money I would earn depended on how many tourists would spend $15 for color copies of views of New York. To me, the pictures didn't have marketable value. But in America, you can sell or get whatever you want to, from old batteries for one dollar to the cheap pictures I was selling.

I remember how I stood at the corner of forty-six street and Broadway. That day tourists came over to my table. They started to ask who was the salesperson and how much the pictures cost. I suddenly turned red and was not able to say a word. The tourists asked louder because they were ready to get it. I was standing aside and looking at them. They noticed me because I had nowhere to run from myself. I hardly said the price when, at that moment, I was ready to give them the pictures for free. I made my first $30, half of which I had to give to my Russian boss.

As time passed, I couldn't succeed in sales. It wasn't in my nature. I felt sorry for myself because I knew that my parents invested so much money in my future and would not be happy to find out that I was working on the streets. I worked six days a week. I slowly started to earn money. Sometimes I earned $500 per day.

Andrey e-mailed me every day. I sent him my picture and he framed it and put it on his desk at the office. He couldn't wait for me to come back to Russia. He wrote me that such a strong feeling had never happened in his life before. Andrey couldn't work because all his thoughts were about me. He was honest with me. But I couldn't tell when I would return. I didn't know. I couldn't tell him the truth about the job I did. I felt ashamed. I even lied to my parents and told them that I worked as a manager of art. Technically, I didn't lie. It was art. The art of being a good salesperson, the art of putting the pictures on the table in the right order for a marketable look.

I decided to stay in America. I called Tomsk and told my parents that I would remain. I felt like it was my time and I was at the right place. My parents were upset. They knew that, even if they didn't agree, I would do my own thing. So I applied to change my visa. I got a tourist visa which you can get for half a year and then you have a right to extend it four times. I worked a lot.

Once a group of Japanese men came up to me. They found out that I am Russian and said, "Russian beautiful! But no money, no honey!"

They asked to have a picture taken with me. I laughed about it. But then all the Arab, Spanish, and Chinese tourists began to come up to me and asked for a picture with me. I decided I could make money out of that. I started to charge $10 for having my picture taken with regular-looking tourists, and $15 from guys who looked rich. So after that, even when the business was slow with art sales, I still made a $100 from taking pictures with all nationalities. I worked like that on hot or rainy days for a year. I hated America and all the streets of Manhattan.

At the end of the year, as a result of all the hard work and from carrying all the heavy stuff, I got a kidney infection. I had terrible pain but I couldn't believe that it was my kidneys. I was always very healthy. That is why, when you get sick or something doesn't work in your body, you usually don't believe in it at first.

In October, right in front of Times Square I was taken by ambulance to the hospital. I didn't have any ID with me and was very thankful about that. While I was in the ambulance, I made up a false name and social security number. I was Valerie Modlo, my grandmother's maiden name. The social security number was my mother's birthday date. These were facts I couldn't ever forget. The one truth I told them was my billing address. I was curious to see how much they would charge me. They kept me only one day in the hospital. Two weeks later, they sent me a bill for $8,000. I was shocked. It was for nothing. I was glad that I lied because sometimes lies can save you.

I got an e-mail from Andrey again. He wrote that he wanted to see me in Moscow when I returned. I lied to him and wrote him that I got a prospect for my career and that I didn't know when I would be back. Andrey asked for my address in New York and said that he would come to any place on earth and take me from there.

I didn't work any more as a salesperson. I found a job as a babysitter in a Russian-speaking family. They paid me $500 for six working days. The family I worked for seemed very strange. The woman laid around the whole day, or she'd be in a bathtub full of sliced cucumbers. She said that after she delivered the baby, she needed to care of herself. Her poor husband worked three different jobs and came back home deathly tired and not able to do anything.

His wife gave me orders every moment and kept me busy. She wore expensive clothes and tried to look beautiful while I worked. Once when I was changing the diaper for her nine-month-old daughter, she came in and said that she felt like the child was hers and mine. At first, I didn't pay attention to her words. Half a year later, she tried to kiss me. She said that she fell in love with me and would give me everything I deserved. I was shocked. I never went back to work, even to get my paycheck.

Andrey asked for my address again. He wanted to come and take me back to Russia. I gave it to him. I thought that it was just a joke. A week later, he stood at my door with a huge bouquet of red roses. We spent two weeks together in New York. We didn't leave the apartment. We made love with only breaks for food. The time came for him to go back. He asked me to go with him and to marry him. I couldn't agree. I liked America and my independence. I had a difficult life, but I controlled it. We held hands and couldn't say goodbye to each other. I couldn't believe the happiness I had for two weeks was about to disappear from my life but there was no guarantee that we would have a future.

He flew back. I cried for a week. He called me and said that he was in love with me. He asked me to be his wife and promised to give me the best life. I loved him very much, but I didn't want his money. I liked America and I wanted to accomplish everything myself. I was dying from the desire to be with him, but I couldn't make the right decision.

My period was late and then it didn't come at all. I was pregnant. Andrey wrote to me five times a day. I didn't respond to him. I was afraid that he would think that I needed his money or connections and decided to marry him because I wasn't successful in America. I couldn't have an abortion because of my health condition. But I didn't even want to think about it. I explained the situation to my mother. She said that they would help me out but that I should let Andrey know that he would be a father. We had enough money to raise the baby without his financial help.

I decided that I wanted to remain in America until I had a big belly. I always had positive emotions about America and told my mother that I wanted to stay for a while. I promised her that I would deliver the baby in Russia. Also, I needed to stay in America because of my health. A gynecologist told me that I was at risk of losing my baby. She wanted to look after me, at least for the first few months when the baby goes through the important phase of developing. My parents sent me money from Russia. I also had savings. I lived all the months trying to think positive. I went to all the possible museums, theaters, etc. I wrote Andrey that I was coming back to Russia at the beginning of February. He asked what made me reach the decision to leave America, which I loved very much. I didn't tell him.

On February 23, I arrived in Moscow. I went to my aunt's house. I was there no longer than five minutes when there was a knock at the door. I opened the door and there were two policemen. They asked for me and said they needed to talk to me. They asked me if I knew this man and showed me a picture of Andrey. I said I did. They questioned me for over an hour and a half. They wanted to know what I knew about his business affairs and what he did. I didn't know anything and I told them so. At the end of the interview, they told me that Andrey was in jail for an offence against the State and that it would be unlikely for me to see him again.

I asked where he was and if I could contact him and they suggested that it would be a very bad thing for me to have any further association with him. They said that it was an absolute fact that was necessary for my well-being if I remained in Russia. I realized at that time that I'd made a tremendous mistake. Moscow was no longer a safe place for me.

I called my parents and was ready to go home to the comfort of their loving arms. But I faced even worse news. My father had refused to pay off the local crime bosses. Both of his stores were vandalized on the same day. Much of the contents were destroyed. The same crime bosses came back to my father and asked him to reconsider. He said that he would think it over and let them know in a week. They told him that he didn't have a week. He told them that he wasn't sure he was going to comply. The next day, it was reported that there was a car accident and my father was killed and my mother was in the hospital on life support. In all probability, she would not regain consciousness.

Russia, unlike America, does not keep people hospitalized for a very long period of time because the cost is very high and the state can't afford it. I knew I had no place to turn. I stayed with my aunt during the delivery of my wonderful baby, Nastya. Then, I started exercising and getting into shape. I was as attractive as before I had the baby. Indeed, I was courted by a number of men in the neighborhood, but I knew there was no future with any of them.

I had some small savings, which I used for necessities, but I needed to find a way back to America. I didn't know what to do. One of my girlfriends told me that there was a service called "Svetlana." They introduced girls to nice American men at parties and arranged marriages where there could be a happy life for the girls, and perhaps even for her child or children. I felt that I should at least explore this possibility. I paid a fee of $300 to attend the parties. At the third party, I met Roger. He was not young, he wasn't handsome, but he was very nice to me. He told me of the good life I could have with him in Saint Louis. He owned his home.

He had people to clean the home and a swimming pool. He would make a good place for me and my daughter. We would vacation often and I would be able to have the nicest things in life for me and a good future for my daughter.

I was taken with his kindness and his sympathy. I overcame my doubts and said that I'd marry him. Roger paid the Svetlana Agency $2,000 and they did all of the paperwork necessary. Two weeks later, I was flying on a one-way tourist ticket on Lufthansa Airlines to Frankfurt, then to New York and finally to Saint Louis. My husband-to-be met me when I got off the plane and we went to his house, which was in fact an attached track home in a condominium development area with a community pool. That was not how he had described it, but I was happy that Nastasya would have a home and someone who would care for and look after both of us.

For our honeymoon, we went to Las Vegas and stayed at the Stardust hotel in a room he had managed to get for $49.95. I've never seen anything like Las Vegas. I enjoyed what I saw which mostly consisted of three meals at the buffet, which was offered to slot machine players and their families. Roger spent all of his time at the slot machines and left me on my own. I did enjoy the weekend. Shortly after we consummated our relationship, he left to play the slot machines and the card games. So there was my honeymoon.

When we arrived back in Saint Louis, I found that life wasn't as previously pictured. Roger said that we needed to save money for our future and Nastya's education. He said that I was to do the housework so that we could save even more money. Of course, I did the ironing and the cooking. At first, I didn't realize this would be every night. He told me that he worked quite hard, which, of course, I accepted. But often, he came home late at night with liquor on his breath. When I asked why and asked what he was doing, he told me to shut up and that I was just a damn Russian bitch.

There went the illusion that I had about my happy marriage and a loving husband; it was all fiction. And yet, I needed to stay at least long enough to get my green card. With luck, such a process can take a year. Roger was often not willing to go to appointments with me and help with the process on a timely basis, so it took almost two years to get my papers. Roger, I'm sure, felt I didn't have a place to go and would stay no matter what he did.

After I received my green card, from that day onward, I was his willing slave. There was hot food on the table, no matter what time he arrived. His cigarettes were always by the couch. When he watched sports on TV there was hot buttered popcorn on the coffee table. When he wanted sex, I was available for him to fulfill all of his varied wishes and experiments. I was the perfect Barbie-doll wife content to stay at home while he went and got drunk or anything else he wanted to do. He would tell his friends that he had broken me in and that I was the best wife in Saint Louis. Once he even brought me home some candy, although it had been opened and some pieces were missing. I carefully managed his money while shopping, but I was always careful to put a few dollars aside each time I could, to add to my own small savings which I kept under the lining in the corner of my suitcase.

There was nothing he could ask that I would not do. As soon as he woke up in the morning, I rushed to start his breakfast and brought him coffee in bed. I always had a smile on my face. He seemed happy with me, but still was mean to me. The greatest luxury he ever gave to me was every month or so, he took me to a movie and for a steak dinner at a restaurant called Sizzler. Six months to the day that I got my green card, I cooked him the most lavish dinner I could make, including a soufflé for dessert. That night I performed every sexual act that he had taught me, but this time I did it to flatter his ego, pretending to be overwhelmed with his manliness.

The next evening when he came home from work, Nastasya and I were gone. All our things were gone; all traces of where we went will never to be known to him again. I believe that for the rest of his life, he will wonder what happened to us, and he'll suffer knowing that no one will ever give him what I gave him. He will admit it was real, but not know what on earth had happened. Now I am teaching at a kindergarten in Brooklyn, where my daughter attends school. We live in a condo in Brighton Beach and my life is just fine. I am happy at last.

Chapter 14
THE LONG ROAD HOME

I was born in Saint Petersburg, but I was too little to be able to remember my life in Russia. When I was two years old my mother married my father who was a forty-year-old immigrant from Saint Petersburg named Paul. He moved us to America. In Russia, my mother worked as a travel guide. She showed foreign tourists the places of war and architectural glory. My mother said that they lived a good life in Russia.

When I was seventeen, I found an adoption certificate among my mother's important documents. I was confused and deceived because it said that Paul wasn't my real father. My mother explained that Paul was fifteen years old when his family migrated to America. Twenty-five years later he came back to his native land to recapture his childhood memories. He met my mother and found out that she was a single Russian lady with a one-and-a-half-year-old little daughter and he began to court her vigorously. They dated for a while and passionately fell in love. He wanted to have kids, but he couldn't have them because of his health condition. My mother knew that it would be hard for her to give me everything and that's why he adopted me.

Although she explained, I was hysterically upset. I didn't understand why she had deceived me all these years. Paul loved and spoiled me. I would have never thought that he wasn't my real father. My mother told me that a real father wasn't the one who made me. A real father was the man who gave me everything, was always near, and took an active part in my upbringing.

My mother finally told me that my real father's name was Tolik Anatoly Vasiliev. They studied at the same university. They were friends and started dating. After one of the parties, they made love, and later my mother found out that she was pregnant. When she told Tolik, he said that they were too young to become parents; they hadn't set their lives yet. He was a child himself and wasn't ready to become a father and take on that kind of responsibility. He recommended that she have an abortion. But the doctor told my mother that if she had an abortion, she would never be able to have children again. If by chance she would become pregnant, she would lose her unborn child in a few months.

It was their last year at the university. My mother decided to have me. In the evenings, she worked from home and was paid for writing synopses for lazy students. During her ninth month of pregnancy, she was studying hard for her final exams. She was afraid that she would deliver me in front of the professors from the university. They were scared by her big belly and wouldn't ask her any questions in fear that it might make her nervous or upset and induce her labor. The professors automatically passed her through all the final exams.

Tolik helped in the beginning, but disappeared later. He transferred his documents to another university and started to live a new life. My mother remained full of pride. She didn't try to find him. She knew she could raise me by herself because she had never met her own parents. She was an orphan. She was sure that I would always be around her, and a single mother with a daughter could be a happy family.

My mother had a younger girlfriend, Lusya, from the university. She helped my mother and sat with me while my mother was running around the city trying to find a job. My mother wrote a synopsis for her as well. So it was a-favor-for-a-favor relationship, and both were happy and comfortable with that. Then my mother found a job as a guide and ran with tourists around the city. Lusya helped and received souvenirs from thankful tourists, which were in the former Soviet Union.

I was an attractive young girl with bright blue eyes, curly red hair, a thin waist and big breasts. Men always liked me. At that time, almost every boy liked me because I had a woman's desirable body and it drove them crazy. I started to date boys early. When I turned eighteen, I partied in a company of older guys and students from Baku. My girlfriends and I felt like they were sponsors and fun company.

There was one guy that I liked named Paata. One spring evening there was a party at his house. I had been drinking, and kissed Paata. It was an exciting feeling. I felt my pulse race throughout my whole body. He took me to a different room and started to take off my clothes. I realized that he was ready to make love to me. I was in a panic; I shouted and started to cry. He was strong enough to hold me down with just one hand to keep me from moving. He didn't react and ignored my shouting. He just whispered something like: "Bad girl, don't play around. I know that you want me." He kissed me passionately and then he fucked me. Later, he apologized for what he had done. He didn't know and didn't believe that I was a virgin. I was ashamed; I hid that incident from mother and everybody. I was in pain and I cried into my pillow all that night.

At the age of forty, my mother and Paul found out they were having a baby. They thought it was a miracle and were very happy. Paul was absolutely against us living in Brooklyn, which is where we lived at that time. He said that a baby needed a quiet atmosphere and fresh air. He said that we had a car and could come to Brooklyn any time to visit. I was against us moving. I had all my friends and my computer classes in Brooklyn. My parents decided not to sell their apartment and they let me stay. Paul and Mother bought a house in Upstate New York. They would visit once a week or I went to visit them. My mother would give me enough money to buy food and necessary things.

After hearing my mother's story, I decided that I wanted to look into the eyes of my biological father. My mother and Paul were against it. They said trying to find my father was like looking for a needle in a haystack. I needed money badly. My mother wouldn't give me the money if I was going to use it to find him. I couldn't work during the day because I was attending school. I wanted to earn and save enough money to go and find my real father in Russia. I was calculating how much I would have to pay for a flight, hotel, and to hire a detective.

When I was nineteen, my mother and Paul went to Europe for a month. They left me behind because I had exams. I thought it would be the perfect opportunity to find my father. I sat with my girlfriend and we looked through the newspapers trying to find a job. We saw an advertisement where they invited girls to visit a health club and spa. I went the next day. There was a security guy at the front door. When he opened the door, a steam aroma met me. I went into the room and met a very sweet and charming American woman named Jessica. We liked each other from the first minute. She walked me in to another room where four other girls sat and I found two of them to be attractive. They explained the job to me. It was simply to give a massage, nothing difficult. Before that moment, I knew only about medical massages. I finished school, but I didn't enroll in a college. I didn't want to waste time and I started working right away.

During the first week, the girls had taught me the art of massage. They told me what men liked to get from us and what they didn't. There were four rooms with music, massage tables, mirrors and a shower. I was working with the name they gave me, which was Stella. I wanted to be a Lolita, but they had one already. There was a Tina and a Barbara too. Before I started to work, I was nasty and rude to men. But while I was working I became a pleasant feminine woman in all my professional relations. My earnings seemed huge at that time. I made five to six hundred dollars per day. I worked that way for three months until one day the police came and we got busted. They came and pretended they were normal clients dressed in regular clothing. They showed us a fake ID and when one of the girls walked her client in a room, asked him to get comfortable and pay money, he showed her a police badge instead.

I was taken in with other girls to the police department. It was scary. They put us in different rooms separate from each other and started to threaten us. Then another police officer came in and started to act like a nice guy. He promised to let us go if we would cooperate and tell them the truth and the names of our bosses. Thank God our bosses reacted very quickly and paid someone off for our release. The police let us go without a record. That day, I smoked four packs of cigarettes, and lost four pounds from stress. Needless to say, I quit that job.

During the next five months, I was running from one spa to another with hope to earn fast money, but it never worked out like it did at that first spa. I was upset. I got addicted to the large sums of money. We sat in a little room with a television set. Some of the girls applied makeup, others got dressed. We were waiting for a call from the "phone girl"; she was the one who booked our clients.

Someone would ring the door bell and we had to search them at the check point outside, through a window. We had to make sure they didn't look like police. They came in and we checked their ID. They had to choose two girls from the four of us. These were Arabs who looked at us carefully, and they chose me and Tina. We walked our customers to a room. My client put two hundred dollars on the table for a regular full body massage. They didn't want to pay much money, but they all wanted to get a good service. That client tried to put his fingers in my panties. I removed his hand from my thigh. I hit him on the head and he passed out and fell off the table. He told me that he just wanted to make me aroused. But they were all just money to me. He was disgusting and I threw him out.

Nobody wanted to pay extra money or tips for the service. Forget the fact that we ran around the table all day long. Everyday, a girl usually had about eight customers. At the end of the day, we were so nervous and emotionally off-balance. Some girls smoked and some drank just to pull themselves back together. There was nothing to do while you waited for another client. That was the hardest thing for me.

One night, a regular customer, who was an Italian man in his forties, raped me. He was very controlling and demanded everything be his way. He was a big, solid man with a large penis. When he was done, he left me a lot of money, I guess to help me forget about the pain. I couldn't. But who was I to complain? We were prostitutes and what we did was illegal. There is no doubt that some of the girls would give blow jobs and fuck for extra money. Some customers had their different peculiarities: sadists, gays, and people who loved to be humiliated by women. I understood one thing. No matter what's happening in your life there is always a normal way to solve any problems. God suffered in order for us to have that chance. The main idea is not to put your life at risk because of money. Money ends and your health will eventually take you down. Money is only paper and you can't buy your health back.

After that client, I quit that job. It wasn't easy because my bosses were Italian Malfiosos and they said that if they found out that I went to work with a different agency, or stole clients from their agency, I would be in huge trouble. I knew that it wasn't a good idea to play games with them. I didn't violate their rules, and I took a break from that lifestyle.

I started to live by a normal schedule and return to feeling like a normal human being. I would go to my favorite place at Starbucks in Brighton Beach and write in my diary. One day, I arrived there and a handsome American guy there asked me to share a table with him. He kept staring at me. Then, a few minutes later, asked why my eyes were so sad and empty. I pretended I didn't hear anything. But he continued on and said that he would do anything to make me feel happy. I smiled. He said that my smile was the best smile he had ever seen. He asked what I was writing about and I started to cry. I was so depressed and consumed by the idea of finding my father that everything in my life seemed unfair. I was ashamed and hated myself for what I had put myself through.

We began to talk that day. Larry was a twenty-five-year-old successful real estate investor. He was from California and came to visit his friends on that weekend. He was happy when I told him I was Russian. He told me that he always wanted to have a Russian girlfriend with her different emotional world and views on life. He said that our life was like a zebra. We all have black and white lines. So at that time I had a black line and the next line to come is supposed to be white for good luck. We started dating. He would come to visit me in New York two times a month. I would go to visit him in California every other weekend.

Later that year, I became a big sister. My mother had delivered a baby girl and named her Melissa. Paul was happy; my mother cared very much about her newborn daughter. They became very busy and didn't concern themselves about my life very much. But one day, my parents invited us over for dinner at their home when Larry was visiting me. It was a wonderful evening. In the middle of the dinner, Paul took me to a different room in the house and gave me his approval of Larry. He said that Larry was the best man for me, he would take good care of me and was a very knowledgeable person. Then it was my mother's turn and she asked if I loved him. At that time, my life was so crazy; I wasn't sure how I felt about him. Everything changed in a half year.

On my twenty-first birthday, I went with Larry to Saint Petersburg. He was shocked by the style of life Russian people lived. We found my father through his mother, who was still alive. She gave us his address. I was too little to remember how the Russian middle class lived. My father lived in a two-floor building with old and scratched painted walls and no light in his bathroom. He looked terrible to me. I could not say that he was my father. He couldn't remember me either. But when I told the story about my mother, he started to cry and apologize. I didn't need his apologies. I was curious to see him and I did it. There are no regrets. I know I don't look like him in any way.

I remember when I was younger, I didn't appreciate Paul after I found out about the adoption. I wanted to find my real father and look into his eyes and ask one question. How could you give up on Mother and me? Now, I am adult, I am smart and my biological father will always be a fucking son of a bitch. This terrible phrase I practiced in front of a mirror as a teen and for a long time after.

I realized I belonged to Paul and he will always be my father. Not that stranger with the swollen face from drinking. We had nothing to talk about. I had nothing to ask. It wasn't a pleasure to observe the remains of what was once a normal human being. My father had turned into an alcoholic with shaking hands, terribly bad breath, and an awful body odor. All he had in his refrigerator was some old eggs, half of the dark bread loaf, and some milk. We did not even have lunch with him. Before we left him, my father said to me: Since you said you are my daughter would you give your poor father a few rubles to buy a celebration drink. Larry gave him a hundred-dollar bill and we left.

Larry asked my parents' permission to allow me to go live in California with him and try to enroll me in UCLA. For my parents, it was the best prospect I could have. For me, it was a chance to spend all my time with Larry and to get my education. We decided I needed to go, and we lived in a wonderful comfortable apartment. I started to study journalism at UCLA. We lived very happily and we never fought. After a year of living together, Larry proposed to me. At that moment, I couldn't imagine my life without him. He had done everything for me and now I was ready to enter into a marriage and start a new family. I knew our relationship would grow and be even better. I was proud and told everybody that I was engaged. I couldn't wait to show the ring to all my girlfriends.

In July, we celebrated our wedding. My family was happy for me and they came to help. I was happy too, but my past didn't give me the chance to feel absolute happiness. I knew I had lied to my future husband and always would. I was very disappointed after visiting my father. It was not because I met him in that horrible condition. It was because I realized that I had become a prostitute because of the strong desire to meet my real father, and he wasn't worth that. He didn't even remember that I existed and I suffered trying to find him.

At twenty-two, I became pregnant. Nine months later, I delivered twins who looked absolutely like Larry. He is the best father, he gives us oceans of love and cares for me and our kids. Melissa started to walk slowly and said her first word, which was mama. My parents are happy about that because they know that she loves them both. They are perfect parents. I am still studying at the university. Larry helps me with the kids when I need to go to my classes.

Now my life seems perfect to me. One thing which bothers me a lot is that my husband doesn't know about my past. Sometimes in my dreams, I see my past life with all those lustful clients. It's impossible to forget, but what is worse is that I have to pretend it never happened. I still wonder why I wanted to meet my real father. Why didn't I think that he could possibly be dead already? Maybe he moved or just got lost somewhere? If I thought these things, I would not have done that job to earn enough money to be able to meet him. I stood on a lonely road of sins. I feel like I will always live with a sin if I continue to lie to the man I love and the father of our children. I know that this may sound like an excuse, but I am sure that if I didn't place meeting my father as a main goal and priority, I would never have been in that world of sin. I have all these regrets. I try and make up for the mistakes in my past by giving the best that I can to my family. "The road that God sends you down can never be known until you have traveled it."

Chapter 15
WHO NEVER RISKS, NEVER TASTES CHAMPAGNE

Every person has uttered the words "I love you." Most women ask themselves, "Why do I love this man?" We also wonder, "Does he love me just as much?" We conjure up all the positive qualities about his character. We try to find an explanation for our love by examining all of his attributes. Then we find a path to love and, if necessary, forgive him. It's always interesting to ponder who is capable of loving deeper—a man or a woman? Again and again, we say, those three little words as we snuggle into his shoulder. But what exactly is love?

I can't say that we can always distinguish the real feeling from a mixture of dubious feelings. It happens very often that a feeling which seems like love is, in reality, quite lightweight without any serious commitment or consequences. For instance, when you have a high temperature for him and he says that he loves you, but he can't come to you. Or when he dreams about a vacation house in Italy, but, in reality, he can't even spend a weekend with you at home. Or when he gives you constant promises, but when it's time to put his money where his mouth is, he can't commit for any indefinite period of time. People say that it takes three years before you have a real knowledge of someone's character. But do you think it's always possible to be that patient when we're talking about a fire that can't put itself out?

When you are in love, you can't easily determine real love from mere empty words. Often, we don't build solid relationships.

We're sure that a real and better love is waiting for us in the near future. Later, we realize that the chance to meet our second half, our soul mate appears only once in our lives. It's very scary if we lose that chance. Many people really want to embrace a perfect match.

People say that a woman's happiness depends on being near the man she loves. But, for most women, their dream man has become the one who owns the latest model luxury car, wears a fine suit and has a fat wallet. The time has come when a comfortable future has overthrown any need for a deep love. Yes, times have changed, but they still haven't changed the minds of women who still believe in ideal love.

For a smart woman, even if she is a thousand times more beautiful than the rest, real happiness is not about marrying a millionaire, moving abroad, or establishing a great career. The most important thing is to meet a nice and intelligent man who will be good to her and become the loving father to her children. Of course, every woman dreams about a glamorous wedding dress, white limo, and an expensive ring with a big diamond. But is this so important for a future family life?

I was born in Moscow. My parents had a good income. My mother was a talented artist. My father was a jeweler. These two professionals weren't important or well-paid in the former Soviet Union. However, during the 90s, out of necessity, my parents began to work as hard as bees.

At that time, the brigades appeared in Russia. A brigade was a group of friends or "brothers" who built businesses based on criminal activity and became rich and important. People called them "new Russians." It was a prestigious to be called a "new Russian." Like "new money" in America, they were well-dressed, dined elegantly, and lived in well to do areas. In other words, they spent a lot of money.

To accommodate the wealthy newcomers, my parents opened a small studio. My mother painted the portraits of the new Russians' wives. My father made gold and diamond rings for the same customers. My parents became image-makers for the new

Russians—at least they kept them looking cool. The wives of the new Russians were exchanged rapidly and thus so was the portrait order. The new brides added more diamonds to their rings with my father's help. My parents were busy from early morning until late at night. But even during those busy times, parents never spoiled me with material things. Sometimes their clients paid with quantities of cheese and sausage from foreign countries. Such food was unknown or very expensive for Soviet people. That is why we always had high quality food and delicacies on our table.

My parents dressed me differently from the other children my age. Many years ago, my mother made a portrait of a woman who was a private seamstress. She took orders and made clothes from a rare magazine called "Burda Moden." My mother and I wore all the dresses, and I earned my own money. My father and mother didn't believe in luck. My father used to quote the proverb: "Spend lots of time on your work first and get an hour for rest later."

At age seven, I started to assist them at the studio. I helped my mother mix the paint and refill jars. I helped my father weigh the gold and count the diamonds. I also had to keep the shop clean. That was how my parents made me get used to working. As a reward, they put money in my piggy bank. We had a deal that I would not open it until I was twenty-one years old.

I was a good student in school. I wrote wonderful compositions about my childhood. When I was in high school, I worked part-time at a newspaper for teenagers called "Youth." I wrote articles about sporting events and other competitions for Moscow students. When I graduated, I knew that I would study journalism in college.

I enrolled at Moscow State University. It was interesting for me to study there. I imagined myself being a journalist and nothing else. Often, successful journalists and television personalities came to our classes and shared their personal and professional experiences with us. However, when a producer named Leonid came, I fell in love. For the entire week, I went to a class where he talked about the errors and successes in the world of television. I asked virtually all the possible questions. At nineteen, I wanted him to remember me and distinguish me from the crowd.

Finally, Leonid paid attention to me. One day, after a seminar, he came up to me and asked if I wanted to visit the television station. I almost passed out from the thrill. I went to a beauty salon. I colored my dark brown hair black. I ordered a black business suit with pants and two blouses with English collar. I wanted to look perfect. I knew that Leonid was my opportunity. I couldn't lose him. It was a window to a career.

I wanted to prove to him that I wasn't merely a curious young lady. I was gifted and wanted to learn much more than what was offered to me at the university. I showed up at his studio on my twentieth birthday. I had straight black shoulder-length hair, eyelashes with mascara and red-colored lips. I looked older than my age and I loved it. Leonid had a new project. He wanted to do a reality show about teenagers and their relationships. He asked me to look for interesting stories and characters who would agree to take part in the show. It was my first television work, and also my birthday, but nobody except him knew about my birthday.

I sat with him and learned. He was so handsome and solid-looking that my heart was racing. I was 5'7" and he was 6'2" with blond hair. We could be the perfect couple; I thought Leonid was very interested in my ideas and opinions. He gave me a few suggestions for the beginning of a story, and few hours to do it. The first two months, I worked very hard and tried my best. The first show was set. Leonid asked me to his office. He praised me. He said that he didn't make a mistake when he chose such a creative employee, and beautiful young lady. I felt very proud of myself. I hadn't spent my nights at the disco, but rather writing stories.

It wasn't for nothing. Leonid's was the best praise that I had ever heard in my life. That same day, Leonid invited me for a cup of coffee in the downstairs cafeteria. He told me that he wanted to offer me a position as a journalist. He said that he liked me a lot. We both understood that the success of my job depended on our personal relationship. I knew that I needed him more than he needed me. He offered to meet me after work to celebrate my birthday.

He said that he hadn't congratulated me because he didn't want to interfere with my work attitude and create a feeling of intrigue from the first day. I understood. We went to a restaurant and had a bottle of champagne. We talked and laughed. Leonid was interested in my private life priorities. I fell in love with his sparkling eyes. I had never been in love before. Lots of men liked me, but I never paid attention to them. They were like kids compared Leonid. He showered me with compliments that evening. He wondered how he could have lived for thirty-three years and never meet such a charming and beautiful lady.

While he paid for dinner, I called my parents and told them I'd sleep over at my girlfriend's house. I couldn't let our evening end. Leonid came out of the restaurant with a bouquet of roses. After that, I was ready for anything. He asked me if I was in a rush to go home. I said no. We drove slowly and held hands. We stopped at a hotel and took a room. I was scared. I couldn't tell him that I was a still a virgin. We went onto the balcony. The view of Moscow was beautiful at night. Leonid kissed me and told me that he had been looking for me his whole life.

Later, I found myself on a wide brass bed. Everything happened so quickly and painfully. He asked me why I didn't tell him that I was a virgin. I didn't answer. It wouldn't have changed anything. I was glad that he was my first lover. After all, he was the handsome and famous Leonid. I knew that everything between us was waiting ahead. I fell asleep while he was telling me all his dreams about us. I woke up the next morning as a young and very happy woman. Leonid brought me breakfast in bed. We drank coffee and ate fresh baked croissants. Leonid told me that no one should know about our affair at work. It was against his work ethic. I agreed with it. I didn't want any gossip.

I took the subway and went to work. Leonid, the boss, took a cab. Our passionate affair continued for almost a year. I graduated from the university and continued to work at the station. I loved

Leonid more with each passing day. I didn't know why, but for his part, he became colder and busier. On the weekends I missed him very much. I counted the days until our next meeting. We always went to the same hotel, and, most of the time, even the same room. In the morning, we took different means of transportation to work. My parents didn't notice anything unusual. They were too busy with their jobs. I was still a very good daughter. I cooked, cleaned the house, studied and worked.

My twenty-first birthday came. I was excited. I waited for a surprise from Leonid. I had no friends. Girls were envious of me. Guys seemed to me like little kids compared to my Leonid. On that day, I got an offer from the television company. They wanted to send two people to America for a few months. We had to film and write about Russian immigrants who were successful in Russia and had achieved the same in America. Leonid recommended me and Misha. Misha was a photographer. Our travel department applied for visas.

That evening, Leonid gave me a real birthday party. At first, we went shopping in the Moscow boutiques at a local mall. Afterwards, we went to a rented country house for a weekend. This was the first time during our relationship that Leonid had spent two days straight with me. It was heaven. He took care of me. He declared his love. But he always told me that he was so sorry that he met me too late. I thought that he was talking about the twelve years age difference. I smiled, kissed his forehead, and said that everything would be just fine in our future. I wanted to have a child with him. Every woman wants to have a baby with the first man she loves.

I regretted that I had applied for a visa to America. I couldn't even imagine how I would live so long without Leonid. I wanted to give up the business trip, but Leonid told me it was a great opportunity to build a career faster and to make more money.

As the saying goes: love comes and goes, but we always want to eat. I understood this. My parents taught me well. When all is said and done every person has to rely on himself and work hard his whole life. I had worked since my childhood and was never afraid of any job. I remember once when Leonid gave me a couple of hundred dollars for my personal expenses, I felt insulted. I was used to earning money on my own; I was capable of supporting myself. In fact, that caused our first serious fight. I was young and full of energy. I didn't want to ride on somebody else's shoulders and turn myself into a mistress who needed to be kept.

During the entire trip back from our weekend, Leonid was sad and held my hand. But we decided to continue our celebration. First, we went to a bar, then we finished a bottle of champagne and, to my surprise, Leonid asked me to go to his house. This meant a lot to me. It was one more step closer to him and a stronger relationship. Leonid was finally inviting me to his castle. To me, this meant that I deserved his trust and respect. We came to an elite building in Moscow and we went upstairs to his apartment. I was burning with curiosity.

As soon as I walked in, I noticed a portrait of a beautiful woman painted by my mother. Then, I was shocked to see framed pictures of his wife and two little sons. I was struck dumb.

Leonid was ashamed of himself. He asked me for my forgiveness. He said he didn't know how to tell me either. He admitted he wasn't brave enough. I knew that a person can't be happy forever, but I didn't expect such a blow. I walked up to Leonid and slapped his face. As I drew back to slap him again, he stopped my hand and said, "Don't do that." Crying, I dashed out of his apartment. Once outside I ran for the bus, and then the train that would take me home. It was two o'clock in the morning when I arrived, I cried the entire night. The next day I couldn't go to school or work. People say that love is something that often winds up hurting deep inside your heart. I felt hurt that day to the fullest, my whole body hurt. I loved Leonid so very much. I was sure he was mine from the first moment we met and I was certain that he felt the same way.

Within a week, I was to graduate. I couldn't eat. I lost fifteen pounds. I didn't go to work. I was dying without Leonid. I felt sorry for myself and I can say with all honesty, I felt the same for his wife. We were both victims. Neither of us knew about the other.

Leonid showed up with flowers at my graduation ceremony. I skipped the celebration that followed it. We talked and walked the embankment as he again asked for my forgiveness. He took the blame for falling in love with me. He never thought of taking back the job he had given me. On the contrary, he felt guilty that our relationship was doomed from the start. He tried to open doors for me, but I couldn't be near him. I couldn't pretend that we were just co-workers or acquaintances. I wanted to kiss him, but I didn't. I continued to live without the man I loved.

I was twenty-two when my visa to America was granted. Misha, Leonid's photographer, and I started to pack our suitcases and prepared for our trip. Leonid was upset all time. I felt that he missed me very much. Yet, I stopped missing him. I was thankful that he was my first lover. But I wanted to go to America and change my entire environment.

I said goodbye to Leonid and we parted as good friends. I could see the hurt in his eyes. I felt offended by it. Before my flight, my parents and I broke the piggy bank and somehow there was $600 in it. I was glad that I didn't have to ask them for more. They were pleased with my prospects.

From my earliest childhood, I don't remember seeing any visible love and warmth between my parents. They loved their jobs, money and me. But all they did was sleep, eat, drink, work and count their money. They were interested in politics, news and travel. They lived in their own world and it was comfortable for both of them. That is probably why they stayed together and didn't get a divorce. They just never disturbed each other.

In the plane with Misha, we made a list of food we promised each other that we wouldn't eat. It included hot dogs, pizza and French fries because we didn't want to gain any weight. We spoke only in English during the entire flight. I saw myself going to America on a business trip as if it were another city in

Russia. I wasn't as excited as Misha. He kept telling me that America was a country of dreams and opportunities. We landed. People from the New York-Russian affiliate station met us at the airport. We lived in a rented apartment in Manhattan Beach in Brooklyn. We wanted to be closer to the people we came to write about. The first few days were difficult for me and Misha. We went to the supermarket and tried to convert the prices. We didn't buy any food and went to bed hungry. To us, the prices seemed outrageous. We were shocked that a loaf of simple white bread cost the equivalent of six loaves in Russia.

Later, we understood that there was no sense in comparing prices. We decided to work, earn, spend the money and get by the best that we could. I already liked New York and I associated it with Moscow. It had similar shops, restaurants, and high-rise buildings. If you have money, I thought you could live any place in the world.

Our apartment was near a place where Russians hung out. Many were from the Mafiosi organization in Russia and were doing the same kind of thing in America. They drove expensive cars, wore modern clothes, and ate at the finest restaurants. They lived in America and many were American citizens, but they were still Russians in spirit and mentally. They received and spent American dollars, but they still created a small Russia in every state. Many of them were racketeers and had done machinations in Russia. They had learned how to steal huge amounts of money from the Russian government and then had immigrated to America. They bought the same elite palaces near the ocean. They lived in America the same way they had lived in Russia.

One day, Misha and I went to one of the birthday parties of a Russian Mafioso at the restaurant in Brighton Beach. It was a real treat. We had almost spent all of our money on souvenirs and clothes. But our stomachs missed Russian homemade food. We found just what we wanted on the menu and even got the chance to try something new. The party was absolutely perfect. The tables were served very exclusively. I can say that there was just no holy magic water on the tables. Everything else, you could easily find on the menu. I ate broiled duck stuffed with oranges, smoked eel and marinated calamari in a sour cream sauce.

But I didn't like the new Russian Americans, they lacked a sense of humor. Still, learning about them was my job; one that I didn't choose. Every man smelled of expensive fragrance, had a manicure and groomed hair. They were dressed in suits and shirts from Armani, Hugo Boss, and Gucci. They bored me. They flattered each other the entire evening. Misha and I had to wait for the vodka to kick in for them to get honest. After that, they forgot all about their inhibitions and began to tell the real stories of their lives in Russia and America. Their conversations were about comparing their lives before and after immigration.

This particular party honored a Mafiosi boss named Pirate. He was a short man with a big stomach and a patch on one eye. He got his name because of his appearance. He wore expensive brand name suits with striped shirts, and in fights used only knives and swords as weapons.

When these new style Russians got totally drunk, they gave me a chance to join them at the tables and talk openly about the topics that I was interested in, but after a while I almost fell asleep. Misha woke me up insisting that I was an absolute fool. He said that there were so many rich available Russians here that I should open my eyes. He thought that I was stupidly sitting around and missing my chance for a good life. To me, after the painful experiences with Leonid, all men looked shallow and like deceitful liars.

I didn't want to become anybody's slave, mistress, or remedy for stress. I was used to earning my own money. I never had the mentality of women who choose a man based on the amount of money in his bank accounts. I explained this to Misha.

At the table next to me sat a man who appeared to be thirty-five. He looked at me with obvious interest. I felt uncomfortable, even offended. Did he think that he was Superman or some kind of judge of people's fate? He was probably sure that his bit of attention made me happy. Misha went to take pictures of the dancing Mafiosi. The man politely asked if I would mind if he joined me. I smiled. Oh well, I thought he might be someone interesting to speak with, maybe I could get some interesting information.

The man's name was Marat Gorky. He was the owner of several dental offices called "Smile" in Brooklyn, Manhattan and Queens. I started to introduce myself, but he stopped me and said he knew who I was. We chatted and he said he was amazed by my talent and my extraordinary way of thinking. I thought he wanted to become a hero on Leonid's show. I asked if he would be able to come to Moscow. He countered that he had a business offer for me. He wanted me to become his wife. In a very delicate way, he said he hoped I didn't mind him making the offer. I looked at him as if he were an idiot. I knew and read a lot in my twenty-two years, but never had I heard about contracting a wife that fast. I rudely replied. He was probably a lunatic, or he hadn't been lucky in the past relationships. I knew that men's fantasy lives were rich, but not this rich.

Nevertheless, I was curious. Marat went on rapidly. He said that I would live in his house, a palace like those from a fairy tale. I would attend all possible intellectual classes. I would go to the gym and always look perfect. In addition, I had to be the perfect housewife and create a cozy atmosphere in our house and sometimes cook. Marat said that it wasn't a problem for him to find one-night girls. Well, there were no doubts about that. Marat was very stylish and handsome. But this man was looking for marriage.

The party was over. Misha and I went to our apartment and studied the pictures we had taken and the information I had gathered. The party was one of the last pieces of work we had to do before returning to Moscow. I had noticed that I had enjoyed America very much. I liked the fact that I didn't know a lot about American people and their laws. I always loved to learn something new. For me, the unknown is always something interesting.

I told Misha about the offer that I received at the party. He looked at me and said that if I passed it up, he wouldn't talk to me for a year. He thought that this was the perfect opportunity for me to find out if I would make a good wife without having to be a wife at all. I didn't think that I would be able to live with Marat in the same house right away. It would be important to determine first whether I liked him enough as a person.

I caught myself thinking that I did like him somewhat already. He was tall and blond, my type, and he was obviously well-educated and intelligent. I just couldn't understand why he didn't want a real family based on real feelings. I didn't know why he wanted to have a fake relationship with a woman. I had a few ideas. Finally, I came to the conclusion that he was gay and probably didn't want this fact known due to the business interest and popularity. He wanted a make-believe wife to hide his homosexuality.

The next day, Marat called me. I didn't know where he got my phone number. This time he politely asked me if I was ready to be his wife for $7,000 a month. I answered nervously that I might be almost ready, but that I first had a few questions. The salary he offered me was bigger by almost twenty times my salary in Moscow. But wouldn't I be selling myself for money? Then again, I was going to work for that money. Like an actress.

I calmed myself down with the thought that if something went wrong, I could always cancel the contract and live my own life. After I married Marat, I would apply for a green card. I would then have to live with him for two years to get my card. I felt better when I thought about that in two years I would earn $168,000. I wouldn't have to worry about my financial situation for the next few years. I considered how I would feel about giving up my TV career, then said, "Oh the hell with it," and told Marat "yes."

I called my parents in Moscow and told them that I got a job offer from BBC and had to remain in America to build my career. I told the same lie to my friends and to Leonid. Leonid was very happy for me. He said that he was proud of himself for the decision he made to hire me originally. When I lied to Misha about the BBC, he was glad and envious. He went back to Moscow.

Marat gave me a room in his mansion with an ocean view. He was at work from morning until night. Considering how big the house was we could avoid irritating each other. It was a three-story building with eight bedrooms. My day as a hired wife started every morning at 5 o'clock. I woke up and cooked breakfast. Marat liked fresh-squeezed juice, freshly brewed coffee, and butter sandwich with red salmon caviar. Of course, he had maids, but, true to his Russian mentality, Marat didn't trust any strangers. He would never let any maid stay overnight. After breakfast, he left for work. I took care of the house and my appearance.

I realized that the life of a Russian American wasn't such heaven as it was written about in the newspapers and magazines. Not only did I have to rise early and always look good, but I had to supervise maids, compose menus and lists of items for the shopping. I had to supervise the gardener and manage all the domestic expenses. The most difficult thing for me was visiting the beauty salons, boutiques, and gyms. One might say that it's what every young woman dreams about. Maybe it seems like a life of pleasure, but I hated walking around the house in high heels and elegant dresses.

Even after the shower, I had to wear an expensive silk robe from Roberto Cavali and sleepers with kitten heels. I wanted so much to rest at the end of the day. I wanted to wear old jeans and a sweater and be able to lie down in front of the television with no makeup and without my hair being done. I just wanted to take a bag of popcorn and watch a movie or read a book. I hated the responsibility of always having to look good. Marat's answer was to send me to study psychology and hot stone massage techniques.

In the evenings, Marat wanted us to sit on the balcony. We drank tea, looked at the sunset and discussed a variety of different topics. He had a tough character. All the time he found things that I had done wrong. He always reminded me that it was my job and I got paid for it. During the first six months, I planned to annul the contract every day. I wanted to go back to Moscow and stop being controlled all the time. But still, every morning, I woke up and cooked breakfast for him.

Soon, my efforts at the gym and the beauty salons began to pay off. I became more attractive. I turned into a really elegant lady.

We began to go to theatres, restaurants, museums, and social functions. Other men looked at me with admiration. Women whispered enviously. My pictures appeared in local newspapers and some were also published in Moscow. I was afraid that my lies would be blasted and my acquaintances would recognize me. I was ashamed, but, at the same time, I was proud of myself. I found myself in the company of the most stylish wives in the Russian community of New York.

One afternoon, Marat called and said that he would be late from work with the possibility that he wouldn't come home at all. I said "Okay" and hung up the phone. Panic started to set in. I began to cry. Slowly, I had been transformed from a hired woman into a real wife with genuine feeling of concern for my marriage. It was a mistake. I had violated the conditions of my contract. I had made a business proposition into something personal. I was jealous. I couldn't understand how he could go from a woman like me, even though we did not have sex, to sleeping with someone else. I felt offended. I didn't have to worry that after he hugged another woman, he would touch my body. Our entire intimate relationship consisted of a simple kiss on the cheek. From time to time, we even slept in different bedrooms. That night Marat didn't show up. I couldn't sleep the entire night.

In the morning, I realized that I loved him. I knew that six months ago the agreement of his business offer wasn't simply a wish to make a lot of money. I liked him and that is why I agreed. If in his place was some fat or old man I would never have agreed for any amount of money. Marat returned around 11:00 a.m. I met him as usual, but with a sense of sadness. He pretended that he didn't notice anything.

My work became a real torture for me after I realized that I was in love with him. I couldn't quit. I wanted to be near Marat even if only as a simple hired employee. He was always polite, but cold. I tried to be even better than I had been. I began to cook a tastier breakfast. During the day, I baked his favorite oatmeal cookies. I wanted him to come home from work and drink a cup of peppermint tea with me. I wanted to ask with real interest if he had a good day. I tried to look better than before. I wore the best dresses even at breakfast. I enrolled in psychology classes as he had asked. I wanted to be taught how to become the only woman for the man of my dreams. Marat noticed the changes. He added a $500 bonus per month to my bonus. It humiliated me. Once on the weekend, I heard how Marat flirted over the phone. He joked and laughed. It made me angry. He never did this with me. I understood that he had no feelings for me and that we were only partners.

Once, after he had been flirting on the phone, I went up to him and through my tears told him that I was annulling the contract because I couldn't live like this anymore. He looked at me and asked what caused this shift in me. I cried so hard that I couldn't say a word. He came up to me and hugged me. I snuggled up to him. I told him that I had fallen in love with him and that I couldn't hurt myself this way anymore. He kissed me deeply and passionately. He said that he had waited for this moment for a long time. He had also driven himself crazy over me. He had thought my feelings about him were only cold and businesslike.

He had been waiting for me to confess my love to him since we had made our arrangement. He had prepared a romantic setting where we would consummate our love a long time ago, but I just thought it was one more guestroom. All night long we made love. We stopped only long enough to tell brief stories from our past lives. I told him about Leonid. He told me about a few women in his life that only needed money and position from him.

The next morning, Marat woke up at 5:00 a.m. He made me scrambled eggs with sliced tomatoes, fresh brewed coffee and juice. On the tray, he placed a little jewelry box. It was a diamond ring. Again, Marat proposed to me, but this time it was for real. I accepted. I can't imagine how I ever lived without him.

We went to Moscow and we got married at the Vasily Blajenny church. My parents were there and were happy for me. Marat ordered a portrait of us from my mother. It hangs in the hallway of our house. My father made us gold hearts with diamonds. He said for us to wear them always. I have a blue heart and Marat has a pink one. Marat's friends joined our celebration from all over the Soviet Union and from New York. Before we married, Leonid called me. He told me that he was ready to leave his wife and kids in order to be with me. He wanted to start everything all over between us. It was kind, but he was now nothing but a distant memory.

Recently, Marat and I returned home to New York. The only thing we dream about now, and work hard for is to have a baby. What could be better than this?

Chapter 16
THE SECRET LIFE
OF TWO SOULS

The birth of a baby girl is always the first chapter of a unique and unimaginable story. Every woman has secrets embedded deep within her heart and soul that can never be shared. Men used to think that women's lives and the stories of their fates were dramas not to be taken seriously. Many men think that our lives are just long-lasting repetitive soap operas filled with love, sorrow, tears, insults and partings. If you feel this is something true in America, then I can assure you it is considered an absolute truth in Russia.

In reality, the story of a woman's fate is the discovery of her own dreams and sometimes her nightmares; the story of her heart and soul, which she can never share. We are always trying to find a point to our lives. We sometimes even seek to find it in the predictions of fortune tellers. There is a belief in Russia that a mother's fate will repeat itself as a mirror in the lives of her daughters, granddaughters and beyond.

We want to understand why we came into this world and in what manner we will leave it. We want to live our life without any regrets for what we did; satisfied what we did not like the fork in the road we did not journey down. Every woman fights for her personal happiness and to have a soul in harmony with all that is good in this world. We all have secrets and emotions that are not for sharing.

People say that memories help a woman to survive and to suffer loss. Love is the most important thing in a woman's life. She can love. She can be loved. But when she experiences both at the same moment and, of course, by the same man, only then is she truly happy. And a woman is beautiful when she has a man's love within her heart.

A woman is usually unhappy if she gives her love for the sake of material gain, financial benefits and the comfort of a carefree style of life. This compels her to divide her life into two different segments and live parallel yet separate lives. It's a life of two halves.

She will play one role in the fake life she chooses, and another in her true life. She may write the story of real life and true feelings in her little diary, or at least this was so with my mother. It was her secret. She would always feel sorry for herself.

A man can never find out about his woman's heart. He will be thankful to her, because she has lived her life with him, given birth to his children and made him a happy home.

My mother, for instance, never told me about her real love. She kept her whole true life a secret from me and my father. All mother's daily notes were preserved. I found them in her dairy after she died. It was hidden in an old shoe box in the corner of her closet.

My mother was a simple woman. She was a musician. She married my father just to have some advantages in her life. My father was forty-five years old, twenty years older than my mother. It was the perfect time for both of them to get married. My father was a general and he needed to have a wife who would be absolutely happy. Father needed to have a wife and child according with his status. He wanted a child while his age still permitted him to do so.

My father loved my mother very much. When they got married, my mother quit her job as a violin teacher at the musician conservatory. She turned herself into a very proper general's wife. According to that status, she had to control the maids, take care of all her husband's wishes, and always look classy and intelligent.

They met each other when my father moved to Moscow. For all his years of hard work, the government installed him in a four-bedroom apartment in downtown Moscow and gave him a good new job.

My father had an average appearance. He was well-shaped with a little gray intertwined with his brown hair. He asked every question with directness. He answered simply and sharply. He almost always talked to people as if they were under his command and treated them as if he was giving orders to one of his soldiers.

My mother at twenty-five had graduated with honors from the Conservatory. She had good manners and, perhaps most importantly to the men in Moscow, a thin waist. She was an attractive and shy young lady with musical fingers and a perfect ear.

My parents met in front of the cinema theater Rassvet. There was a long line there. There was no romance in their relationship on her point. Generals know how to win a battle in a war, but they don't know how to win woman's heart. After the movie, they went for a night walk around Moscow to have a cup of coffee and some ice cream in a café. There were no declarations of love, no poems and no romantic music.

Instead, my future father told my musical mother about tanks and life in the army. My mother nodded as a knowing woman would and agreed with him about everything. But, in reality, she had no idea about, or interest in, what he was saying. The most remarkable observation I found in mother's diary was her admission that she felt sad and empty. *"He looked into my blue eyes and he told me that they are very sad and empty. I didn't say a word in reply. He was right. Everything shouted out inside me. My soul was breaking into small pieces, I wanted to run and never stop. I wanted to fall down into some place where nobody would ever find me."*

My father walked my mother to her house. Three days later, he knocked at her door and was in her life again. He was dressed in a military cap and a green well-ironed general's uniform. He appeared suddenly and said without preamble, "Aleftina, I thought a lot about us. We have to get married. I am not young, and for you it's also the right time. I promise to give you a wealthy, carefree life. In exchange, you'll be a good wife and give me a son."

My grandmother, my mother's mother, acted very quickly, as was usually the case in my country in those days. Grandma agreed for my mother and a wedding day was set. My mother cried on her pillow for a week, but, nevertheless, she married my father.

My grandmother was very strict. She worked her whole life as a heart surgeon. The one thing she was concerned about was that my mother must not bring shame on the family name. They were a famous dynasty of respected doctors. My mother had fought with my grandma because she didn't want to be a doctor as my grandma had wished. My grandma survived World War II and thought that a doctor's profession was important both in times of war and peace. My mother would have passed out at the sight of blood. She couldn't imagine herself with a scalpel in her hand.

One day my mother brought home syringes for injections from the hospital where she worked. She exchanged them on the market for an old violin. That was her display of character. She would stand under the window of the music school where they taught a violin class.

Later, my mother enrolled at the Conservatory on her own. Grandma didn't talk to her for two weeks. For those two weeks, my mother didn't have money for a bus or for lunch at the Conservatory. It took her three hours. She took apples from the trees of the farms she walked by for snacks in order to have something to eat.

The teachers in the Conservatory thought my mother was a very gifted student with great prospects for her musical future. Once, they had an international musical festival devoted to the music of Tchaikovsky. It was an important event. My mother was then just twenty years old, with large blue eyes and an open smile. She dressed like everybody at that time, in dark colors. It seemed like all woman wore dresses made from the same fabric.

One could see ten women walking on the street dressed in the same color and the same model of dress. Poor women tried to look different from each other. They sewed collars on their dresses, shortened them and added brooches. It wasn't considered polite to live better or dress better than everyone else. In communism, everything was supposed to be equal.

At the festival, there was a performance by a twenty-year-old black man. His name was Bruno. He spoke Russian pretty well. He too was a professional violinist. When my mother and Bruno looked at each other it was an instant love duet. The festival lasted one week and a half. My mother and Bruno spent almost every minute together. My mother wrote in her diary about Bruno: *He is so different and extraordinary. He is not like the others. His eyes are bottomless. His pupils remind me of shining stars. I adore his white teeth and heartfelt smile. I remember his thin fingers which caress both his violin and my heart with such perfection. I think I love him. My mother will kill me if she finds out.*

Every day, my mother and Bruno listened to Jimmy Smith and Cannonball Adderly records which Bruno had brought from America. Bruno introduced jazz to my mother. In the 1960s, the violin went through a rebirth as a jazz instrument. But nobody in Russia knew about that or wanted to know. Russia was a closed society and, in the Soviet Union, popular American music was frowned upon.

One day, my mother and Bruno were walking in the park and holding hands. They met my grandma who made a terrible scene and took my mother back home away from Bruno. Grandma threatened Bruno saying that if he didn't leave her daughter alone he would be in serious trouble. She asked if Bruno would be able to play his violin without fingers? My mother knew that grandmother would be able to make bad things happen to Bruno, especially because black people were disliked in Moscow.

After all, she was a famous surgeon and had friendships with many people from the government. And then some bosses of the Russian crime families. As punishment, my mother was locked in her room and wasn't allowed to come out until the end of the festival. My mother cried all those days. She ate nothing.

Bruno went back to America. He left his mailing address at the Conservatory. My mother wrote letters to Bruno. She also got letters from him. Bruno wrote that he couldn't forget her. He loved her and promised to come back next year for the festival. My mother was counting the days until then. She put a big calendar on her wall and crossed off the days with a marker.

That year passed. My mother became even more attractive. That was her graduation year. Grandmother bought her a new white dress with black pearls to perform at the exam concert. Bruno came, but stayed in the background. My mother was happy.

They decided to be more careful this time. They secretly met on the corner of Malinovskaya Street and quietly walked, hiding themselves in shadows, away from the eyes of passersby. Everything was done in secret. They couldn't allow themselves either to lose each other or to be caught. They loved each other too much.

After the festival, Bruno went back to America. He promised to bring my mother there as soon as the political relationship between Russia and America would allow it. My mother was ready to wait. They swore to each other that no matter what happened or how long it took that they would be together.

Three months later, my mother noticed that her breasts were swollen and stomach had become bigger. She felt sick all the time. At first she couldn't even think that she might be pregnant. Bruno was her first lover. They made love only once. And for all these three months, she continued to have her period on time.

My mother passed out one day. Grandma took her to hospital. My mother at twenty-one was three months pregnant. The doctor told her that sometimes women have their period until the fifth month of their pregnancy. My grandmother had connections in that sphere. She arranged an abortion for my mother. It would have been an unbearable shame on the family for their Russian daughter to deliver a black or colored child.

Love couldn't be exposed between these two absolutely different people from different worlds. Russia has never been a place for tolerance even among its own citizens. It was a cause for great shame just to have a baby out of wedlock. Nobody at that time talked about it publicly. It was a forbidden topic not only for conversation but even for personal thoughts. It would have been easier for my grandmother to kill her daughter than to let her deliver that baby.

After the abortion, my mother fell into a deep depression. She would cry for whole days and play the Brahms Lullaby on her violin for hours.

A few years passed, and it didn't hurt her quite as much. But Bruno's memory still wasn't absent from my mother's heart. Grandmother forbade my mother to have any correspondence with Bruno. All her coming and outgoing letters were confiscated by the Post Officer and given to my grandmother. She probably burned them all the while enjoying her power and ability to determine her daughter's fate.

Yet slowly, my mother came back to life and started to work in the Conservatory as a violin teacher. She still hoped that one day she would reunite with Bruno. But there was no word from him. He didn't show up at any of the festivals in the following years. Mother dreamed that Bruno would come again and they would be happy. She believed that day would arrive if she could just stay patient.

I can only guess what Bruno's feelings were. Did he feel betrayed that mom never wrote to him or answered any of his letters? Was all this not my grandmother's awful revenge? These answers I do not know. Years passed. My mother, like any normal woman, had to think about her future plans, family, and children. But you can't command your heart to love somebody. My mother didn't like any man. In fact, most of them irritated her.

The evening my mother met my father, she had gone with her co-workers to the movies. Her girlfriends had noticed that the general liked my mother and they had become envious. It was a great success to marry a military man of such a high rank. It meant she would have respect, honor and wealth for the rest of her life. It meant living in a large comfortable apartment, wearing expensive clothes, having a private driver and freshly cooked and seasoned pork on the table.

My mother didn't think that it was as wonderful as her friends did. She was ready to live her whole life with Bruno in a dormitory if necessary. She was ready to give up sausages, to eat plain boiled eggs and to drink her tea without sugar.

My mother married my father without a huge celebration. They got married quietly and began their life together. My father brought my mother expensive dresses and boots, hats and gloves.

But it wasn't enough. I remember when my parents had fights, my father would always say: "Aleftina, why don't you ever appreciate anything I've done for you? I am trying my best to make you happy, but you still have the same sad and empty eyes you had many years ago."

Now I understand that the answer was a simple one. My mother never loved my dad. Of course she respected him, but for her whole life, her heart was faithful to another man.

When my mother died, I found her diary hidden in a corner of her lingerie drawer. I was shocked when I read it. I couldn't understand how my mother could be so strong-willed and could control her feelings for all those years. How could she hide her secret diary and never share her thoughts with anybody? She was the only one who knew her secrets. She had never given my father any reason to feel shame.

My grandmother had died one month after my parent's wedding. I was the last female in the line.

*　*　*

My childhood to me seemed to be very interesting. I was good at ballet and graduated from ballet school. Later I enrolled in Moscow State Ballet College.

I remember how much my father loved me. Despite the fact that he was a general, he was a loving and caring father and husband when at home. He always brought me the best. The rarest delicacies such as sausages, imported Swiss cheeses, smoked fish and the finest yogurts were always on our table. I wore fashionable clothes. My friends were envious. I don't even remember any dress

I wore longer than one season. My father would always buy me new ones. He thought that his lovely ballet dancer, Arina, had to have the best. Surprisingly, I didn't grow up spoiled. It happened probably because my father's love mixed with my mother's coldness and strictness. Now I understand, with the passing time, that my mother had turned into her mother, with the same demanding and commanding tone. I never had a close relationship with her. She wasn't my girlfriend. She was my boss. When I had any problems, I was only able to talk to my father.

When I think about my childhood, I always remember my birthday celebrations. We had them in our huge, expensively furnished apartment. I invited the whole class with my favorite teachers. There were about forty people. My mother cooked all the dishes on the table herself. She would cook twenty-four hours non-stop. She was pleased that I was grateful to her. I knew that my mother cooked everything better and it was tastier than if anyone else had done it.

On the birthday table there were always several varieties of cooked meat, like fried duck stuffed with apples; chicken stuffed with dried plums; pork; and steaks with cooked cheese and sliced tomatoes. There were usually ten different salads. My mother took all the recipes from foreign cook books. My father got them from his foreign friends. That is why nobody could cook anything similar to my mother's dishes. She liked being the best in this sphere. For dessert we would have apple pie, three different types of cake, sliced frozen pineapples and ice cream.

All the children I invited loved my birthday and were waiting for it every year. They took dance classes and practiced before my birthday. I had a strange party list. I did not invite friends on my birthday. I invited just kids who danced well and looked beautiful. That is why my birthday party was more like a final performance. In order to be on my birthday list and be able to eat all the delicious dishes, my classmates would have to work on their dance skills all year round.

I didn't like to go to anyone else's birthday party. I would always come back hungry. From my early childhood, I was very fastidious. It was important for me to observe how food was cooked. I needed to know if the preparer washed his hands before he cooked and if he coughed or sneezed. My mother would send me to other birthday celebrations because she wanted to know what food was on the table and how many salads and desserts they had. It gave her pleasure to be sure one more time that she was the master chef.

When I enrolled in the Moscow State Ballet College, my life consisted of long hours practising and preparing myself for exams and the performance. I wanted somebody to notice my talent and invite me to perform at the Bolshoi Theater.

During the second year at the school, I performed in a University of International Friendship Nations. I danced in *Swan Lake* with other girls.

After the performance, a few girls and I decided to stay longer at the banquet. It was great fun. The students were from different countries. The one thing which united us was a wish to live, to dance and to have fun.

In the middle of the evening, I began to pay attention to a young man. He did a break dance in front of the admiring students. I came closer and decided to add my ballet flexibility to his crazy dance. We made a wonderful duo. The audience squealed. We were quickly covered with sweat.

His name was Smith. He was a twenty-two-year-old guy. It was his last year of studies. I liked the fancy way he was dressed. He wore a white t-shirt, Levis jeans and white Adidas sneakers. All his clothes looked perfect on his dark skin. I felt excitement in my heart. It happens sometimes that at first sight you can say that this is the one and I don't want anybody else.

Smith told me that in a year he would go back to America. He had a big family there and a chance to earn more money than in Russia. We dated for one year. I wasn't brave enough to introduce him to my parents.

We loved each other very much. We walked in Moscow in the autumn and danced on fallen leaves. We walked in Moscow in the winter and threw snowballs. We were happy to be together. I taught him Russian songs and he taught me American rap. I had a feeling that he was my second half, a part of my soul.

I told my parents that I was dating a man named Sasha. I said that Sasha was very shy and our relationship didn't even reach the level of meeting parents.

During that year I was invited to dance in the Bolshoi Theater. I got a featured role in the *Nutcracker* and *Giselle*. It seemed like good luck was on my side. I had a man I loved, a job I did well and healthy parents.

Smith left Russia after a year. I was lost and sad. I had a feeling that half of me had died. He promised to visit me twice a year and call me until I graduated. He even learned a Russian phrase without an accent. He could say perfectly: "Hello, can I talk to Arina, please?" There could be no possible suspicion from my parents. We had a maid in our apartment. She always picked up the phone. After she heard my name she would call me and get back to work around the house.

I knew that my parents would never accept Smith. He always would be a stranger to them. I hid his pictures and letters in the lowest shelf of my table. I knew that after my mother married my father she had never again taken a violin in her hands. Even when we would have a dinner with a guest she would sit the whole night in the kitchen with a light on and lock the door. I knew she wrote in her diary and opened her soul there. I remember I read a phrase there: *How my life could look like if Bruno and I were together? He still didn't show up in my life. He didn't find me. I am proudly respected as a general's wife. But I am hiding my tears under expensive sable furs. I have deceived myself all my life. But it's impossible to deceive my own heart.*

One year after Smith left, I was invited to dance in a Broadway show. It wasn't my favorite ballet, but it was a chance to be near the man I loved. I was very happy. Smith had waited for me. My parents weren't against it. My father thought that it was a big

175

success for me with prospects for a star future. My mother was hesitant at the thought of me leaving.

My departure day came. My father hugged me in the Sheremetievo airport and, as a general would, commanded me to be a good soldier and to remember my native land. My mother was nervous. She handed me a little box and asked me to throw it in the ocean when I had time.

I opened it in the airplane. There were two scratched record disks: of Jimmy Smith and Cannonball Adderly. But now I understood my mother. She was saying goodbye to her dream of seeing Bruno again.

Smith met me and we started to live together. He taught me English. I quickly picked up some words. I don't remember exactly why I liked America. I probably loved it because I was with Smith. We started the life we had been dreaming about. I danced in the show.

He worked as a therapist in the Maimonidas Hospital in Brooklyn. In the evenings, we would walk in Manhattan or sit at home with a bowl of popcorn and a rental DVD. In the mornings, we couldn't make ourselves get out of bed.

I called my parents and told them about America, but not about Smith. My old father was interested in every detail of American life. My mother would ask about my health and diet. I had a job contract for one year. When the contract was supposed to expire, my visa allowed me to travel around America for more months. One night, I twisted my ankle at a performance. Around the same time, I found out that I was pregnant. Smith didn't want to hear anything about abortion. He used to say that if people love each other they have to welcome the fruits of their love. I thought: I'll never be able to go home again. I didn't know how to tell my parents about such happy news for me. It would be a serious blow to them. I knew that they wouldn't understand. It was impossible to lie because they waited for me to come back to Moscow.

I decided that I would talk to my dad and he would prepare my mother for the news. Surely the most important thing was that

I was a happy woman. Smith gave me an engagement ring and said we should get married right away. It's funny because in Russia, you don't swap rings before you get married, the "wedding ring" is called the "engagement ring" and you are given this on your wedding day. We got married and had a small celebration with just the two of us. I thought it was strange when Smith put the ring on my left hand. In Russia, you only wear the ring on your left hand if you are a widow. Otherwise, it is customary to wear the ring on your right hand. Smith and I got married. We had a small celebration for just the two of us.

His parents didn't accept me. It all came out when we went to dinner with his family. They had french fries and freshly made hamburgers from McDonalds. I had never eaten that food, plus I knew that it would be bad for my future child. His family felt insulted. They gave Smith an ultimatum: choose them or me. He chose me.

When I was three months pregnant, I called home. I told my father that I wouldn't come back soon. I asked them to come to America and visit me and Smith and our newborn child. It was a big scandal. It was the first time in my life that my father had shouted at me with words: "I won't let you do that!" My father couldn't deal with the news that his grandchild would be black. He hung up on me.

I called him right back, but the line was busy. I thought that he would calm down and I would talk to them again. But in a week my mother called me. She said that my father, who was seventy-two, had died from a heart attack immediately after he had talked with me. I was shocked. I couldn't come back to Moscow right away because we had just applied for my permanent papers. I didn't want to deliver a baby in Russia. I knew it would cause a lot of problems and a long-time separation with Smith.

My mother talked to me very rudely. She said that she had found pictures of me with a black man. She shouted in the phone that I couldn't shame the honor of my dead father. I asked if she knew about everything. She said that she didn't. I had to truthfully tell her the whole story. My mother told me that the doors of my Russian home would always be locked for me. She gave up her unborn grandchild. She said that I wouldn't be her daughter anymore. She asked me not to call home and bother her ever again. That was the last conversation I ever had with my mother. I still continue to call and talk to the maid.

Five months later, I delivered my little black Anastasia. She is my little lovely bit of coal. Smith and I decided that we would teach her both English and Russian. Smith helped a lot with our baby. He saw how hard it was for me to suffer from my father's death, from the angry damning words of my mother. Smith let me sleep at nights, awaking himself for our little daughter. He changed diapers, reheated bottles and put her back to sleep.

We had lived together for four years when Smith told me that he was having an affair with a co-worker. We applied for a divorce. It was difficult for me. I was hurt a lot. I loved him but he loved another woman. I know that if a man stops loving you, there is nothing you can do about it. I decided to be respectful toward Smith. I wanted Anastasia to still have her father around. First, I lived with Nastya only with the money Smith gave to us. Later, I found a job in a pre-school as a ballet teacher. I can work there and be with Anastasia near by. I also give a lot of private lessons. My weekly salary is usually about a thousand dollars. Smith pays for our apartment and gives me seven hundred dollars a month for Nastya's expenses. It's enough for the two of us. Anastasia understands Russian better than she speaks it.

Not long ago our maid from Moscow called and told me that my mother had died. I took a flight with my daughter back home. People around us gave me condemning looks and whispered about my black daughter. After I had been there a few days, I understood how much I loved America.

I will never go back to Russia. I am so sorry that my parents died and didn't get to see my little sunshine. I felt hurt when I found my mother's diary. It was scary for me when I thought about the life she had lived. I still don't understand why she treated me like she did. It's strange how often parents forget that long ago they were little kids too. They also wanted something. They were forbidden sometimes. It doesn't hurt so much when it's only about a toy. It hurts when it's about love. You never know which love in your life is your last. My mother, too, was a teenager and she and Bruno were in love. They hid something from their strict parents. They were upset when their parents didn't understand them.

The last phrase my mother wrote in her diary was about her personal life: *I hope that one day Arina will forgive me for not being understanding. I want her not to be angry at me. My life is my fault. I didn't fight for my happiness and love. I swam along the river current; the same river that had carried my mother. I turned absolutely into my mother. I hated for twenty-five years. I turned into her in the years that followed. She had made me cold, a suffering and submissive woman. Arina may repeat my fate. I absolutely hope and pray this will not be so. Perhaps she will take the ability to preserve from her father.*

I can't stop thinking about it. What if my mother had given birth to a boy and the father had been Bruno? How would her life have been? It was a path that was not taken.

I made a decision to try to find Bruno and tell him about my mother's love song that always played in her heart just for him. It never ended. As I read my mom's diary, I can hear it still.

Chapter 17
TALES OF THE
PINK PANTHER

I came from Moscow two years ago to live in Boston, Massachusetts. I wanted to finish my college education at Boston University and receive a degree from an American university. I had never in my life dreamed of permanently living in the United States because my family in Russia was very wealthy. I had no reason to want to leave my native country. My life was good.

It was easy to get my visa. I was from a family with a high income and net worth. Father easily proved that his income was more than thirteen thousand dollars per month. My parents were always generous. They were happy to spend money on me and ensure my future. They sent me to various prestigious private schools in Russia to learn foreign languages, music and sports. My father was a very successful businessman, the owner of a commercial building complex. My mother was a housewife who didn't work outside the home. Her main concerns in life were to oversee my education and to maximize her beauty.

Father worked constantly. He almost always came home late, but sometimes he didn't come home at all. My mother and I surmised things, but we kept silent because there was nothing we could do. Russian men pretended they were away "on business" when they were really with prostitutes and sauna girls. This was accepted by almost all Russian women. We knew for sure that he who pays the girl, chooses her dance. We completely depended on my father's income for the cost of my travels and my college education. All of this lay on his shoulders and he provided well for us. My parents had a warm relationship. I do not remember them ever fighting, but I knew that they no longer loved each other. I was certain they stayed married just for me. It is said in Russia that habit is worse than love.

I enrolled at Moscow State University in the department of foreign languages. I drove an expensive car and dressed in expensive designer clothes. During my third year, I was given a chance to transfer to an American college and graduate in two years. My father thought that this would help secure my future. So I came to America. I flew here business class through London, with British Airways.

The first year, I studied well. Everything pleased me, my new country and my new life. I absorbed knowledge like a sponge. At the end of the first year, I called home as I always did on Sunday mornings and learned of a terrible family tragedy which would change my life and my family's life forever. My father's competitors had burned his business complex to ashes. Dad would have to sell what was left of the property so he would not be destroyed by his debts. It was absolutely clear to me that they no longer would be able to pay for my tuition and living expenses. This news put me in shock because by this time I had fallen in love with America.

I am now twenty-two years old and it already feels like I have lived a long life. In the beginning, I worked during the summer in order to earn money to pay my tuition. I didn't want to stop my education in the middle, or worse—not finish at all. I thought of the huge amount of money my parents had already invested in me. I lied and told my parents that I had been awarded a grant for my tuition. I didn't want to concern them as they had more than enough to worry about already. At first, I worked as a dishwasher and as a cleaning lady in a night club after it had closed.

Before long, I met the strippers who worked there. Later, I became close friends with one of them. We became roommates to cut down on our expenses. At that time she had been dancing in strip clubs for more than two years. One day, she asked me why I didn't work as she did or at least give it a try. We were sitting at home and I tried on her dresses and high heels just for fun. I thought I looked good. I started thinking about it and I decided it was a good way to make money.

However, in Boston it was hard to break into this business because there are only a few clubs and a lot of competition. There is not even any guaranteed salary. The owner of a club doesn't pay the girls. On the contrary, every stripper has to pay the club one hundred dollars for every night she works. Some of these clubs charge even more and raise what they charge the girls on weekends. There are no days off and if a stripper doesn't show up, for no-matter-what reason, she has to pay anyway. Sometimes she can come to work and earn nothing or even put herself in the red, which means owing the owner and driver. Both expect to make money.

In any event, I found a job, which entailed working in the bar area, around three hundred men assembled during the course of a night on a weekend and about half that many during the week. Most clubs have about fifteen girls and each dances a five-minute performance every hour. While one dances on the stage, the rest of the girls are down in the main room or at the bar where, for twenty or thirty dollars, they sit down with the men for a few minutes. In almost all these clubs, there are so-called "private rooms," separate special places where a man, after paying one hundred and fifty dollars, can have a girl entertain them with a lap dance for fifteen minutes. But half of the initial sum the girl receives goes to the club.

I enjoyed performing at bachelor parties, the night when the groom celebrates with his friends before his wedding. It's fun, absolutely safe, and usually there are just ten to twenty men. I danced wearing a wig, which changes my appearance so much that I cannot be recognized on the streets. It is also interesting to work at "hen parties," where the girls give you your money for doing absolutely nothing truly sexual. You sit and drink with the girls, smoke and talk. Sometimes the girls ask you to teach them how to move their asses and strip. They are just having fun. As soon as we start taking off our dresses, they all start howling and whistling. Some of the girls themselves dance and undress in time to clapping and laughter.

It is interesting that the girls never demean us or make us feel cheap or ashamed, unlike men who talk to us and try to seem cool in the eyes of their friends. They do not understand that to us they are simply money. Most of them are pathetic losers who come into the club and pay money just so some girl will keep them company and pretend to find them interesting. They are unable to attract normal girls. When they are in the club and they pay us money, they feel like the owners of life itself. However, when they run out of money and leave the club, they turn back into the real losers that they are.

Sometimes they try to touch us and put their hands in our panties. When you tell them "no," the pathetic slobs get offended and surprised, because they think that we're having fun and getting pleasure from them. Think again! What's the pleasure? I meet you today for the first time in my life in this bar! I come up to you between dances, not because you look like Johnny Depp, but because money is burning in your pocket and I am the one who'll help you to spend it all. I am not looking for love or a boyfriend. In fact, you are usually the tenth or twentieth I hustle that same night. You may take pleasure in it, but I take pleasure only in your money.

Generally, men are weirdly wired. A few minutes earlier, one may have been cool and courageous at his office or at home with the family, but now, here with me, he is naïve, stupid, and as foolish as some dumb punk. Like beasts, he sees your breast and ass and suddenly nothing else matters to him. He begins to pretend that this is a love relationship, that I give a rat's ass about him, but where is the romance and the intimacy?

I bullshit such men by talking any nonsense I can think of. The fools open up their ears and listen, spending money like crazy, deceiving themselves, leaving behind telephone numbers and coming back night after night. All the while, their girlfriends or wives sleep soundly at home. The bastards would be better off with them instead of going to clubs to be shaken down by the likes of me. For this very reason, I do not have a boyfriend. As soon as I become acquainted with a man away from the club, I draw parallels with my clients and instantly I disrespect them and view them as losers.

Sometimes, I realize I am becoming nervous and evil because it's so hard to work at night and study during the day without days off. I wonder what will become of me. Some of the girls start becoming street sluts rather than upscale whores which seems stupid to me. Others become drug users. At first, they use drugs as a stimulant in order not to fall asleep, and then they begin to work only on narcotics. But, no matter what men may think, there are strong girls with moral characters who work hard to pay for their tuition and who are not addicted to bad habits.

For many, money becomes the only important thing. When these girls see money, it's no longer important what price she has to pay to get it. The girl rushes after it and the moment of truth when she gets it is not important. A person gets accustomed to money very quickly and only the smart ones understand what it's necessary for and how to save it. Many girls earn good money but they do not have a dollar in their savings account. They spend everything. They get accustomed to a new standard and, with a proudly raised head, they go shopping at expensive stores, attend pricey restaurants, and live for today. I have goals: to pay my tuition, to save a little bit and to send some home.

When I come to work, I put on lots of makeup, I wear a wig, and I become another person. I even have a stage name: the Pink Panther. But there is no me in that person. Therefore, I simply do not think about the job that I do. I am the Pink Panther and I am so different from my real self that I do not have a soul or a heart. When I am working, I'm not black or white, good or bad, shameful or not. The Pink Panther has no genuine mood. There is no personal relation. Feelings are absent. There are only moral standards I don't let myself step over. For instance, some girls let somebody touch them or kiss them for an extra dollar. I never speak to the clients in earnest and I do not look at them as real men or as potential partners. For me, they are associated with banknotes. Period.

Before every lap dance, I imagine the man as a hundred-dollar bill with the face of Franklin. I don't even remember their real faces. Every working day, each man is as a newcomer to me. There are no thoughts of meeting any one of them afterwards under any circumstances. I remember only one thing. After work it is necessary to take a taxi, go home, have a shower and go to sleep.

Usually, in the taxi, I start to become myself again. The main thing is to exceed the expectations of the place where you work. Like a hangman who doesn't have any emotions for the work he does, I do not show my real face. I always must seem vulgar, sexy, and with no expression of intellect. The men in the strip clubs do not like normal faces. I understood that the main thing is not only to undress beautifully, but also to possess the skill to take away some of the weight from a man's wallet.

To learn in a class how to dance is not necessary; we learn everything independently by just looking at other girls or on a video. It is important always be in top form and not to let yourself go. Overweight girls cannot earn much money. They are not pretty enough to the men. I do not know why, but modern men have their own ideas about a women's beauty. She must be thin.

I knew one somewhat overweight girl who attempted to be a dancer in a strip club, but over the course of two weeks, she spent all her work time alone at the bar and got drunk. She hardly earned a dollar. Unhappily, she returned to her previous place of work as a salesperson at a bakery.

I was never afraid to dance and then to appear in public places. I was no longer dressed as the Pink Panther. And, besides, psychology plays a role. Even if someone recognized me on the stage, he would not remember where he had seen me. But if he does remember, he will not say a thing; he would be afraid of being mistaken. He thinks what if it's not her and I end up insulting her? Instead, I look boldly into the man's eyes and smile sweetly.

I don't have close friends except possibly my roommate because there's always competition and the fight for survival. My parents also have no idea how I live. I tell them that I work at the college and that it's enough for me. I don't think that they would understand. To them, it would be the same or worse than their daughter being a thief. I don't dispute this because, to some degree, they are right. The fact is they did not raise me to be a topless dancer waving her breasts in front of the noses of sleazy men.

Yes, in reality, the workload is heavy, dirty, and, at moments, I hate myself. But when you do not earn money at night it offends you doubly because you didn't sleep and also did not increase your income, but showed your body to losers and degraded yourself for nothing. Indeed, strip dancing to a certain degree is like prostitution, especially when everybody treats you like a prostitute. However, it's better not to think about that because you will drive yourself mad. It is a blind alley.

The most important thing is not to believe that you are this stage person. A prostitute could pretend to be the Pink Panther while she is working, then she is spitting on the cartoon character and not on her true self. I always remember that I am not here forever and I will earn a necessary amount of money to end this way of life.

Sometimes when such moments come, I hate my clients and myself so much that no amount of money can give me any pleasure. I also hate the Pink Panther that possesses me and sells me for money. I tell myself, "Stop!" I take a bottle of champagne, a pack of "Marlboro" cigarettes, and I sit down by the window and begin to plan my future. I remember that there is a little bit of time left before my college graduation and that I must earn just a little more money.

Then I will take a tour around the country and will go back home to my mom because my father has left her. I know that with my life experience and an American college degree, I will easily find a job and my mother and I will be happy. And, by the way, I will have nothing to be ashamed of because in Moscow no one knows and will ever know what I did in America besides study. The main thing is that I will arrive with lots of green bills which I can use to buy everybody and everything. I already have my airplane ticket to Moscow for July 1, 2006. I have no regrets.

Postscript: When I returned to Russia, I realized that it's my country and that I love my land. The first week I spent with my mother, I saw my father twice. In two weeks, I realized that I don't have any friends and all people with whom I had a friendship before had changed and now treat me as a stranger. But I found a job as an interpreter in a political organization.

I hate and I love men. I hate them because they are pitiful cheaters with all their brains in the small head between their legs. I love them because they give me the money I need to live my life. I still miss America very much. I thank God for Uncle Sam because at least he is one old man in America who I won't have to fuck. I think about going back. But this time, I would bring my mom. My number one goal would be to find her an American husband. I do not know what tomorrow will bring, but I know that I will survive.

Chapter 18
THE DATING GAME

I always believed that I was born into the absolutely wrong environment for the kind of person I am because I have very good genes, from quality people. By the time I was five years old, I knew that I had to get away from the kind of life I had. It was a typical Soviet environment, even though we weren't poor.

I was born in Tajikistan, in the former Republic of the USSR. My mother was a Kindergarten teacher and ran her own small daycare for young children. My father was basically a criminal, but, as I said, he had good genes. He was highly educated, from a very good Georgian family, and had a respected name reaching back into the Russian aristocracy. But he was greedy for money and possessions and the finer things in life. These were hard to come by in the Soviet system even if you were a lawyer as he was.

My parents divorced when I was still quite young. My earliest memories of them were their fighting and screaming all the time. After they split up, my mother and I moved to a small city in Southern Russia to live with her mother. There, we had a small apartment inside an ugly house in an area of town full of ugly houses. The surrounding streets were block after block of old houses with no architectural style whatsoever, mansions subdivided into apartments. Our neighbors were working class people who, for the most part, slaved their lives away in factories. They were simple folk. We all ate potatoes, Russian borscht and, occasionally, caviar as a delicacy. Yes, caviar.

The winters in southern Russia were brutally cold, below zero every day for weeks on end. And the summers were fiercely hot. We had automatic heat, but no air-conditioning. No one had air conditioning. We had a television with the official government channels. There was a movie theater in our city, but I don't remember ever seeing any American films. Our theater only showed lots of long Indian movies.

My maternal uncle traveled overseas all the time on business as he held a high position in the Soviet government. His family had very beautiful things because he could afford to collect them. For instance, they had gorgeous rugs from Iran and home furnishings and clothing that all the other regular Soviet people just couldn't afford. I never had any of the things my cousins had and I wanted them.

A Georgian last name in a Russian city makes life difficult. I spoke Russian clearly. I was in school with the same group of kids from the time I was seven years old, but they most likely overheard their parents' racist comments and took them out on me. I am half Jewish and half Georgian and I looked different from everyone else. I knew I didn't belong there. All the kids constantly made fun of me. It was very painful. I had a different kind of look that they weren't used to. I'm now 5' 9" and weigh one hundred and twenty pounds, but as a kid, I was an ugly ducking—tall and skinny, very awkward. I just did not fit in. Where I lived was not where I wanted to be.

I played the piano constantly and was quite good at it. I used to read classical Russian books all the time, trying to escape. My favorite writer was Chekhov and, by the time I was thirteen, I had read everything he ever wrote. I fantasized that I was an aristocrat from the nineteenth century. In reality, I was so awkward that I was an easy target for my classmates. I wanted to wear the finest clothes, silks, satins and furs. Such things I didn't have. I wanted to look like a princess. I had this image of myself in my head. My mother could have afforded better clothes, but she refused to buy what I wanted. She didn't pay attention to these fantasies of mine. I was a funny little homely thing. My mother was sensitive to my emotional needs, but she was very protective of me and always worried about what I ate. All in all, she made me crazy, like a typical Jewish mother, but she took care of me the best she could.

I was very naïve, living inside an Old Russian novel in my head, completely pure inside and out. I felt like that ugly duckling for so long. And I longed to soar. If I wasn't pretty, how would I meet my prince? These were the types of thoughts I had in my head all the time. I wanted more than anything else to look pretty, but I couldn't afford the right clothes or makeup. I did have one short miniskirt that got me a lot of attention. I was young and I had pretty legs. I noticed that men noticed me when I wore that skirt.

I was wearing it the day I was raped. That day changed my life forever. I was walking down the street alone. I was sixteen years old when four men came up to me, surrounded me, walked me to their car and made me get in. They were in their early twenties, known members of a Russian-style gang. I knew enough to be deathly afraid of them. I had a choice: they would either beat me up, maybe to death, or I would give them what they wanted. I gave in without a fight. Four men altogether and they raped me one after the other in that car. Afterwards, I did nothing.

If I had gone to the police, they wouldn't have believed me. There was no justice in the former Soviet Union. The men who raped me were powerful and I was very afraid of them. I was too embarrassed and ashamed to tell my mother. Maybe she would have helped me. I'm sure she would have tried, but I just couldn't bring myself to tell her. I felt like the whole thing was my fault; maybe for wearing that goddamned short skirt in the first place.

This story is not unusual at all, I am sorry to say. Almost every girlfriend of mine from Russia was raped at some point in her early life. I'm thirty-one years old now, and most women I know in my age group who grew up in Russia had something very similar happen to her. Almost every single one of my Russian girlfriends has had an abortion. It was a very harsh life, a very fucked-up way to live. When these things happen to you, you blame yourself. Society won't do anything to help you. That was our reality. It was a terrible way to grow up.

After the rape, I started to tell myself that I was a very bad girl. And I believed it. People started to gossip. I came to think it was deserved.

I no longer cared about myself at all. By the time I was twenty, I had a full-blown case of what some call a dichotomy inside me. There was a terrible conflict raging there that really disturbed my self-image. I didn't see myself as I really was. I felt ugly all the time when I really wasn't. I felt totally disconnected, like I was living somebody else's life. After the rape, I had many, many instances of undesired sex. None of them was enjoyable to me. In many parts of Russia, at least at that time, this was the way young girls were often treated by Russian boys. You were lucky if they said, "Thank you."

After high school, I attended college and studied music. I had been playing the piano since the age of seven and had some talent. By the time I was in my senior year, everything felt wrong. My professor, a brilliant musician and teacher who made twenty-five dollars a month, was not very encouraging about my prospects for a career in the music world. I felt absolutely useless, like I had the wrong education and nothing to look forward to. There was a huge pain inside me; I was living the wrong life. I had no boyfriends, and very few girlfriends. I was sick physically and emotionally; I was pretty much suicidal.

I worked teaching kid's music after I graduated from the conservatory, scraping by on about ten dollars a month. That was a very poor life. I was young and even though I was very disturbed, I still badly wanted pretty clothes and makeup and things. That desire never went away. I wanted a lot more than I could get teaching kids how to play the piano. I met an older woman who worked as a madam. She was kind to me. If I had a father figure at home, if I hadn't been raped, perhaps I wouldn't have fallen into the trap so easily. But I felt dead inside. I had nothing to lose. I thought, why not? People already called me a whore.

She put me to work at a very prestigious hotel in Moscow and that's where I met my clients. These clients were high government officials who paid me at least one hundred dollars every time I saw them. Suddenly, I was a prostitute. But at least I was one who was making good money—four thousand dollars to five thousand dollars a month, but I couldn't manage to save anything. I spent like crazy. I wanted to buy things for myself to make me feel better, to try to fill the hole inside. I bought clothes, cosmetics, jewelry, and all the things I wanted so badly when I was growing up.

* * *

When I was twenty-six years old, I felt that I could no longer live in my country. I had never felt like I belonged anyway. I was completely played out. My Russian madam got me to America where she also set up her business. I flew from Russia to Mexico City, where some Russian citizens who lived in California met me, drove me to Tijuana and arranged for me to get across the border. They charged me ten thousand dollars. It wasn't as dramatic as it sounds: I sat in the back-seat of a car, and got waved through as they drove across. After what I'd been through, I didn't feel afraid of what might happen to me next. I had nothing to lose.

Getting to America was very expensive but it was worth every penny. I had no idea what life there would be like; I had no plans and no expectations. I just wanted things to change. When I was quickly caught by immigration officials in America every word I told them was true: I was raped, I was humiliated, and there was nothing left in Russia for me. Maybe this story helped my temporary immigration papers to go through smoothly while I waited a decision about whether I could stay. After I arrived to America, I felt for the first time like maybe God was going to start helping me. In Russia, I had felt completely forsaken and abandoned. I found some hope when I arrived in America.

My Russian madam handled my career as a prostitute in America. She charged three hundred dollars per date and took half. I could see four or five people a day. Lots of men here had money, and for the most part, they were very happy to help a poor little Russian girl. It was just a job to me. But it gave me money to buy books and hire a private tutor to teach me English. And of course, I picked up English from my clients.

My big problem was obtaining a green card. I found an ad in a Russian language newspaper for an agency that said they could help anyone get a green card. I met with them and made a deal for six thousand dollars instead of their asking price of ten. They would find me a make-believe husband. And they coached me to memorize a list of the questions INS might ask me and how to give satisfactory answers.

I would pay my so-called husband three thousand dollars for marrying me and for letting me keep some clothes and personal belongings in his apartment. And I would pay him a thousand dollars a month until I got my green card and two thousand dollars more payment when I actually received my card. I would, of course, pay all the expenses of travel to a couple of places for photos of the happy couple, etc.

The whole thing including the lawyers would cost me thirty-five thousand dollars. This was certainly worth it. I met my husband-to-be, Lester Jordan, and I guess it could have been worse. He was a forty-year-old divorced prematurely balding man who worked for a messenger service in L.A. He was about thirty pounds overweight and dressed poorly. Still, I had been with hundreds of unattractive men, what difference did it make?

It did not go smoothly. On our first photo trip, our honeymoon weekend in Las Vegas, he told me that we would have to share a room he assured me though nothing sexual would happen. We got waiters to take pictures of us toasting each other with champagne at Drai's restaurant. Then we went back to our room across the street at the Bally's hotel where I had found ninety-nine-dollar-a-night room rate. That night I got fucked in more ways than one and had to pay for the non-pleasure. As time passed, whenever I needed him for pictures or to do something for the lawyers I knew that I was going to be pushed into giving him more freebies. It kept getting worse. Implied threats became clearly stated. This guy reminded me of the kind of men I left Russia to get away from. And I was paying for this! I needed a way out.

A couple of my Russian girl friends told me about a special provision in the marriage immigration rules. If your husband hit you, you were eligible for immediate green card status. He did not have to be convicted or even told that you had filed for this status. Of course, this procedure was taken advantage of and the INS was now investigating each claim more closely. I decided I needed to find out of this marriage and this was it. I was sure that I could provoke Lester into physical violence without great difficulty.

Back in L.A. we began to live separately. One time when he called he said he wanted me to come over. I told him we should be seen out in public and that I would buy him dinner at a nice Italian restaurant in Hollywood called Madeo's. I ordered a bottle of wine and encouraged him to drink saying that he couldn't keep up with me. Then I ordered a second bottle. When I could tell that he was feeling the liquor I decided that this was the time to strike. I said every nasty thing about him I could think of. I told him he was a rotten bastard, a faggot, a cock-sucker, a mother-fucker and every terrible insult I could think of. I did not even know what all of them meant. Some of them were just what I had heard on HBO. I was amazed at what happened next and how swiftly it happened. Lester started to cry. He was sobbing and agreed with me that he was all those things and he begged for my forgiveness! So much for plan. I even felt sorry for the bastard.

That night I stayed at his house a few hours while he cried and begged my forgiveness. He did not even try to have sex with me. He told me he loved me! Now I was really confused. When he called me three days later and starting threatening again and trying to blackmail me regarding my green card, I was actually relieved. It was time for a new plan. As some of my girlfriends say, "Desperate times call for desperate measures." And these were desperate times.

The next time Lester called, I came over and followed his commands unflinchingly. I gave him more than he asked for and he promptly fell asleep. After about an hour of fearful indecision I did what I had to do. I stood up on the bed over his unconscious body with one foot on each side of his barrel chest and then I let nature take its course. As he awoke, at first I think he thought there was a leak in the roof, then he opened his eyes and saw the stream of liquid coming from between my legs. Instinctively he drew back his arm and knocked me off the bed.

I got up and immediately left the apartment hastily throwing on my pullover dress on my way. I knew I would never have to look at him again and I knew what my last memory would be. Ten minutes later at the police station I showed my bruised shoulder and thigh and told the officer filing out the report how my husband had knocked me down. I truthfully told him the entire story except for one detail. And to take you to the ending, within the next ninety days I had gained my papers and desired legal status. You may ask if I regret my awful behavior in this matter. No.

So I didn't have any money problems now and most people were nice. My lack of English was my main problem. I was very isolated. I found the Russian people I met in America very different from "real" Russians. A lot of them had come to America when they were twenty or so to study and wound up doing very well for themselves. They were different, softer, more American than Russians now. I found them all to be quite settled and boring. With my limited language skills, it was hard to make American friends. But despite the cultural shock and loneliness, I started to feel like a human being again.

After several years in America, I gave up prostitution. My self-esteem had grown to the point that I just didn't want to do it anymore. I started to feel distant and unfriendly and my clients sensed it. I feel superior to my clients now. I no longer want to be in a situation like that. I want to be appreciated as a woman now.

I constantly tell myself that I deserve to have a good and happy life. This is hard to do because my mother always made me feel like I wasn't good enough. She was very stingy with her love. I never felt spoiled or admired. She made me feel that I wasn't ever good enough. I just didn't have enough of anything—ever. I also never had a father around to love and protect me. Even now, I can never have enough things because I didn't get enough of anything as a child.

I still talk to my mother once or twice a week, but she refuses to take money from me. Fortunately, she doesn't need it. I play the piano for pleasure and I teach children in order to make money. If I had been born here in America, I believe I would have been very successful. I imagine I would have gone to Harvard or Yale or Julliard to study piano. I might have married and had kids. But I can't blame myself for what I've done or how my life turned out. I lived the life I had to, given my circumstances. I am living my life for myself now—that's it. I'm dating a nice guy at last. He does some sweet things for me sometimes. I like him and may marry him. Isn't that a happy ending?

Chapter 19
CHRISTMAS KNIGHT

I was born into a good Soviet family in the city of Krasnoyarsk. It was the same kind of simple looking Soviet Union city as any other which you can find on the map. It had the same three- to five-story house, the same long gray lines at the grocery shops, and the same modest stores that sold ice cream cones for three pennies.

My mother worked at the passport office. It was a special government organization where she drew up passports and registrations for people. Her job was prestigious and respected at that time. Her job could be dangerous because criminals and thieves who came out of prison and needed documents in order to live could apply. She worked with different kinds of people, from teachers to bandits. If my mother denied them papers, we went through "scary years." "Scary years" is a slang phrase that appeared after World War II when people always lived in fear. During that period, my mother's organization asked the militia patrol to walk her to and from work. My father was employed at a weapons factory.

I was a late child. My mother had me when she was almost forty years old. I don't remember much about my father. He died at the factory during a gunpowder explosion when I was five. I do recall that he loved me very much and spoiled me with ice cream every day. However, I didn't really love my mother. And after my baby years, it was mutual.

I now understand that she couldn't give me the warmth and love that I expected. She suffered starvation during the war and then had this demanding job. Life forced her always to be ready for one kind of battle or another, often in a defense mode. My mother cared about me as a baby, but as I grew up I never got anything like laughter, praise or obvious love. She did buy me good quality clothes and she enrolled me in pioneer camp during summer vacation. But she had a trait that I hated. She shouted at me and humiliated me in front of my friends and strangers. In some ways, mother was cruel. She thought that there was only one correct opinion: hers. Anybody who tried to prove anything to the contrary was placed on her enemy list.

I remember when she came to see me on parent's visiting day at camp. I was seven years old and very homesick. I cried and asked her to take me home with her. I told her that once for break- fast they gave us rice cereal with cockroaches. My mother went to the kitchen to find out what was going on. It happened that I took fried brown-colored bit of chopped onion for cockroaches. But I was a child. I didn't know anything about cereal cooking. In front of my teachers, camp acquaintance and everyone else, my mother slapped me on the face. She said that I humiliated her, a govern- ment worker, in front of low-class cooks.

I had a stepsister. My father was a widower with a child when he married my mother. His first wife died in childbirth. My stepsister Natasha was seven years older than I. The most vivid memories I have of her are from New Years celebrations. I remember how early on every New Years' morning, I would look under the tree excited about my gifts. At that time, most presents contained candy, fruits and book. But I always found packages opened and almost empty. Natasha had got to them first. She had ripped open the gift wrap paper and eaten the chocolate candy and the tangerines, leaving behind the rind in the gift box. My mother always defended her. She felt sorry that Natasha first lost her mother and then her father. But everybody forgot that he was my father, too.

I was a perfect student. I picked up knowledge quickly. I was talented when it came to languages. After high school graduation, my tutors suggested that I enroll in college and take English classes and I did. I studied to become English teacher. More than anything else, I wanted to leave my mother.

It was considered kind of "cool" at that time to correspond with foreigners. We met them through school, friends and other innocent minors. We exchanged letters, presents, packages, and post cards with each other. I found this interesting. It was an expression of friendship among students and others all over the world. I had a correspondence with a captain from Latvia who sailed great distances. He sent me scarves, calendars, and foreign stamps which I collected.

Once, he came to visit me in Krasnoyarsk and, to my astonishment, proposed! My sister was already married to a simple electrician. They couldn't have children and were unhappy. I didn't know Vladlen well, but I accepted his proposal. I knew that he'd be gone sailing for weeks and months. I believed from our correspondence that he would never irritate me, he would provide for me a comfortable life with fashionable clothes and free vacation. But it wasn't money that made marriage attractive. I wanted to run away from my mom's control. I hoped that I would get used to Vladlen and would fall in love with him one day.

I lived with Vladlen in Latvia for six years. Then, we immigrated to Washington in America. To me, America was a strange country. I had no friends, no job, and no interests. Even my little knowledge of English had disappeared. I didn't understand anything. Further, Vladlen wanted to have children, but I couldn't get pregnant and he still sailed. I was dying of boredom. When he came home from his trips, I created arguments out of nothing. I found everything in my life tiresome.

One day, Natasha called me and told me that mother had died. She was washing the bathtub, fell down, injured and suffered fatal bleeding in her brain. I didn't cry. I felt sorry for her. I didn't feel at all happy about it, but I didn't cry.

When I was living in America all the relatives remembered me, Natasha among them. She would call and list all the clothes she wanted to receive. I explained to her that I couldn't afford all those presents because I didn't work. I didn't even have them myself. She shouted in the phone that I had to help and support my relatives because I lived better than they did. At such moments, I remembered my New Year's presents that she ate every year. It seems strange to me that people in Russia think that people in America collect money like leaves from trees and that their lives are one perpetual vacation.

I was twenty-six years old when Vladlen came home from one of his trips and didn't bring me any presents. He didn't even send a post card saying that he was coming back. I knew that this meant something. He walked into our expensively furnished apartment with a sad and guilty look on his face. He used to sail frequently to Newport, Rhode Island. He reminded me that he always dreamed of having children. He said that in Newport he found a simple Russian student from Novonikolayevsk. He charmed her and she got pregnant.

He wanted to file for divorce, but was leaving me everything. I went into a rage. I threw plates and frying pans into the wall. This is a particular expression of character by offended Russian women. I couldn't believe that my Vladlen would leave me. I cried for an entire month. But, in a way, when I thought about it, I didn't feel offended that he was leaving. He had wounded my feelings of rightful ownership. As usually happens with women, in her mind she is convinced that her man is supposed to love her during his entire life and be under her feet. In any case, he must never be seen with another woman, even if he leaves her.

I thought that everything that was mine was supposed to be mine forever. As the days passed, however, I became stronger and decided that it was time for me to come out of my nest. I started to look for a job. A few months later, I began to work at a travel agency. I felt alive again. I had a good salary: five hundred dollars per week and, after all, Vladlen had left me an expensive apartment.

I befriended a co-worker named Janet. We went out and had fun. Still, something was missing in my life. I felt lonely. Janet advised me to find a man through the internet. She thought that it was a solution for loneliness for a temporary reduction in my finance and for other problems which divorced Russian woman encounter in a strange country. I knew for a long time that getting acquaintances through websites was absolutely possible. But I set conditions for myself: only intelligent, rich, and handsome men would be invited to write me.

I looked at myself in the mirror. I knew that I was pretty and interesting looking. Surely men would go crazy for my sky blue eyes and my thick ash blond hair that fell below my hips. Yes, I was short only 5'2", but, I was slim and had good breasts. I thought that my height was to my advantage. Short men, too, would go for me. Plus, I didn't look twenty-seven years old. The clerks still checked my ID in liquor stores and bars. As the Russian saying goes, "A little dog in his old age is still a puppy." In addition we say, "A little woman decorates a big man." A big man in every sense of the word "Big" is what I wanted to get and decorate.

People always want to believe and hope for the best. I wanted to find a man I could truly love. I believed that the Internet was the best method to meet my soul mate. Slowly, I started to choose men who fit my requirements. I had normal requests. The most important things were intelligence, a good sense of humor, and a good income. But, on the other hand, I knew that everyone would say that about themselves.

I wondered who all these hunters were on the internet. They could be newcomers, professionals, searchers, even men after prey. They would all send their pictures and information with hope. But, their hopes could be different from ours and we women might never find out about them until it was too late. Anyway I placed my application on a website. I attached my most attractive pictures and described myself in the best way I could while still being honest. Maybe I just added half a size to the description of my breasts. My goal for meeting a man, I wrote, was friendship, love and marriage. Mostly, I asked for a man who matched my desire about how he looked and my other requests. I knew it could take some time because, as the saying goes, "The first pancake is a lump."

I took every man as a separate case because each of them had different life experiences and lots of complicated baggage. With my first case, I had a correspondence that lasted for more than a year. His name was Aaron. He was in his forties. In the beginning, we exchanged lots of intense e-mails. Later, we sent fewer. Aaron was the head of a small fire department in Massachusetts. He was very proud of his uniform which consisted of a helmet and a sand-colored costume. He had two grown daughters. They lived with his ex-wife. He had a compact house for which he paid a mortgage that equaled two weeks of his salary. He had a computer and flowers that he was lovingly growing on his windowsills. He expressed loneliness in every e-mail. He wanted to be needed by somebody.

At first, I was struck by his ideas about love, romance, and poetry. He wrote how our meetings would be candle-lit dinners, and beds filled with white rose petals. I didn't understand how a fireman could be so romantic. I couldn't understand how his wife could have left a man full of warmth and love. However, his e-mails bothered me. I couldn't sleep or work. I imagined our love-filled future and family. By nature, I am an impatient person. I wanted to know everything.

I decided that since we matched so well and dreamed about the same things, why should we postpone anything? I was even willing to fly to Massachusetts to meet my prince. As people say, "Strike while the iron is hot." I tried to get closer to him through phone calls.

But my would-be partner in romance didn't want to come out of his dream state and turn it into reality. I began to feel he lived in an imaginary world and felt warm and comfortable there. The more we wrote to each other, the more I was sure of it. Aaron was a virtual Romeo. I didn't want become his virtual Juliet. In addition, I feared that he would eventually want to have phone sex with me. This prospect didn't make me happy at all. I wanted to have real feelings. I dreamed of meeting a man who I could touch, a man whose eyes I could look into. I tried to imagine how wonderful Aaron's virtual roses smelled. The unreal world he lived in and conversations about love began to irritate me. I still wrote to him, but I kept my eyes and Internet site open and started to look for a man again.

I chose a few men and started to exchange e-mails. But these men came to mean nothing to me. I met them, but usually, I never went out with them again. People say that the first impression about a person is usually the most accurate. One has to have a keen nose and know what smells good and what is disgusting. After quite a few meetings, I saw it was enough for me to look at a man once to know if he was worthy of being anywhere in my future. I would set up a meeting at a Starbucks. But I would check the man out before I sat down. Sometimes I didn't even approach my candidates. Some showed up with their messy hair, wrinkled t-shirts and scruffy shoes.

I did meet a lot of annoying men. They bored me with their stories about victories, successes and all the positive features of their characters. I was always curious about why their wives had left such a treasure in hope of finding a mate. Sometimes I asked them outright. The men were seldom at a loss. They complained that they were too young when they stupidly married a doll who turned into a bitch after the wedding. They would say she became a vampire and sucked almost all their blood, nerves and hard-earned money. Nothing surprised me in such men but their rudeness.

Then I met and sat down with Steven. He was married and didn't hide the fact that he wanted to have some sex on the side. He talked about his incredible intelligence and honesty for hours. He thought that if in the beginning he told a woman not to depend on him as a possible future husband, he could save his moral face and remain faithful to his family. He was Russian and, like most Russian men, he had only right and truthful opinions about everything he thought. Physically, he was a dark-haired and muscular man. He had a beautiful white smile and dimple in his right cheek. Usually, such men don't stay unnoticed. But I was interested in compatibleness. I decided not to test myself. I sent him an e-mail saying that I had found my soul mate and was no longer available.

But I decided I was definitely looking for a sexual partner, one that I could drop at will. Right after Steven, I found a weird case. His name was Tom. I gave him the nickname: mystery advisor. He told me that he worked at The White House as a personal advisor to a very famous official whose identity was a big secret. It's possible that his name was not Tom, but who knows? It was impossible for me to contact him because of his sensitive professional duties. In the beginning, he sent me e-mails every day at the same time in the morning, afternoon, and night. The e-mails were long and all about how important and busy he was.

Later, they became shorter with simple stuff like: "How are you?" "Thinking about you," etc. Then he asked for my phone number. He explained that he was so busy that he had no time to write long messages. But he could call me at any time and at the same time do other things like drive a car, smoke, or have lunch.

Somehow, I believed him. He always called around one o'clock in the morning and bullshitted me. I listened to him talk about his job. He said that the agenda of the White House depended on him. After I got bored and fell asleep with the phone on my pillow. Tom wanted to see me at the same moment he called me. So, in his opinion, our meetings were supposed to be around two o'clock in the morning and would take place on the other side of Washington. I asked him not to call me anymore. He replied that I would regret losing him. But I didn't.

Of course, I had some pleasant meetings as well. A few times, men invited me to a restaurant, bought me ice cream desserts and took me to the theater or a movie. One elegant gentleman even gave me a red rose. He was an immigrant from England and wasn't spoiled by the American lifestyle. But something went wrong in heaven because we didn't continue our acquaintance. I wasn't attractive to some men and vice versa. But it was all a big and interesting adventure, and I did learn some lessons. Still, I wanted to meet the one man I would love. I wanted to share my life with him. I still believed at that time that loneliness could depart from me forever.

He seemed to have appeared. His name was Michael. He said he was thirty-five years old, tall and skinny with blond hair and big brown eyes. He was a lawyer who defended children's rights. I fell in love. All day long, we sent each other e-mails. The e-mails were about poetry, novels, and interesting questions. He seemed smart, kind and funny. Michael respectfully replied to all my thoughts. He wrote wonderful poems and songs. Only I didn't feel comfortable about the fact that in every e-mail, he stated that our first sexual encounter would be the most blissful moment of my life. According to his predictions, it was supposed to be that start of a healthy and romantic relationship between man and woman.

In the beginning, he was shy with his ideas about our intimacy. But soon, he offered to meet with me and "light the candle." To light a candle is a reference to a romantic night without any expectations or commitment. No, I couldn't stop thinking about Michael. He had a respectable job as a lawyer, composed beautiful poems, and played the piano. I always asked myself if he was the one I was dreaming about in my lonely bedroom when I was so horny. Didn't I say his name a thousand times into my pillow and didn't it become my favorite name in the world?

But it's surprising what jokes our fantasies can play on our mind; how cruelly our fantasies translate into realities. It wasn't enough for me to have all those virtual conversations and offers of sexual entanglement. I wanted to know it all for myself. You'll say that I am a promiscuous woman, but I am normal. How would you react if in every e-mail he asked and died from impatience, promising you heaven? Could anyone resist the sinful temptation? By that time, it was almost four years since my body had experienced the warm feeling of a man's hand.

Still, we met five more times before anything sexual happened. Every meeting made me think that we were born for each other. I came to the conclusion that we were also born to make love. He wasn't a stranger any longer with whom I jumped into bed like a whore. Finally, after yet another dinner, he invited me to watch a movie, *The Notebook*, in his apartment. Everything was beautiful. He cried as he watched the movie and made comments that such love as in the movie would be ours.

Every woman falls in love with what she hears. I was no exception. Every word of his made me fall in love with him even more. He kissed my neck. Suddenly, everything happened. Actually, I had felt that nothing had started yet, but already it was over. I've never been a sex machine. I never had any pretensions about my life. I wasn't that experienced, but Michael tried to assure me that everything was supposed to be that way. It should take three minutes and in only one comfortable position for the man.

But I had been married before and knew that there were other theories about love-making. Partners were supposed to bring pleasure to each other. This was the only way it could work. I was shocked. On the one hand, I was so much in love with Michael that I was prepared to forgive him any small issues and share with him all of life's difficulties. But on the other hand, I was a young woman with whom he didn't want to allow a normal, healthy sex life. I needed satisfying sex to keep the balance of my body and my mind. I felt deceived.

Very delicately, I asked him if he was incapable due to circumstances. It could happen when the man had a stressful day, worried a lot, or wanted sex so much that he got it over with quickly. But Michael's eyes grew even larger when he told me that this was the best sex he ever had! He explained to me that for sex like this, he needed to be inspired. And a woman like me was in charge of that inspiration. But I was not willing to become the casualty of such thinking. It wasn't enough for me to live only on the basis of spiritual harmony. I knew that love was not only an attraction of the soul and mind, but also of the two physical bodies. It was supposed to be harmonious all the way around.

As the saying goes, "It's better to be hungry than to eat garbage." I told Michael that I had to go away for six months on a business trip to England. I gave him lots of compliments. I told him that a man like him deserved a better woman than me. He looked at himself in the mirror, smiled, and probably silently agreed with me while imagining himself with Claudia Schiffer. I told him that I wouldn't ask for any promises from him to remain faithful. I said that I understood that he needed a woman near him and not one who traveled frequently to other countries. Michael listened to me, feeling from the look on his face, that he had made his case successfully. I probably gave him too many compliments, but it must have made him happy. He said that he was sorry to lose me. He kissed me on my forehead and we got up from his bed.

To tell the truth, this was a big loss and disappointment. I suffered for a while. It was that rare time when I had felt my soul was in harmony with a man. I was sad. I sat at home and looked through new e-mails. I was in the middle of feeling I was a loser and I had lost interest in life. But, again, I noticed a posting that got my attention. Perhaps it would save me from missing Michael and eating myself up inside. At this time of my life, I was wondering if I was too demanding in bed or if all men were just looking for the easiest method to please themselves. I was curious if there still was a real lover left somewhere.

The posting was clear and simple. It stated everything. Richard wrote that he was looking for a woman and could make love with any woman at any time. The bold ad made me smile. I could feel it in my body. I had to find out if I was still able to turn on a man in a way that meant something to me. With Richard was almost no correspondence. After the second e-mail, we decided where we would meet, what time, and how we would be dressed.

Richard didn't want to describe the way he looked. He wrote that it would be his pleasure to surprise me. He wanted to recognize me himself. According to the ad, I sent him my sexiest picture. I was in a solid red robe and wore high heels. He replied with one word: "Wow!" I liked him from that moment. It warmed my heart that he so valued my beauty.

We decided to meet in front of an art gallery. Richard came up to me. I was shocked. He was a fat, bald, and short man. But in a way he provoked my respect. After all, I was a small and delicate woman. I wanted to snuggle into his strong shoulder. I don't know how everything happened, but I found myself in his car going nowhere. He talked without pausing about his business. He explained that he was owner of a big restaurant in downtown Washington. Why then was he driving an old green Toyota? It was damaged on the outside and dirty on the inside. But, I told myself, rich people are often very simple in their lifestyle. They don't care about expensive clothes and the other outward joys of life. Also, a car was not necessarily a luxury, but a means of transportation.

Richard told me about his mentally ill wife who was very annoying and refusing to have sex. He tried to look into my eyes as a fellow and not as an animal. He maintained that he would never leave his wife. He thought that he was a decent man. They had children who were his responsibility. It was amusing to observe him. It's curious what I remember from that meeting. He didn't ask me questions, which he was sure would work in winning over a woman. Maybe he didn't actually believe it, but he had a satisfied and secured face of a male.

We stopped at a deserted park near a little lake with scum along the bank. It was close to Washington. The weather was very hot, almost a hundred degrees. I turned to look at the lake. Within seconds, Richard had taken off his old jeans and t-shirt. He stood there in Mickey Mouse underpants. They didn't appear to be clean. Richard jogged off into the lake. I got out and stood on the shore. He played in the water like a child and demonstrated to me his swimming skills. He couldn't drown because he was round as a hot air balloon as he came out from the water.

I was amazed and yet horrified by his shameless effort at communication. I didn't understand at that time that my new friend didn't have morals, intellect or tact. He came up to me and hugged me without warning. He told me to take off my clothes because he was "ready." He took off his wet, ragged underpants. I could see that he was *really* ready! Other women might be frightened by such behavior. But I felt amused, I could hardly contain my laughter. I said that I was an intelligent woman and I couldn't have sex on the sand. He jumped into his car. He tried to find any scrap of a blanket. He was absolutely sure that everything would happen between us very quickly. After all, there were three e-mails.

I couldn't be serious anymore. I started to laugh hysterically. I cried from the laughter and gasped from lack of oxygen. I was dying from laughter when I noticed how his face had changed. He tried to find his underpants in the sand and then washed them in the lake. I imagined a police car passing by and seeing this self-styled decent family man, Richard, and how he would end up in jail for nothing. I calmed down. I was somewhat thankful to this odd little man. A big part of my insecurity disappeared with my laughter at that unknown lake. Silently, Richard delivered me to the gallery where we had met. The only words he spoke were for me not to write anything about him on the Internet and frighten off other lonely women.

I continued searching the Internet. But I no longer hoped to meet the man of my dreams. I understood that men are even more defenseless and easier to hurt than women. I began to associate men with children who don't understand what they are doing and don't have any sense of responsibility. Yet all of them were in some way attractive to me. Each of them taught me something and gave me emotions.

Suddenly, everything changed. After the situation with Richard, I became more secure. I started to reply differently to the e-mails. I demanded more and gave back less. Men started to send me more and more e-mails every day. I didn't answer them, but when I did, I was mysterious and brief.

At the end of 2005, I decided to quit this question-and-answer game over the Internet. I came to the conclusion that there I would meet only losers. It was all lies that the men were so busy with they didn't have time for truly personal communication and subsequent meetings. It was a convenient excuse. If a man had the time to look through the pictures, read ads, write and read letters, then he had a lot of free time! He was just lazy and insecure. I stopped checking my e-mails from unknown people.

The Christmas season had arrived. I decided that I would celebrate the holiday in my proud loneliness. I didn't feel bored. I had a lot to think about. I wanted to analyze all the correspondence and all hopes. And I made a food list for my holiday table. More than anything in the world, I loved fried potatoes with mushrooms, dill pickles, home fried lamb, and a bottle of chilled vodka. Of course, it could seem like the party of a lonely alcoholic, but would bring me pleasure. I could afford to eat this food and drink my vodka only when I was alone, otherwise people would judge me. As I was leaving, Janet called and invited me to Christmas party that night. But I had given up. I didn't want to go anywhere. I wanted to rest. She even announced that there would be ten available men, but I still refused.

I went to the neighborhood supermarket and to liquor store. On my way, I stopped at a pet store and bought a small puppy. I named it Knight. This way, I had company for Christmas. Knight and I bought all the necessary food for our dinner. Before leaving the store, my little Knight pulled his leash from my hand and ran out. I went after him with plastic bags full of food and caught him on the sidewalk. I couldn't let one more man leave me alone on Christmas.

I showed Knight my apartment. He could sleep on the coach, but he wasn't allowed to make a restroom out of my apartment. We understood each other. I cooked and served dinner. I played *The Bodyguard*, my favorite movie. In the Russian tradition, I placed the bottle of vodka on my dinner table and lit a candle. My frying pan sizzled with potatoes and lamb and smelled heavenly. I was happy. I drank the first shot of vodka. I wished for good health and happiness for everyone and for their dreams to come true. I knew that everything was well now in my life. Nothing had really changed during all the time I had wasted to become better (or worse).

During my dinner with Knight, my doorbell rang. I thought perhaps it was Janet and hurried to open the door. I was in my pajamas with the puppy in my hands and at the door stood a man. He had a Slavic appearance. In bad English, he asked if my name is Valentina Lomskaya. I said: yes. He proceeded to tell me just how he had located me. He said that he had found my wallet in the grocery cart. He couldn't stop himself from returning my wallet on Christmas. He was afraid that I was worrying about it instead of enjoying the holiday. He thought that, instead of celebrating, I was sitting at home and calling the company to report my lost card.

I smiled and told him that, in reality, I didn't even know that I had lost my wallet. This man introduced himself as Igor. I spoke to him in Russian, which made him happy. I invited him to come inside and celebrate with a drink of vodka in Russian tradition, even if New Year was the Russian holiday. He was shy, but finally he agreed. He had nowhere to go in a hurry. He appeared lonely. As I learned later, he had recently moved to Washington from New Jersey. He didn't have any friends yet, only American co-workers. He had been working at a Bank of America for only a week as a translator and hadn't gotten close to anybody. He wasn't invited to any holiday celebration.

We sat, talked and laughed until six o'clock in the morning. He was interesting and funny. He said that he never saw such a beautiful woman in his life without makeup. The whole night, we remembered different stories from our youth and life in the former Soviet Union. The most amazing thing was that Igor had lived for a time in Krasnoyarsk, my native city. More than that, we were neighbors and lived in the same part of town. He stayed and slept over in my apartment. I didn't want to let him go at seven in the morning. He didn't want to leave either. Sparks had flown between us during the second minute of conversation.

We dated three times and found our attraction for each other increased. When people ask me and Igor how we met, we laugh and say that we had to cross half the globe and come to America in order to find each other.

With great appreciation, I remember every one of my acquaintances who, for a brief time, became my hope, friend, or object of love. They taught me a lot. They taught me about myself. They showed me myself. They showed me my options and abilities. I learned to be patient. After all that, I met my other half, my dear Igor. And I met my "Christmas Knight."

Chapter 20
GOODBYE CRUEL WORLD

Once upon a time, I lived in Kazan City. You may ask why I say *lived* and *was* if I am still alive.

There is no more *me* in this life. There is nothing left of that happy woman with childlike, playful eyes. The woman with a loving husband and little twin girls no longer exists. I drowned in my sorrow on a tragic autumn day with my dear daughters. It was the bloody year 2000.

People say that even after the death and betrayal of loved ones, life goes on. Psychiatrists tell me to look forward and continue to live. But please tell me, isn't it a treachery to start everything from the beginning when it's already behind you? We are all guests in this world, but how could life be so unfair and cruel?

My husband, children, and I got into a car accident. Our one-and-a-half year old daughters, Liza and Masha, died instantly. My husband got a concussion and broke a few ribs. I turned into a disabled person; an animal no one needed.

We were coming back from our dacha, a Russian country house. Alexander (Sasha), the girls and I had celebrated our fourth anniversary. We spent the weekend as it was supposed to be—the whole family together. We went boating on the lake. We had a pork barbecue. We had two beautiful and last nights of making love. Sasha made a wonderful fuss over me. He kissed me on the forehead and said, "Thank you for your warmth, my dear."

I remember that I slept very badly during that rainy night before the tragedy. I dreamt that we were planning a vacation with the entire family. We packed our suitcases when suddenly our twins boarded the plane, but the flight attendants didn't allow us on board. The plane took off without us. Our daughters flew away.

I woke up crying. Quietly, I went to our children's room at the dacha. My girls slept hugging each other. I lay down on their bed when Sasha came in. He lay down also and hugged the three of us. He said that in that bed were the dearest three women in his life. By evening, we needed to head back to the city. The girls were wide awake and played half of the way. Later, they fell asleep. We drove down the road and quietly recalled our own childhoods.

On the road ahead of us came a huge long-range truck. The driver was drunk. He came at us full speed and ran right over our little white 1999 Toyota. I don't remember anything else. All that's left of me is sitting in a wheel chair now. The driver is in prison, but I don't care; it won't bring back my children and my happy marriage.

My husband survived. Slowly, he got better. I experienced a clinical death. When I opened my eyes, I was hooked up to countless medical devices and IV's. Sasha sat next to me; he looked thirty years older. His hair was gray. He wasn't shaven and he was blue under his eyes. I asked about our daughters. He wept uncontrollably and screamed that our babies were dead. I passed out again. I went into a neurological shock. From that stress, I became paralyzed below the waist. I remember that I came back briefly and lost consciousness again.

Suddenly, I plunged into my carefree youth and a happy childhood. I remember when I was seven or eight years old and my parents and I went to the lake. It was a summer tradition for all of us to go on a picnic every Sunday. When I became older, we took Maxim with us. Mama wore a green dress with a strawberry print. She dressed me in an identical dress. My father dressed in the latest style jeans and a blue t-shirt with yellow stripes. We took an old blanket and a thermos of iced tea. My mother boiled potatoes and eggs, sliced tomatoes and cucumbers, and fried a chicken. She took all that food for our outdoor lunch. After we ate all that food, we played badminton with my father and then a game of charades.

In order to get to the lake, we needed to take a bus from our house and a train from the railway station to Zamorskaya station. When we got off the train, my parents bought me fresh carrots from an old woman. I had to eat them while we walked to the lake. My father called me a little rabbit. We chose a spot for our picnic and my father ran into the lake. He dove like a walrus and swam with a funny snort. My mother couldn't swim. I played in the sand nearby with the other kids. It was a wonderful time and made happy memories.

I was a loved and cherished child. My parents loved each other with a correct Soviet kind of love. They always had the same opinion about everything that happened in the world. Every morning, my parents woke up at 5 a.m. and did their morning exercise while listening to commentary on the radio. Then, for breakfast they each had a boiled egg and tea with a slice of lemon and one and a half teaspoons of sugar.

We lived in a little one-bedroom apartment. But nobody imposed upon my freedom. My parents trusted me. My mother was a short and delicate-looking woman. However, she was very strong on the inside. She worked in a local hospital as a nurse. Her nice looking appearance was very helpful when it came to reducing fear in patients before treatment. As long as I can remember, my mother always wore braided hair and lined her eyes with my drawing crayon. She was always smiling. She believed that we have to live and hope for the better, no matter what.

She brought needles and a white nurse's uniform home from work. I wasn't interested in girl's stuff. I didn't like learning any women's skills whatsoever. I don't even know where I learned to cook, do housework, and supervise our kids. It just came to me when I married Alexander.

My father was a retired military man. He was strong-willed. He had a huge long Cossack mustache. It made him look like he didn't have any lips. He had deep-seated sparkling eyes and a powerful, commanding voice. When I was a little girl, I was a tomboy. I liked everything connected with knives, weapons, catapults, service caps, and war memorabilia. It was a great deal of fun for me when my father took me to work at the army base. A few soldiers entertained me with military songs and ran around the iron barriers where they trained.

My father earned enough money that my mother didn't have to work. But mother couldn't put upon father's shoulders all the family needs and responsibilities. It wasn't in the character of a Soviet woman to provide a supportive shoulder to her man.

From my childhood, I befriended only boys. Until I was seventeen, I didn't wear any bows, flowers, or earrings. I had a best friend named Maxim. I called him Potty because we were friends since we were toddlers. We climbed trees and did a lot of construction on underground tunnels and the like. I remember how I once fell down from the apple tree in the back yard. As I fell, I twisted in the air. At the last moment, I grabbed a branch and it saved my life. I could have fallen to my death. God saved me. My parents observed the scene in shock from the balcony of our apartment. That day was the first time my parents ever punished me. They stood me in the corner of the living room. I stood for three hours with heroic endurance. I didn't cry and didn't ask for permission to sit. I studied the lives of cockroaches. They lived in the wall cracks underneath the wallpaper.

My parents always gave me freedom. This helped me realize that life wasn't easy. In addition, they knew my friends and didn't worry. We weren't interested in drinking, discos, or breaking windows. The worst thing we did was cut roses from the Kazan flower beds and bring them to our teachers on examination days.

Sometimes, during the summer, my parents sent me to pioneer camp. It was terrible. I always ran away after the first week. After my third attempted escape, my parents finally realized that I didn't like it there and eventually stopped looking for camps. It made their lives easier too. But, of course, there were some good memories from the camp. I had my first love experience.

I was ten when I fell in love for the first time. It was in a pioneer camp. I didn't declare my feelings to the cute twelve-year-old blond-haired and blue-eyed boy. His name was Kostik. I quietly suffered from love 'til the end of the camp season, but I tried different ways to get his attention. Like any child, I wasn't really successful at it. I probably chose the wrong methods. I collected spiders in a glass jar and let them out in his bed. I tripped him up and threw a bucket of water at him. I took his pants off in front of other children. Everybody laughed, but he turned red. So, my first love was a disaster, but I thought that I was on top of the world. Kostik must have guessed that I wasn't indifferent to him. I was a quiet child who said little but acted out more.

When I became older, I couldn't fall in love with anyone unknown to me. When I was in the ninth grade, I fell in love with my potty friend, Maxim. Everything happened so strangely. We had shared a school desk since the first grade and, at fourteen, feelings appeared. I was a very amorous girl. I would leave him all the time and come back again. In the first year, he was so much in love with me that when I told him that I would sit with Vasya Ivanov, he didn't come to school for three weeks. His parents were summoned to school. His mother asked me to please sit with Maxim again. He was on a strike. He said that if I didn't sit with him, he would never come to school again. This way, we dated for three years until graduation. To tell the truth, like every boy at sixteen, he wasn't interested in holding hands, hugging, and kissing. Before graduation, he wanted to experience adult love and become a real man. I wasn't ready at that time. I mean, I was curious but I didn't feel like I was ready. In addition, my breasts started to develop late and it hurt very much.

Maxim broke my heart right before graduation night. He broke up with me and came to the graduation with a freshman college girl. I went with a classmate. He gladly accepted my invitation. My mother sewed me a long rose-colored dress with chiffon bows and flowers. We curled my long black hair. My mother applied mascara to my eyelashes and put lipstick on my lips.

I looked terrific. Everything became evident when after the ceremony we all went to walk on the embankment. I was the most beautiful-looking girl that day. Somebody brought a bottle of champagne. We crawled into the bushes and drank it. Maxim came up to me and said that I looked amazing. We talked for a while. We came to the conclusion that, no matter what, we would always be the best and closest of friends.

About a month after my graduation, my father died from a sudden heart attack. My mother lost herself as a woman. She went from always being positive and smiling to sad and melancholy. She sat at home and looked through the photo album of their past. For a few years, she burned from anguish and died without having any health problems. I was nineteen years old and in my sophomore year at university. Maxim was very supportive at that time. He helped me a lot.

We enrolled at the same university and the same language department. We were supposed to be linguists after graduation. I lived alone in my parent's apartment. I always had parties with my school friends. Something happened to me during the first year at university: I became feminine. During the summer, I grew out my hair. On my vanity table, mascara appeared. It was a little box with solid paint and a little brush for eyelashes. In order to do your eyes, you had to spit in it until the paint got soft; then you had to apply it quickly.

I had a lot of admirers at the university. I can't remember their names. During the second year, I met my future husband. As I said, I had many student parties in my apartment. We sang, played the guitar, smoked and talked. One day, Alexander came. I once heard that the name Alexander, translated from Greek, meant a wall, manly, and a defender. He was different from the rest. He seemed stronger and more single-minded. It seemed, judging by his strong character, that he could achieve everything and anything. He was very charming and affable. But I did not notice it at our first meeting. I read that "Alexander" was able to go through all barriers, to protect weaker persons, to love warmly and care for a person in need.

From the beginning, I didn't like him. But I didn't have anything against him either. He looked like a hippy. He was dressed in inexpensive clothes and used English words in conversations. He was strangely relaxed and always smiling. I took this as a self-acknowledged genius. But he had a good sense of humor and I valued that quality in people more than anything. That is why I probably I had a good friendship with Maxim for so many years. We understood each other without words and laughed about the same things. If somebody told me at that time that Alexander would be my husband, I wouldn't have believed it!

A whole year went by before I saw Alex again. One day, Maxim reminded me about him and offered to invite him to a party. He liked him and thought he was interesting. I became curious. I wondered why I didn't like Alexander if he was so special and wonderful. I took a closer look and fell in love. After graduation, we got married. But I had a choice.

It so happened that Maxim and Alexander proposed to me at the same time. At the moment, I felt that Maxim looked upon me only as a friend. But Alex noticed the woman in me. He used to say that he wanted me to be very happy. Maxim would stay over my apartment after parties. We slept in the same bed but nothing ever happened. We didn't even kiss. I knew him like the back of my hand. When he told me what a fool he was in school, I just laughed.

Of course, when I began to date Alexander, he began to sleep over at my apartment without Maxim being there. But I still had a friendship with him. Alexander joined our friendship. Everybody called us The Saintly Trio. The three of us were inseparable. We were very different and that is why we complemented one another. Maxim had short blond hair with blue eyes. He was tall and muscular. He always smiled and blinked a lot when he lied. I had long black hair and green eyes. I had a thick waist and a big butt. I always looked serious and deep in thought. But in reality, I always felt humored. I found something to laugh about in every situation. On the other hand, Sasha (Alexander) had light brown shoulder-length hair. He wore glasses and stylish clothes. Alex had nice lips and astonishing eyes. When he shared his thoughts, he always brought his finger to his temple and started a phrase with the words: "I don't want to seem very brilliant, but." Our love blossomed suddenly. One night, he stayed over after a party. Nothing happened. He laid down on the floor and rolled into a blanket. I was lying on the bed. We both dreamed about our future and shared our plans. In the morning, we finally kissed. It happened just because he was frozen on the floor and asked to lay with me in the opposite direction. After that night we never separated, not even for an hour. Sasha transferred to our student group. He passed all the required exams.

We sat at the same desk, all three of us: Maxim, Sasha, and me. Sasha and I kissed during class breaks, in the parks, and bus stations. Sasha came to study at our university from Samara. His mother worked somewhere in the government and that is why he lived at the dorm. During the school year, he earned money by selling jeans. It wasn't legal, but he was too young to think about that. It gave him a good income. Sasha almost constantly lived with me in my apartment. Maxim didn't date any girl seriously during all those years at school. He tried to spend every minute around me. But it happened less and less. Sometimes he tried to talk about his love for me. When Sasha wasn't around, he came and reminded me about our friendship. One day, they both proposed to me. But I gave up on both of them.

The first was Maxim. It was unexpected because he knew that I dated Sasha. I told Alexander. He woke Maxim up in the middle of the night and brought him to me. He said, choose him or me? I told them both to leave and not to start a circus performance. They left. Alexander came back two hours later and proposed himself. I agreed, but, in exchange, he would cut his hair. We applied at City Hall. We went to meet with his mother in Samara. She was wonderful, a little fat but a very wonderful woman. She looked like a hippy herself. She had a short haircut, bright make up, and red nails. She liked me from the first moment. She said, if you love my son, I am glad. But never lose your self-respect and know that you are the best. Remember kiddo, if a woman doesn't love herself, nobody will.

We went back to Kazan. We applied again about six more times at City Hall for a marriage license. I tore up a marriage application in a fit of anger and Alex did the same in a fit of jealousy. We had a very emotional and passionate relationship. It was much better than any Latin soap opera today.

Max went crazy when he received the wedding invitation. His feelings for me became even stronger. But people are stupid fools. They understand everything only when it's too late. But, as the saying goes, when we have it, we don't care; when we lose it, we cry. In other words, there is probably no simple friendship between a man and a woman. It's possible from the woman's point of view because we choose to be understanding and supportive. We don't care about physical attraction when choosing friends. We can separate sexual attraction from friendship. But for a man, it's more difficult. Max began to compete with Sasha. He lost, but very suitably. At the wedding, he toasted us and said that I would always be his friend; he would always love me and care about me.

I chose Sasha because he was new and interesting. Max suffered, but we still remained friends. However, with each passing day, it became harder. He couldn't get used to the idea that I was a married woman and a wife while he was still free and available to go everywhere at any time. It hurt his feelings that before I would call him and say, "come over, I am depressed." Then, everything changed. He understood that I had a new shoulder to cry on—my husband's. I saw that Max needed me and I worried, but I had a family I just started. Our friendship lasted six more months, until Max got an offer to work as a translator in an American court. He moved to America. To tell the truth, he didn't care about his career prospects, he just couldn't watch Alex and me being in love and happy. It was too painful.

We said goodbye to him and promised to stay in touch. But, as is often the case, a new family has its problems, things to do and needs that demand time and attention. Slowly, we lost touch with each other. But Maxim still called from New York and congratulated us on birthdays and anniversaries. After two and a half years, I got pregnant. At the time, Sasha had a clothing store. He flew to Turkey to buy modern clothes and goods for the Russian market. We sold the apartment I had from my parents. We risked it all and invested the whole amount into that business. The first few months, I went on buying trips with Sasha. We couldn't live without each other. But, when I became pregnant, Sasha was very worried and forbade me to help him. I started to teach Russian kids how to speak English. The children were spoiled, dissatisfied, and never heard the word "no" for any of their requests. Young Russian fathers paid me in dollars. They were quite polite and, because of my health condition, sent me drivers who picked me up at my house and drove me back after the lesson.

The delivery date came. It happened that Sasha was on a plane coming back when the flight was delayed. Maxim, under the happy circumstances, became a witness to my delivery. He cried when I delivered twins girls. He became their godfather. When Sasha came, he filled my hospital room with flowers and balloons. We came back together with the girls to a new apartment with a decorated and furnished nursery. Maxim helped Sasha prepare everything beforehand.

Then, Maxim flew back to America. I was back in my house with my loving husband and our lovely babies. Later, we found out that Maxim married a Russian woman who had recently emigrated from Moscow. He usually didn't say much, so we weren't terribly surprised. When I asked him if he was happy, he gave a positive reply and made it brief.

Sasha idolized me and our daughters. When the babies cried, he got up himself in the middle of the night and let me sleep. He wanted me to be rested and healthy. The girls felt his warmth and their loving father's hands. They loved him very much and, within a minute, they fell asleep when he sang to them. They reached out their little arms when he came home from work. They made Sasha happy. He pulled me into his arms. He kissed me and said that I was the best woman in the whole wide world. During those three years, Alex went from a funny hippy to a perfect husband and father and a successful businessman. Every day, I was waiting for him to come home from work. Some people say that it's hard to deal with the first child. But for me, it was easy with my two babies. I loved them very much. I loved everything about them. I enjoyed playing with them, reading to them, observing them, walking with them, taking pictures, and all the rest. I cooked different dishes for Sasha. We had a wonderful life.

In the mornings, I usually woke up early too. The girls also woke up with their father. While he kissed them and changed their diapers, I cooked breakfast for all of us. For the girls, it was milk or mashed fruits and vegetables; for Sasha, a buttered sandwich with red caviar and a fresh brewed coffee. I was busy around the house, with the kids and Sasha. But I never felt like I was a housewife. Everything I did brought me pleasure. I felt like a loving wife and mother.

After the car accident, when I became better, the doctors let me go home. Alex took me home. For the first few months, he cared and looked after me. Later, his mother came from Saratov to help us. She felt sorry for me and tried her best to give me good care and lots of warmth. Sasha tried to be strong as well, but he needed to earn money for my treatments and medical necessities. It was terrible to pee in my bed in the presence of my loving husband, being a smart and dignified woman of twenty-six. It's scary not to be able to be in control of yourself or your body.

With each passing day, Sasha felt more and more distanced from me. People usually say that problems bring people closer than they were before. Together, they are a force. But our problems only multiplied. I wanted to share with him my pain. But he wasn't ready to hear it. Sasha began to come home from work later and later each night. He barely stopped in my room to say hello, or ask how

I felt. His mother covered for him. She lied to me, saying that Sasha had called and said that he would be late because the store needed repairs, it was tax season, had meetings, etc. She saw the hurt in my eyes. She quietly cried, feeling sorry for me. I remembered how much she loved me the first time Sasha introduced us. She was sure that I was the best woman for her only son.

A nurse from the hospital came and checked on my health, gave me injections, and pills. Sasha stopped coming home altogether. He began to buy new ties; it was the first sign that he fell in love. I knew it. I cried all the time. I understood that he was young and had no use for a disabled wife for the rest of his life. Suddenly, his mother died. There was nobody to take care of me. For a few days, Sasha sat with me. But we had nothing to talk about. He felt guilty and uncomfortable. I was ashamed of the way I looked, I was hopeless and helpless.

One day, he came up to me and said, I am sorry, but my life has to go on and I need to set my priorities, maybe I will get a new family and kids. A few weeks later, he took me to a nursing home for disabled people, with one suitcase and a wheelchair. I lived there absolutely lonely among other disabled people like me. I wasn't even Tanya any more. I was an essence of her; I ate, drank, and peed in bed. I didn't care about anything or anybody. I cried twenty-four hours a day. I waited for Sasha's visit. I couldn't believe that he had betrayed me so and gave up fighting for me that easily. The first week, he came to visit every day. But he did it out of a sense of duty. He was still my husband. Slowly, he showed up with a guilty face three times a week; then once a week. I saw that he was in love. I asked him not to come any more and filed for a divorce. We lost all communication with Maxim by then.

As it happened, he had called all that time while Sasha's mother looked after me. She thought that it was one of my lovers. She lied that we had moved. It was cruel. I turned into a simple animal, moved into the status of being forgotten by everybody. I tried to commit suicide three times, but somebody always saved me and brought me back from another world.

One day, the most unexpected news came. Max had waged a campaign to locate me when he got word of my whereabouts. He called the nursing facility and screamed into the phone that he couldn't find me all this time. He asked what was wrong with me. I replied that there was no more me alive and hung up the phone.

Max immediately got on a plane and came from America. He found Sasha in his store. When he learned what had happened to me, he beat Sasha to a pulp. By then, Sasha lived with a young woman from St. Petersburg. He planned to marry her and start a family again.

I always wondered how some men can wipe out their past so quickly and start all over again. Max found the nursing home where I had been housed. He met with my doctors. For me to walk again, I required radical surgery. It was very expensive, more than $50,000. Max wanted to help me.

When he came to my room, he found me sleeping in my wheelchair in front of the barred window. I was rail-thin and old-looking. He fell to his knees. He kissed my hands and cried. I cried too. Max tried to persuade me to agree to the surgery in America. But even the doctor said that patients who don't want to live never became better, only worse. I was one of them. I refused. I had no desire to live this life. I didn't want to live another day. He asked permission from my doctor to take me to a cemetery, to the graves of my babies. I saw the neglected tombs of my daughters. If there is no mother around for the children, who will tend to them? I knew that men can't bring up and care about somebody else's children, but can they forget about their own?

I felt terrible. I agreed to the surgery. I realized that I needed to live and make an effort. As Max told me his story, it ended up that he got divorced. He still loved me and suffered from the loss of my love. He married that woman because he wanted to forget me. He couldn't. Again, I thought how people so often realize their life's priorities too late. If he didn't act like a silly boy when we were fourteen; if he didn't break up with me, who knows, today we could have been a very strong family. We were soul mates since our childhood. A friendship is the beginning of all things, but if life was so predictable and easy, then it would be boring to live.

Max prepared everything for my flight. He collected all the medical records, statements, and recommendations. We were at the airport. Sasha didn't show up to say goodbye to me. I was hurt. I remembered a long time ago, when our daughters were just born, Sasha and I dreamed of our future. We wanted them to get an education in America. We planned to visit them on vacation. At that moment, I lost myself. I didn't believe that I would find myself again.

I was taken straight from the airport to the hospital. Dr. Steadman headed the team of doctors that performed my surgery. For three whole days, Max sat in the hallway. He didn't sleep and didn't eat. He just smoked. He was afraid and worried about me. This was my second surgery that he witnessed. The first was the delivery of my twins; the second was my rebirth.

When I came out of the operating theatre, Max looked after me every hour. I became better. As it happened, he was an owner of a successful language school for immigrants in New York. He still loved me. Now, for me, he is my old friend and a man's shoulder to lean on.

I can almost stand on my feet now. I know I have a life ahead, but I still miss Sasha and still see him in my dreams. I see my daughters too. Recently, I looked in a name dictionary. I found the name Maxim. It says: Maxim came from the Latin word *Maximums*. It means the biggest; the greatest. Parents, teachers, and friends won't know any trouble with this boy, and believe in his golden future. He has a rich imagination and lots of knowledge. The adult Maxim is not very successful. He is very often insecure. It's good if he's close to an understanding person who can give him moral support and believe in him. Maxim lives with an open heart. He is very sensitive and always ready to help. Maxim starts dating girls very young. Before marriage, he will know all the pleasures of sexual life with a woman. After marriage, he is very reliable.

Usually, when he loves, that love lasts forever. He loves children very much. He is not capable of betrayal or cheating.

I remember how during my childhood, when I was sick, my mother would sit with me. She sat at the kitchen table and sewed. She was always good at it. I sat close to her on the kitchen chair and drew. As long as I can remember, I was always drawing. I can see the window, a very blue sky and a blue-budding tree. That tree was as tall as the fifth floor of our building. It always smelled good. I looked at the window and made sure no insects would fly in. I was especially afraid of bees.

I am still afraid. I can see my mother is still sewing on the machine and singing a song. The soup is boiling on the stove. I feel tired. I feel sad. I want to go to my mother's room and try to explain to her that I didn't eat the soup because I'm not hungry and not because I didn't like it. Once, when I came from school, instead of soup for lunch, I had a fried potato. I was so happy. I thought that it meant I became an adult and didn't have to take a nap. I want that life very much. I want to be seven years old for whom every new day could be the start of new miracle.

With that, she closed her eyes and fixed a gentle, knowing smile upon her face. She was home once again. The caretaker summoned Maxim and conveyed Tanya's sentiments. Yet again, he understood.

Chapter 21
STORY OF A
PRIVATE DANCER

I was born in what is now the Ukraine, in Kiev. My father was a hard worker. He did construction and made decent money, and my mother stayed home with me. They were quite young when I was born. We lived in a typical Ukrainian apartment, a two-bedroom with central heat and air conditioning, a fairly modern kitchen and a big balcony. We didn't have much, but we were never poor.

My life as a child was very happy. I loved my friends and they loved me and I liked all our neighbors. We had just enough money to get by with a few extras. We ate a lot of potatoes and tomatoes and borscht. But there was caviar for special occasions like Christmas, New Year and birthdays. Russian people love big celebrations with lots of food, even when we can scarcely afford it. Everyone brings so much that it can hardly all be carried in. On the big May first holiday there was also food and drinks and good company and outside there were beautiful flowers.

There was a beautiful movie theater in the center of town and my friends and I loved to go see films on weekends. American movies were always a big treat, life was perfect just like it was supposed to be. I attended school for ten years, and studied English for five years. Every student was required to study English. I wasn't particularly good at it and didn't try too hard because I didn't think I would ever have a need for English in my life.

* * *

My first boyfriend became my husband. He was a high school teacher, the first person I was ever sexually intimate with, and he was eventually the father of my son. I met him when I was sixteen; he was twenty-five and we decided to marry right away. That is how it is done in Russia; women get married very young. No one waits like they do in America.

We had a big wedding with all of our friends and family in attendance. The memories are blurry now, I just remember so many people everywhere, but it was fun. All the guests were drunk as they were supposed to be at a Russian wedding. That is the custom. We honeymooned in Yalta for a few days and, after a year, our son was born. I went to the hospital in Kiev to give birth. In Russia, every woman stays in the hospital for ten days after delivering a baby; and that's just the minimum. The doctors and nurses were very kind.

It was a devastating blow when my husband was diagnosed with lung cancer in his mid-thirties. The doctors and nurses did everything they could for him, but I was suddenly a widow with a young son before I had turned twenty-eight. Nearly all Russian people are heavy cigarette smokers and my husband was among that group. With my husband, I honestly believe there was more to it than smoking. I know many people in Russia who never smoked and died of cancer. Even now, I smoke a couple of cigarettes at night.

I needed to completely start over, and provide a better life for my son. I decided I had to leave the Ukraine and go to the United States. Everyone was always talking about America this and America that. It was like a special magical kingdom. I wanted to try it. To get there was not easy.

Some girlfriends who had more knowledge about all this than I did helped me find an American man to marry. It wasn't a love match at all; I had to pay a broker in New York twenty-five thousand dollars for the opportunity. I was thirty-one years old when I received my visa. I flew from the former Soviet Union to New York. I knew very few people in America, but did know a girlfriend, an old schoolmate of mine, who lived in Manhattan.

I had to leave my son behind for what I thought would be a very short time, just until I got settled. It turned out he would stay with my parents for five years. I had never worked outside the home before and I needed money immediately and desperately. My girlfriend worked in a go-go bar and helped me to get a job there too, dancing on stage. It was quick money that I could immediately send home to support my parents to help them raise my son. I was able to send my mom three hundred dollars a month, which was very good money. Most people with full-time jobs there earned something like one hundred fifty dollars a month. They were actually able to buy their own apartment after a while, paying about one hundred dollars per month for it.

I called home as often as I could, but usually about twice a week. My son was able to attend a very good school, where he learned English and French. I also had a heavy debt to the marriage broker. I owed him twenty-five thousand dollars for this new life in America, and I paid him at least one thousand dollars each month. For this, he would pretend to the authorities that we were truly married and promised I would eventually be granted my green card.

Over the years, I worked in a lot of different bars as a table dancer. My customers were Russian, American, Hispanic, Black, Asian, you name it. I saw every nationality as a topless dancer. Everyone has the same dream of life in America: a good education, a good job, enough money, and the freedom to be yourself and live your own life, and, most importantly, to be happy.

I was very focused from the minute I arrived. I didn't waste my time going out and having fun. I spent every waking hour I could working, not because I enjoyed it, but because I wanted to save money.

I have had some very hard times in my life with my husband dying, my mother suffering a debilitating stroke and counting on me, and my child growing up and needing an education.

My first six or seven years in America were a grind. It was nothing but work, work and more work. And it was also degrading.

I saw a lot of dancers succumb to drug addiction and prostitution in the dancing business. I stayed away from all that. Certain bars had set schedules; others did not. But there were many days I worked fourteen-hour shifts. For the first few years, I worked seven days a week. For each shift I worked, I had to pay the house for the opportunity to dance—usually fifty dollars a day—and the tips I made were mine to keep.

The dancers were supposed to encourage the customers to drink, though we made no money on whatever they bought. All these places had separate back rooms for private dances at twenty dollars a dance. Management looked the other way at what went on in the backrooms. I absolutely refused to have real sex for money, but a hand massage was not out of the question. I could get a two- or three-hundred dollar tip for giving a hand job. The money was too good to pass up. I found this arrangement in every bar in New York I ever worked in, and still do. My customers thought we were friends and they wanted sex. But I had other priorities and, to be honest, that was probably where I belonged and was most comfortable.

I heard stories of women making thousands of dollars a night doing this kind of work. It rarely happened to me, but I was making a comfortable living, more than five thousand dollars cash in a good week. Once, I made eight thousand dollars in one week.

If there's one thing I'm proud of, it's how I handled my money. I didn't spend it on clothes or drugs or anything like that. I sent plenty home to my parents and son; they were always my top priority. And I invested the rest. After three years in America, I had paid off my debt and I knew I should put my money somewhere, so I bought a building in Brooklyn. I wanted to be smart; I knew my dancing days would end someday, sooner rather than later. I knew I had to have a backup plan.

I lived in Brooklyn for many years and heard quite a bit about the Russian Mafia operating there. But they never touched my life. This may be because their businesses were something I was just not interested in. I always kept my head down and worked hard and did not look for trouble.

Given the nature of my job, there were men over the years who fell in love with me, or said they were, and a few did become lovers. But most men I met were married or they were very old or they had mental problems, the kind of problems men who live to go see dancers have. If I stayed at a certain bar for a while, I would get regular customers who stopped by to see me every day I was working. I had men come to see me regularly for five years. I knew they were valuable to my livelihood, and always treated them well.

Dancing certainly gave me a different, more critical view of men. Some of them, of course, were really nice. But so many men, I think, are just such lonely, unhappy people. Often, they don't have any family ties and all they do is work, because that's the American style, to work all the time. So the girls they meet in the bars are pretty much their only outlet. They came to see me not so much in hopes of having sex, but to have someone to talk to. They wanted to meet a Russian girl because they weren't like American girls, who the men all complained about because they were so spoiled.

When I was a teenage girl in Russia, my mom would buy me shoes, or I would buy some for myself, and often they were too big or too small or not the color I really wanted. But that's what we all wore because that's just the way it was, no one even thought to complain. In America, you can buy ten pairs of shoes that all fit exactly, and they will be precisely the color, style, size and fit you want. It's such a small example, but very telling. It's just that sense of entitlement that American women grow up with. Whatever they want is easily available to them. They don't have to settle or depend on a man for money, which made the customers who came to see me quite bitter about how spoiled American women are.

I had some unpleasant incidents over the years, where men would say rude things to me, especially comments like, "Why are you here? You don't even speak the language." At first, this was very upsetting to me and I would cry, but I learned just to take it in stride. Of course, my English improved over the years. And one great thing about a city like New York is that so many Americans weren't born in America. Everyone seemed to be from somewhere else.

For the most part, everyone in America comes together and works together and lives together and gets along. I like that part of it. I know there are also many poor people in America who cannot afford whatever shoes they want. But there is a huge middle class in America. Most people here are much freer to decide what kind of lifestyle it is they are going to live, and achieve it.

Most Russians cannot even eat caviar, our national speciality, whenever they want. More and more Russian women are coming to America all the time because they prefer American men. It is an easy choice for a young Russian woman. They do not want the kind of life they are offered in Russia today. American men are much softer than Russian men in many ways. In Russia, the woman does everything: goes to work, comes home and cleans the house, cooks every morning and night, watches the children. It is a much easier life in America.

What I wish for all Ukrainian women is for them to have opportunities and the chance to be happy. Because our government has so many problems, I understand why they feel they must come to the U.S. to pursue a better life. The corruption is particularly bad in my country, though I must say in recent years I have noticed some improvements. The justice system has gotten much better, with public defenders and fair trials and so on. It has become much more like America in that way. I miss my country very much and go back every year to visit.

Over the years, I have made some American friends, but my best and closest friends are Russian, and we are very close. Some of them are happily married to Russians, and live very successful lives with jobs and houses. But it's not an easy life for many others.

I still dance for a living, but my days are numbered as I get older. It's becoming harder every year as the other girls are younger than I am. I've had a pretty long run as a dancer, though I've known women who were still dancing when they were sixty years old. I've known more than one American woman who is still working in her fifties.

But I now own three buildings in Brooklyn and am studying for my real estate license, so I have a second act to go to. My son is now here with me. It was the happiest day of my life when he landed in New York five years after I did. He is now enrolled in college, and he and I have become very accustomed to life here. Most of my hopes and dreams are now for my son, that he finish his education and have a successful career. I want him to be a good, solid, smart man, like every mother wants. It was hard on him the first year. One has to be born here and grow up American to really understand the lifestyle from the beginning. It was quite a shock to live so differently—for both him and me. But I don't think either of us would want to go back. My parents, though old and sick, are happy living in their apartment building in Russia. It's a big building where everyone is like an extended family, very unlike the U.S. They have no desire to visit America, ever. And I am happy to be able to take care of them.

Chapter 22
IT'S NOT OVER TILL
THE FAT LADY SINGS

I was born a long time ago in a land far, far away, but my life has never been a fairy tale. It is almost certain that you know nothing about the city in which I was born and, if by chance, you know of it, you know only a small part of its story.

The town of Sevastopol has a history that dates back more than twenty-five hundred years. Today, it is the capital of Crimea, a beautiful seaport town that is home to about two-hundred thousand women and one-hundred-fifty thousand men. The Greeks first established a town on this land in 1399. It was not until the end of the eighteenth century that this land became a part of the then mighty Russian empire. Catherine II personally ordered the building of a fortress that became the main port and home to the Russian maritime fleet.

The last of the many known and unknown enlargements of the secret city took place at the later part of the 1970s. Its code name was "Object 221," which was to be a secret underground command post for the Black Sea Naval Fleet that was headquartered in Sevastopol. The command center was massive with five underground stories and a hospital that could bed up to three thousand people. Thirty-thousand workmen were transported from all over the country to work on these projects. One of these men—at least according to my mother—was the man who fathered me. My mother's stories of my father were like the weather: they changed with the season, but as I grew older, I suspect they became more truthful.

One day when I was about twelve, I remarked to my mom about the difference in our hair colors. My hair was the color of coal, and my mom's was golden blond. I asked her what color hair my father had and she told me she wasn't sure—he had never taken off his cap. As time went by, I realized the truth.

Most mothers were very careful not to let their daughters out of their sights. We were counseled to never get in any man's car even if the ride was offered during a rainstorm or heavy snowfall. Gradually, as a couple of years passed, after school, my girlfriends started talking about their first sexual experiences. They told frightening stories of being raped by men, all sorts of men: clerks at the grocery store, teachers after class, truck drivers along the highway, a group of boys out for a joyride in their parents' car. The stories were plentiful and awful. More than a third of the girls I grew up with shared this fate.

There was no one to complain to. When a girl tried to report anything, she was ridiculed by the police and usually blamed for having provoked the situation. In fact, for some of us, this came to be considered a rite of passage. Almost all of us were raised by our moms with little or no help from our fathers, who usually traded in a wife every ten years or less for a newer, younger model. In a country where the women outnumbered the men fifty-five to forty-five percent, there was little choice for the women. And Soviet women outlive their male counterparts by an average of twenty years, so most women spend their later years without anyone to chop the wood.

When I was a child, during the summertime every Sunday, my mother would take me to play in the ocean. I would play in the frothy waves and have fun with the other children from our town. The boys would play pirates and the girls would play princess prisoners. The oceanside was covered with caves where once upon a time real pirates would hide their supplies, and—according to legend—their secret treasures.

I would go sometimes with the other kids to explore the caves, in spite of my mother's warnings to stay away from them.

She also warned me to never be alone with the boys. During one of these excursions into the caves, a boy tied me up. I thought we were playing a game. Then, he took off my blouse. I tried to shout, but I could only cry. He took off my skirt soon after and stared at me.

He said to me, "You have no tits." I told him I was only twelve, and if he would wait a few years, I would promise to please him any way he wished. This time, he took off his own clothes— his pants. I saw his penis pointing towards me and suddenly I was able to scream. He all at once looked frightened, and he slapped me hard across the face. A minute passed and nobody came. He started to laugh abruptly, and I began crying again. Then there came a shout that seemed to come from the depths of hell. It was actually coming from inside the cave. There were other noises and two uniformed soldiers, carrying machine guns and flashlights, came running towards us. They took one look at the two of us, and started to shout at the boy.

"You're trespassing! Get out now if you know what's good for you, and take your little slut with you!" My assailant started to run away without even untying me. One of the soldiers walked over to me, looked down, and smiled. He untied me, and said sternly, "Learn your lesson well. Next time you will not be so fortunate." I ran, falling twice on the way out and scraping both knees.

I ran to my mother and hugged her. I told her what had happened in the cave, and pointed out the boy, who was with his family forty meters down the beach. I knew that he would surely be punished. What happened next changed the course of my life. My mother looked at me and said, "Say nothing of this. The boy's father is a military officer. He will ruin us if we say a word." And that was the day I learned the truth of a woman's life in my country. It was the day I knew that someday I would find a better place to live.

Things improved once my mother met a doctor who was vacationing in our town. Soon after they met, they married and we moved to the doctor's home in Kiev. Now my mother was happy at last with her new husband. They had an internal compass and were fearless in the face of any obstacle. When a problem arose, they sat down at the kitchen table. They drank tea, ate strawberry jam, and began a discussion. They called such gatherings "a family conference." Usually, my new father took a blank piece of paper and a pen. At the top, he wrote "problem" and marked pointers on different sides. Those pointers were all the possible ways to solve the problem. He believed that there were no dead end situations. My mother agreed and this was not because she did not want to argue. She simply thought exactly the same thing.

My stepfather was 6'2" and had huge hands. By the time he was twenty-eight years old, what little hair he had was gray. He was almost bald and often unshaven in order to show at least a little hair. He was a pessimist and looked at every situation from the worst case scenario. He was a pessimist and looked at every situation from the worst case scenario. My mother's new husband was the best gynecologist in Kiev. He was certain about the correct way to do his job. This is why he was loved and respected by pregnant women. Grateful parents bought bags of candies, sausages, and bottles of champagne for him. Of course, my mother loved him more than all of those women put together. She too was a successful gynecologist. My stepfather did the actual deliveries and my mother was the assistant to the obstetrician.

I was enrolled in a new prestigious school, but I didn't like it. My school uniform consisted of a brown pleated dress, white cuffs, red pioneer tie, and a white apron. But it was not only because I hated to wear the uniform. In addition, our teacher shattered all the girls' dreams by saying, "Girls, you will have three important moments in your life. First, when you become pioneers, second when you're admitted to Komsomol (Young Communist League), and third when you become a member of the communist Party of the Soviet Union...."

But more than anything, I hated school because I had problems communicating with my schoolmates. There was a period of two or three years when they persecuted and ignored me. During my entire school experience, I was a lonely and reserved person. I never understood why children at school thought I was weird.

But, by the tenth grade, my situation appeared—to me at least—a little better. For one thing, I fell in love with a classmate named Lesha. Then, I felt myself pretty secure among the rest of the students.

I had been invited to a birthday party for the first time in my whole life. In the evening, Lesha came up to me and said, "I heard from Ritka that you fell for me. Did you?" I turned red and nodded my head. He said that if I wanted to dance with him I had to prove that I loved him. Lesha asked if I could eat a whole onion without any dressing. The class looked at me with expectant curiosity. I couldn't lose again. So, I agreed. Heartily, I ate the whole onion! But Lesha didn't dance with me or ever approach me again. I smelled of onion. That smell was inside me for days. Yet, that episode proved to me that I could be unafraid.

I knew after school, I would enroll in a medical university. During the summer, my parents let me work and hired me as a hospital orderly. I prepared for my university entrance exams. I passed and became a student.

When I was in my third year of studies, my parents died in a car accident. I was so distraught that I didn't even want to live. I think my life fell apart at that moment. My family was my castle. I knew that I lived in order to fulfill the hopes of my parents. We always had such a deep, warm love in our house. It's hard for me to put it in words.

My parents were always respected by their co-workers and friends. However, when my parents died, all of their friends disappeared. They forgot about me. With great emotional difficulty, I graduated from university. In college, I had only one friend named Natasha. She was a sexy blonde with a curvy shape and a huge sense of self-importance. She was friendly with me so she could always copy my homework and test answers. She didn't show up at classes often. Natasha was more interested in pursuing men. After graduation, I heard she was married and moved away to Moscow.

In Kiev, not everybody was lucky enough to be hired by a successful private medical practice where the salary was dramatically different from the government. Not every young woman was able to find a wealthy man or a husband. There was even a long standing opinion that there were no normal men left. Most of the normal ones were married or were single and nobody wanted them. Each of us hoped deep in her heart that she would be fulfilled as a woman. I believed it as well. I wanted to have a family with a man who would choose me.

I did find a job at a local Kiev gynecology center. There, I became friends with Irina Victorovna. She was head of the hospital. Irina was a serious-looking woman in her forties. She always had her hair swept up and wore high heels.

In my entire twenty-five years, I had only one man, Vladimir. We met when I went to Anapa in the Black Sea resort area. I never knew that on vacation all married men became single or divorced and took off their wedding rings. In my early twenties, I was quite attractive. I had long chestnut hair, a broad smile, and a dimple on my right cheek. I had considerable natural beauty. I never used any makeup and I had baby soft skin.

Vladimir noticed me when I went on an excursion around Anapa. We started to talk. Later, he invited me to a local restaurant, disco, and the beach. I decided that the time had come to lose my virginity. I thought that my lucky star was shinning upon me. Vladimir had an interesting face. He had red hair and green eyes. His whole body was covered with freckles. I liked him a lot. He said that he was a geologist. I listened to the stories about his expeditions with admiration. At home, I never heard about anything other than child delivery cases and the mechanical peculiarities of gynecological chairs.

During that entire month, I was deeply in love and really happy. On the last day of his vacation, my hero told me that he was married and had children. Vladimir said that it would be great if we thanked each other for the nice time we spent together and now we could go our separate ways. Suddenly, he had turned from a kind and intelligent man into a nasty and disgusting son of a bitch. I slapped him in his face, cried, and ran away.

The next morning, I went to the station and got on the first bus. I went back to work from my vacation with a broken heart. My friend Irina comforted me. She invited me to movies, shopping and asked me to visit her. One day over lunch, she told me that foreign men are the nicest men in the world. She said she knew how to meet the right foreigner and start a family. She assured me that there was a chance for love. I had nobody left in Kiev. I had nothing to lose.

We placed our ads and pictures with different marriage agencies and started correspondences with foreign men. Russian women think that a foreign life is wonderful and cloudless, wealthy, and full. We are sure that foreign men are intelligent, polite, understanding, and generous. But, as the saying goes: It's good there, but only when none of us are really there. I didn't know about that saying, when forty-year-old Mark Simpson wrote me. He said he was a successful doctor in America who found my ad at one of the marriage agencies. But a few days later, I had to make a choice. I received a letter from a forty-five-year-old Englishman school teacher named Glen Brooke. Both men appeared very nice. They both wrote wonderful seemingly sincere letters. But I knew that if you run after two rabbits, you won't catch even one.

I was looking for love, not money. I had to choose one of them. It seemed to me that America was better than England with its smog. The doctor was closer to my own life interests. And an age difference of even five years for me at twenty-seven was a big deal. In addition, I liked Mark's appearance in his photo better than Glen's. So, I chose Mark. However, I didn't want to offend Glen. I thanked him for his time and attention and offered to introduce him to my girlfriend. The Englishman agreed and I gave him Irina's address. Today, Irina and Glen live together in England, and they are very happy.

I started a passionate correspondence with Mark. I hardly could answer all of his letters. He didn't give me a minute of rest. I was so surprised by him. I couldn't believe that such a man still existed. A few weeks later, all my co-workers and acquaintances knew that I was very happy. They thought that very soon they would have to write me letters to America.

From Mark's letters, I learned that he was divorced and had five-year-old and seven-year-old daughters who lived with their mother. He wrote about his job and the hospital where he worked. He told me about the prospects for work there and how we would be able to have coffee breaks together. He told me about his modest furnished house in a prestigious area of Albany, Oregon. He wrote about his interests and hobbies. He even told me about how much he earned. It was $90,000 a year. I was shocked, but not because I wanted his money. I just compared how I could live and be happy on my two hundred dollars per month. Of course, I began to imagine what my life in America could be like.

I wrote in Russian, then translated the letters, and sent him pictures. As a reward for my work, he decided to come to Kiev and meet me. Just three months had passed since we began our correspondence. Events in my life began to change like pictures in a movie. I met Mark and got a nice kiss on the cheek. He was six feet tall, a big man, but without a bit of fat on him. He had wavy gelled blonde hair, tanned body and white teeth. We had a little excursion around Kiev. I took him to my apartment. I introduced him to my co-workers. We exchanged presents, went to restaurants, took walks under the moon, and took pictures. It put me in a perfect mood and created a feeling in me of absolute happiness. Five days flew by like a fairy tale. On the last day before Mark's departure, he proposed. I accepted. I thought I loved him very much.

After Mark went back to America, he started to make arrangements for my fiancée visa. This process took a while because it was following 9/11; all the documents of potential fiancées were checked thoroughly. The waiting period was from four to nine months. My days of waiting began. During that time,

Mark sent me flowers, presents, and love letters. He also helped me financially.

After eight months, I received an invitation for an interview at the American Embassy in Poland. Mark couldn't stand the separation any longer. He flew to Kiev and from there we went to Warsaw to get a visa. We bought airplane tickets to America. The flight was quiet and after eight hours of flying, I didn't even feel tired when we landed. I was full of energy. I wanted to discover America for myself as soon as possible. I wanted to start living here and get involved in a new way of life. I couldn't wait for my new experiences and discoveries and to write about them to Irina and my co-workers.

My first discovery was his old green Toyota. It looked broken down and filthy inside. I was shocked. On our way to house, Mark told me that life in America was very expensive. I tried to see America through the windows of his antique car, but it was almost night and too dark. Mark was nice to me, but he kept repeating that life in America was very expensive.

After an hour of driving, we came home. It was dark and hard to see, but something worried me inside. We went into the house he was so proud of when he told me about it in Kiev. But this little house was furnished with old damaged furniture. The sink was full of dirty dishes and his bed wasn't made. Everything seemed so unclean and old that I didn't want to sit on the chairs, drink water from his cups, or even sleep in his crumpled bed. There were no clean pots, saucepans, forks, sheets, or towels. I didn't want to appear too upset. I reasoned that Mark was a single man and he couldn't deal with all that work around the house in addition to working long hours. I hoped that in the morning some of the things would look different. Morning came and the first thing Mark did was have a cup of coffee. He didn't ask me if I wanted anything. His refrigerator was empty.

We decided to go to the supermarket. I didn't have time to go through all of the aisles nor did I understand the prices. Mark threw into the cart different packages, cans, and boxes and headed for the register. When we came home, I started to unpack the shopping bags. I saw what he had bought was dip, chips, frozen waffles, cooked vegetables, meat salads in cans, ketchup, hotdogs, hamburger buns, milk, water, and different juices in packages to mix with water. In Kiev, people avoided such artificial food. My hunger disappeared. My mood sank.

My first day in America made me suspect that all Mark's stories about the comfortable American life with him were lies or fantasies. The next grocery trip proved it. Again, Mark selected the food and didn't even ask me what I wanted. I told him that I wanted orange juice, fish, and some fresh fruit. He told me that, like he said, everything in America is very expensive and that he would buy the food I wanted when it went on sale. He recommended that I get bananas because they were always cheap and tasty.

In the evening, we had a disturbing conversation. Mark told me that because of all the travels and expenses, we were in a little financial hole. He asked me to be more economical for now and said that next month everything would be fine. I said I understood. I knew that dealings between a husband and wife were a compromise and that difficulties would arise.

After a week, we got married in City Hall and I wore a white business suit I had bought in the Ukraine. I had just met Vladimir in Anapa when I last wore it. There was no celebration afterwards. He told me that we had to hurry because we needed to apply for my green card. I was very relieved that he cared about my future.

I had always thought that a marriage was a legal agreement in contrast to love. There were expenses, incomes, debts and property in married life. It was absurd, but my American husband allowed me to drink one cup of milk every other day. He didn't have enough money for a daily cup of milk, but he had money for his daily ice cream.

Summer was hot. I was dying from the humidity. The only life savers were air conditioners and a little plastic pool. I had left my swimming suit at home. When I told Mark, he said it was not a problem, so we went to Wal-Mart. Like any normal woman, I wanted to walk around and take a look at American clothes. But Mark bought me a hat and a swimming suit in five minutes and walked me to the exit. He didn't like to waste time in stores.

I didn't want to start our married life with arguments. But with each passing day, I liked Mark's lifestyle less and resented the fact that he was imposing it on me. I began to tell him what I didn't like and what I wanted. Mark explained that he was already spending a lot of money on me. He reminded me about airfare, presents, restaurants, the excursion in Kiev, and the money he spent to get me a fiancée visa.

While Mark was at work, I studied English or sat in the baby pool. The first month, I washed and cleaned the entire house. I tried to cook something tasty from the food he bought. For work, Mark dressed in an elegant business suit, white shirt, and a silk tie. He looked like a lawyer in a TV show. But when he came back home, he changed into old sports pants with holes in them and a dirty t-shirt.

It wasn't pleasant for me to see him dressed like a bum and I told him so. Mark looked at me and said for me not to look at him then, but instead look at myself in the mirror. That was insulting. When I tried to change some things for the better, Mark would never accept it. Another thing that aggravated me was that Mark would never take his shoes off when he came into the house. He would lie on the bed or put his feet on the table while wearing his shoes. Meanwhile, I was mopping the floors everyday. I explained to him that in Russia, not to take shoes off in the houses was considered disrespect to woman. Mark replied that he was in his forties and was too old to change his habits.

I didn't want to live in America just because it was called America. I had flown here because I wanted to create a happy family. I remembered how different Mark was in Kiev. That is why I still hoped that I had a chance. But Mark didn't want to change any of his habits. He was comfortable just the way he was.

Two months had passed and when I looked at myself in the mirror, I decided that it was time to go to the beauty salon. I told my husband of my wish, he replied that there was no need to go the hair stylist when we had scissors in the house. He said that he could do a better job than anyone else. I thought he was joking. But he found the scissors and drew close to me. I said "No," but he forced me down and cut a few shreds of my hair. Then he put the scissors back in the drawer and smiled. He said that hair is not like teeth. It grows back. He asked me to think about my behavior. I cried in the bedroom for two days.

I remembered how he promised to show me all of America. He promised to be a good husband and said that he dreamed of a son. I felt deceived. One weekend, we went on a picnic but neither of us was happy. I became afraid of him. Our relations were more and more strained. For instance, I told him that I wanted to work in order to earn money for personal expenses and food. He grabbed my throat and said that my work was housekeeping and cooking.

My only entertainment was shopping and that was under his control. In the evenings, I could watch whatever he watched on television, usually sports programs. He forbade me to call Kiev because, according to him, I had to try and forget the impoverished country that he took me away from. He didn't want to send me to English classes because it was too expensive. I had a dictionary and could learn the language myself, he said.

I began to think more often about going back to Kiev. But I was scared. I had no money and no relatives there. I hated living with those limitations and humiliations, but I couldn't leave by myself. First of all, I didn't have money for airline tickets. Second, Mark had all my documents in his safe deposit box. It gave him the power to threaten me with deportation, or jail, on immigration charges.

One evening, I asked Mark to buy me a ticket back to Kiev. I had thought long and hard before I made the decision. I was ready to explain everything to him. But there were no questions. He simply got up from the couch and slapped me on my face. I fell down. I was frightened. My nose started to bleed. Without a single word, he kicked me once, twice, and then three times. I tried to stand up. I was crying and screaming and yelled for help. But the closest neighbor we had was three miles away. Mark shouted that he had invested so much time, energy and money on me, and he wasn't going to let some simple Ukrainian ruin his life.

I was aware now that many American husbands bring over Russian wives; all they want is a free housekeeper. Mark considered it a real purchase because he had paid the marriage agency $2,000 for me. He calculated everything beforehand. He knew how much money he would save if he ate at home, how much he would save by not having a laundry woman, and a housekeeper, and so on. He had dreamed of getting a cheap robot, but he wound up with a human being.

Mark threatened to complain about me to the police. He wanted to say that I stole a large amount of money or antique jewelry. He tried to frighten me by making me think that I'd end up in jail. I didn't want to go to jail. I wasn't guilty. But I had nobody to go to. I did understand that there was a problem that nobody could solve for me. I had to protect myself. Why did I let him treat me so badly for so long? Because I didn't have any self-respect, I thought. I knew that first of all, it depended on me. Other people couldn't help me if I wouldn't. I never loved myself. If I wasn't positive about myself then I wouldn't have that core which would give me the stability and strength in different life situations. I started to take my first independent steps and take responsibility for myself in America.

The first time he beat me, I couldn't get out of the bed for two weeks. My face was swollen. My breasts hurt. At night, he demanded that I please him sexually. He said I had to work off with sex everything he had invested in me. I hated him and was terribly frightened. I shouted at him about it. He beat me in response. At night, he tied me to the bed and fucked me. One day, he completely shaved my head. He threatened that he would make a drug user out of me and turn me over to the police. When he left for work, he chained me to the door. My whole body was black and blue.

Mark came back home and found my suffering look a turn-on. He jumped on me. I cried and asked him to stop. One night, he had an emergency call from the hospital. I pretended that I was asleep. He left and forgot to chain me. I crawled out of the house and went to the road. I didn't have any friends. I didn't speak English very well.

I walked on the dark night road. I could hardly breathe from my chest pain. But in my thoughts, I became stronger. It was huge contrast in understanding myself. I had taken a step. Before then, I had been scared to even go outside. Suddenly, a black jeep stopped. An older woman got out of the car. She asked if I needed any help. When she saw my swollen face from the punches and the tears running down from my face, she was shocked. She asked if it was my husband. I was scared, but I said yes. She said that she would help me and offered a seat in her car. She took me to the hospital. The woman—her name was Jessica Rimisky—asked me to believe in myself. I cried from the pain and humiliation.

It was very important for me at that moment to believe in something and in somebody. Jessica explained to me that I had to go to the police and file a complaint against my husband. She wanted me to ask the police for protection. Russian women are not used to involving society in their domestic affairs. It's a stupid feature in our character, but we can't put our husbands in jail. It's against our moral standards. I told Jessica that I wanted to go to the hospital first because I couldn't breathe. She took me to the hospital and it happened to be the hospital where Mark worked. He noticed me in the hall and pulled me into this room. He warned me that once we got home, I would be in a lot of trouble. I left the hospital very frightened. I asked her to drive me home. I was shaking. She gave me her cell phone. Jessica said to call 911 if my husband beat me again. Mark came back from work drunk and angry. He started to beat me and insult me with vulgar words. I couldn't suffer anymore. He went to the kitchen to refill the whisky. I went to the bathroom with the cell phone and called the police. Mark heard me talking to somebody. He began to break down the door. I was washing blood from my lip. I prayed to God. I wanted the police to come quickly.

I was ready to risk jail in order to escape Mark's fists. The police came. They arrested Mark. An ambulance took me to the hospital. They documented my injuries and admitted me. It happened that I had a serious concussion and many other injuries. The policeman asked me many questions and they made a report about Mark.

It happened that Mark, although American, didn't know the immigration laws of his own country. He had threatened me. After I improved, the hospital sent me to a shelter for homeless people. They gave me a place to sleep and food to eat. Half the women in the shelter were like me, all victims of domestic violence. Jessica came to see me. She invited me to live in her house. She wanted to help me. We found a center for women in Albany. It was important for me to be among people who understood me and cared. I was a zombie. I couldn't think about anything. I felt nothing. It was just very comfortable and secure with all those strong women. They tried to help me very much. They were very kind to me.

My husband will remain in prison for two years. He will pay me financial compensation for moral and physical damage. The strange thing is that I don't need his money. I won't be able to buy my health or a dream again.

The Office of Immigration and Naturalization drew up papers under the battered wife's law, which allowed me to remain in the country and to apply for immigration papers without an American husband. I receive financial assistance from the government. I have medical insurance and an opportunity to attend English language classes. I have an order protecting me from Mark. He can't get within three miles of me. Recently, my free government lawyer filed an application Form I-360 for me. It gives me the right to get a green card because I was a victim of domestic violence. We attached a copy of the police report, the medical records, and a psychological evaluation from the Women's Center of

Albany. During one of our court appearances, Mark said that when he was freed he would find me and get even with me for what I had done to him.

We all take risks in life. From time to time, we all do stupid, foolish, and reckless things. We wouldn't be human beings if we didn't make mistakes. Russian women are still coming to this unpredictable and far away country. Overall, it's still better than the country we belonged to. We start the next chapters of our biographies as fiancées and wives. We are after tourist visas, green cards or political asylum. And there are a lot of us. Life mixes us all up in a huge pot. And as the years pass, no one knows who will end up happy and who will end up sad. The most important thing is that nobody has the right to use violence on another person. Recently, I was granted a green card. Nobody can insult or threaten me now. As they say about the opera, "It ain't over till the fat lady sings" and after all I had been through, I still thought it was a beautiful song.

Chapter 23
GOOD FORTUNE

I never intended to become a madam.

I was born in St. Petersburg thirty-four years ago. My father was a businessman there and my mother was a surgeon in Bucharest. My parents decided to move to London for the financial opportunities it offered. My mother could make at least five times more as a nurse in London than she could make as a top flight surgeon in Eastern Europe. Because of the Russian political prejudices, my parents' marriage was not recognized in Russia. That was just one of the many reasons my parents felt life outside of Russia could only improve. We migrated to London before the influx or even the creation of the rich Russian multi-millionaires and at the time of the Arab influx in London.

Once we were settled in London, my father would coordinate business transactions for the early, affluent Russian visitors like us. I would sometimes help them with letter writing and translations. Since the writing was so simple, I usually did not ask for a fee, but it didn't matter because they would give me thousand dollar tips—a ridiculous amount of money for writing simple letters. I also arranged visas for the Russians and Eastern Europeans who wanted to visit England. Gradually, I began to expand my services to include the arrangements for their airport transportation, lodging, and many other services.

My father kept an apartment in St. Petersburg, and was found dead there during one of his visits home. I do not know exactly when it happened because we weren't told about it until after my father had already been buried.

The police informed us that thieves had broken into my father's apartment to steal the art he kept there on display. They told us that he must have walked in on the robbery, and ended up dead as a result. The story is almost certainly untrue, but the police needed to have an explanation ready and that is the one they gave us. We assumed they were being paid off by someone who wanted my father dead. That is almost always the way the system works in Russia...and very little has changed. Very few rich people are in jail in Russia, and those who are there have usually made important enemies.

By the time one of these Russian visitors grew comfortable enough to ask me to arrange a female companion for him, prostitution didn't seem to be such a moral issue to me. I was, however, amazed by how easy it was to find so many women willing to sell themselves for the right price. Establishing my own escort agency did not seem like such a stretch when I finally did it. Any other intelligent woman would have done the same thing, and maybe she would have done it sooner.

Today, I run several of the biggest Internet prostitution schemes in London. In a good week, I might earn thirty thousand dollars, but those weeks are less frequent than they used to be, and the competition is fierce. There are now so many girls in London and so much competition that my competitors are selling half hour sessions for one hundred pounds! If you Google "escorts," two of my agencies are always in the top five search results. Of course, I have to pay lots of people: the webmaster, the website promoter, the girls who answer the phones, the photographer who shows off the escorts' assets and Photoshops their shortcomings. I keep apartments year round for the girls who fly in from Eastern Europe for short-term work, but even that has gotten out of hand. In exchange for two weeks' of guaranteed work, some girls are now asking for five thousand pounds. Then they go back to Poland or wherever they may be from, and take care of their husbands, boyfriends, children, parents etc. I even had one girl that said she did it to be able to take care of the family dog.

I am like a mother to many of the girls. They often give me perfume or boxes of candies as a thank you, and even though I know that these are passed on from their clients, I know it is the thought that counts.

I used to enjoy hearing the incredible stories of how Adnan Khashoggi, the Egyptian billionaire, would offer one million dollars to a woman he'd see out at bar if she would spend the night with him. But I think the stories were exaggerated. He rarely spent more than a hundred thousand dollars.

The good girls do well, but perhaps not as well as you might think because of all the middle men. For instance, if a guest at Blake's Hotel wants a girl for the night, he tells the concierge, who then puts an eighteen hundred dollars miscellaneous charge on the guest's room (converted from pounds to dollars). The concierge calls me, and I am paid about twelve hundred dollars. I, in turn, pay the girl six hundred dollars, and she usually has to give half of that her handler (the person who has brought her to London and takes care of her), at least at the beginning of her career. The vast majority of these girls have less than a handful of years of serious earning potential before they become tired-looking and worn out from selling themselves for top dollar.

I call my favorite girls "Firemen" because they never turn down clients even with only a few minutes' notice. "Candy" is one of my favorites. I once forgot to tell her about an appointment and she was still ready in two minutes. And all the clients have good things to say about her. I know this because I give some of my steady clients a discount to give me reports on the girls. Were they on time? Did they do a good job? And, most importantly did they give a private phone number? If they did, chances are I would never use them again. It is also very important that a girl does not list herself with other agencies. If she does, and I was the one who brought her over to London or have given her an apartment, she is through. I will throw her out of my apartment and do what I can to blacklist her with other agencies.

I have never been a prostitute or even promiscuous. I married a very respectable Englishman, though he has become a drunk. I have had lovers on occasion and gone off to Paris for a holiday with one or two of them, but my marriage was already broken, so I have no regrets. We have a beautiful home outside of London in Maidenhead, not far from the waterside inn where we sometimes go for Sunday brunch. Our son goes to a top private school and has a string of unattractive Russian nannies to look after him. My mother is still working as a nurse and she lives near-by.

I love all things English, like ascot and I love attending the royal events. I buy the best tickets to London's poshest events. I, of course, have to hide my money. Much of it is in a safety deposit box at Harrod's. Also, I have invested in several homes by the ocean in Montenegro, and their value is climbing rapidly.

My business in London is getting more dangerous all the time. Law enforcement is starting to crack down on prostitution and other "services" have already been stopped. I have been sent a warning notice, but I think that I am well-insulated as some of my customers would not want me arrested. They have their own self-ish reasons—like their reputations—for wanting me to remain a free woman. I am also growing concerned because my son is getting to the age where he's beginning to understand more adult topics. The other day he asked me, "How much does it cost to buy a girl?" I laughed, but it wasn't funny.

I just came back from a trip to New York. I stayed at the Waldorf, and I have been asked about opening a business there. I am thinking about it. But I would miss ascot and all the royal functions. America does not have the class and traditions I am used to.

Chapter 24
HE THOUGHT THAT
HE OWNED ME,
BUT HE WAS JUST RENTING

How often do you play the lottery? How often do you win? I have always liked people who believe that victory is just around the corner even though they say you have the same chance of winning a Russian lottery whether or not you by a ticket. These people are patient. They will reach their goals no matter what. Nothing can break them. They are strong enough. They have the best chance of getting everything because they are clever.

Our whole life is a lottery and we have no say in how this game begins. We are all players who tempt fate and fortune on a daily basis. Everything in our lives depends on how well we play the game. We have to display wisdom and single-mindedness in order to have the best opportunity to live a good life especially in the shadow of oppression. But where can we learn this? Where do we find the right teacher?

I never knew my mother. I only heard stories about her from my father. I saw her smiling face in pictures. My mother died when she was twenty-five years old, as she was giving birth to me. She had a weak heart. The local Sochi doctors gave her large dosages of morphine injections. As a result, it seems my mother's heart stopped beating. She never saw me. I was her highly-anticipated little baby, whom she carried inside of her for forty weeks. She had already bought me bright-pink dresses. But she never got to put them on me.

It was hard for the doctors to save my life as well. I was not able to get enough oxygen. I came out of my mother's womb the wrong way. But I survived. My thirty-year-old father, in a way, hardly suffered the loss. I was a child who was wanted so much. My father devoted his whole life to my upbringing. Father gave me so much warmth and love that I never felt loss of parental affection and care.

Of course, I was interested in who my mother was. I yearned to talk about her before going to bed. I wanted to learn new things about her. All I knew of my mother is that she had fire-red hair and blue eyes. My parents were together for five years in our town by the Black Sea before they were lucky enough to conceive me. My mother worked in a Sochi section called the Botanic Garden. She learned and cared about exotic plants and trees.

My father used to say that those five years were the best years of his life. My mother was the best woman in the world, according to him. I became second-best woman in my father's life. I gave him the second happiest period of his life. Ever since I could recall, father told me that my mother was taken by the angels to live in the heaven. He said that she was too good and too kind to live here on earth with everyone else. During those moments, I decided that I would never be too good and too kind. I was afraid that the angels would take me to the heaven as well. I didn't want my father to be alone.

Sometimes, when my father said I couldn't do things I wanted to do or didn't buy me something I wanted, I'd frighten him by saying that I would become very kind and would go to live in heaven. When I felt frustrated or angry, I became very good. I washed and ironed all father's clothes. I brought him lunch at his workshop and sat with him until the end of his working day. I wanted to seem good. I helped the neighbors by picking pears and peaches at harvest time. I did all the homework in advance for the week. I helped the old people cross the streets.

But no angels appeared to take me to the heaven. My father told me angels didn't take me because they knew that I was being good on purpose. They knew I wanted to hurt my father's feelings with my manipulations. The angels saw everything. My father spoiled me. I was, in some ways, very selfish and didn't know how to behave any differently.

Though small, the apartment was cozy because it had been decorated by my mother's loving hands. The kitchen, the two bedrooms, the bathroom—all were small. But Father and I were also small people in every senses of the word. That is why we didn't mind having everything so small around us. But we had big love for each other. That was better than a big apartment or a big piece of fried chicken on a big kitchen table. I remember when I turned ten, my father started to put books for girls on my bookshelves. I could learn from them all about girls maturing physically into women.

But I already had heard everything about menstruation and sexual maturity from my older girlfriends. One day, Father explained to me that once a month, every girl bleeds. He said that it was nothing to be afraid of. It was a sign of maturity. As children, we all seem to want to become adults as soon as possible. I waited for my period for years. I would check my panties every time I went to the restroom. When I turned fourteen, I finally got my period. I was scared. I never saw so much blood in my life. I decided to stay on the toilet and wait until all the blood came out. I sat for a few hours and fell asleep. My father came home from work and waited for a while to see if I'd come out of the bathroom. But I didn't. He started to worry and broke down the door. He found me sleeping on the toilet with a girl's book he had given me. He bought me tampons and deodorant.

We had a neighbor named Galya. She was a single middle-aged woman. She always cared about me and my father. She cooked breakfast, lunch and dinner for us every day. She brought it over to us while the food was still hot. She always prepared something different: stuffed pancakes with meat or fish, cutlets, mashed potatoes, or fried mushrooms with beef.

Galya always celebrated my birthdays with me and my father. It was our tradition. We would go to an ice cream shop called Margarita's. We would sit there until we were full of different kinds of ice cream. Afterwards, we would go to the amusement park. We finished the day off with the purchase of a toy or some clothes for me that I liked. Even when I was older, we kept our tradition.

Of course, at fifteen, I felt I was an adult and wanted to drink a bottle of champagne with my friends. We hid in the bushes because I didn't want to offend my father. After all, he tried very hard his whole life to make me happy. We celebrated New Year's together until one o'clock in the morning. Then I left to a party with my friends.

I was always a good student in school. I knew we had no financial ability to pay for my college tuition. So I had to be smart and pass the entrance exams in order to get a grant for a free education.

I was fourteen when I started to flirt with men. Then I met the first love of my life. His name was Vitalik. He was eighteen years old, a handsome guy with blond curly hair and big rosy lips. He was an athlete and professional boxer. We didn't see each other very often. I missed him badly during the days when he was training or competing. In Vitalik's life, his top priority was always the sport.

It hurt my feelings very much, but I never said anything to him. I respected him and could forgive him for everything. For his part, my father was glad when we didn't see each other. He didn't like Vitalik. My father thought that he wasn't intelligent enough for me. In addition, my father thought that Vitalik was a bandit because he had injured fists all the time. To me, Vitalik seemed a reliable and protective man. We dated for two years. It was enough time for me to come to the conclusion that I wanted to be his wife and the mother of his child. In my mind, love didn't look at other options.

Vitalik became my first lover, my friend, and my teacher about life. He used to say that life is one long fight and you always have to be ready for an attack. It happened that Vitalik was told that he had to move to Moscow in order to study there at a sports college.

At that time, I found out that I was pregnant. I told him. He said that he wasn't ready to become a father and support a young family. His words were like a knife to my heart. Vitalik told me that I should understand him. We have our whole future ahead of us for babies, he reassured me. He said that if we had a baby, he would lose the career that he had worked for his whole life. He said that we were too young and instructed me to have an abortion.

I didn't know why he thought that we were old enough to make love, but not to have a child. It was true. We were too young to be responsible for our actions. I had never told him that I was only sixteen years old.

It made me unhappy that I didn't have a mother to go to and ask for help or advice. Vitalik left. I hated him and his unborn child.

That was the first time in my life that I visited a gynecologist. I felt ashamed as I sat in the waiting room surrounded by pregnant women and women pensioners. They all looked at me with what seemed like hatred. My heart was beating fast. I turned red and kept my eyes on the floor.

I did the same when I went into the examination room. The doctor looked at me suspiciously. Rudely, she told me to take off my clothes and sit in the gynecological chair. I never saw one before and didn't know how to sit in it or where to put my legs. The doctor began by saying that all girls like me were fucking like rabbits, and then they came to see her without even knowing how to put theirs butts in the chair. She examined me and was shocked. I was eight weeks pregnant.

I was a teenager and what did I know? According to law, she had to inform my parents in order to get permission for my abortion. In tears, I explained that I only had my father and that he wouldn't understand and would be very disappointed in me. I offered her three hundred rubles as a bribe. Vitalik had given me the money before he left. The doctor agreed and put the money in her pocket. She piled on the insults, calling me dirty, lustful and irresponsible. She knew that I had to listen and couldn't run away.

I wanted to cry. But I knew that I had to go through with it. She performed the abortion without a local anesthesia. I felt everything. It hurt like hell, but I didn't scream. I put my fist in my mouth and bit it. I was ready to die from the pain. Hot tears came down from my eyes. Still, I remained silent. Six hours after the surgery, it was all over and I went home. I felt empty and lost.

I understood one thing at that moment: it was a crime to fall in love. I realized I could not rely on men and could not believe their promises. Men would follow their penises no matter where it led. Whatever a penis needed, a man's legs would take him there.

After that incident, I quickly changed from a girl into a woman. I enrolled in a psychology class at a college. Men started to look at me and admire me. I liked them, too, but I didn't want anything serious. I did not want love, only temporary emotions and short-term relationships.

I met Artem. He was an attractive and smart man and had college degrees in history and business. He had come on vacation to the Sochi after immigrating to America eight years earlier. He had to leave Sochi, but it wasn't his personal choice. He had to run. Artem was twenty-five years old when he got involved with crime.

It was during the time when the former Soviet Union was divided. Artem started to earn money by means of blackmail. At first, he focused on successful businessmen and politicians. His strategy was simple. Artem and his friends would find rich, married Russian men who were concerned about their reputations. Then, Artem would send beautiful girls to meet and seduce them and become their lovers. The girls were glad to stay in the country houses with wealthy and famous businessmen, wear expensive clothes, and perform their services to the unfaithful husbands. Artem would have them take photos and videos of their parties.

He then blackmailed the men. If the men gave in and played according to Artem's rules, then the victim wouldn't lose his reputation, his family, or his status. This is how Artem quietly lived and worked in Moscow, Saint Petersburg, and the Ukraine for a while. It was interesting and it provided him with an income.

Once, he found the wrong man who wouldn't pay up. This man was an official of the federal security services. He ordered several of his employees to locate Artem's gang and to kill them all. They diligently looked for Artem who learned he was a target and, of course, was scared.

He got a tourist visa and fled to America. As soon as he landed, he went to the INS office at the airport and asked for political asylum. At that time, it was the perfect way to get papers immediately. Artem changed his first name and last name. He had no relatives left. His mother had been knocked down by a car and was instantly killed two years before his immigration. He had no other living relatives. So, in America, he transformed himself from Ivan Vorobiev into Artem Russky. His entire past ceased to exist.

From an anonymous Internet site in a library, Artem sent messages to all of his friends in Russia. The e-mail said that the sender—Artem used another fake name—had shared an apartment in New York with Artem. Alas, said the e-mail, Artem had been killed by black gangsters in New York, a fate that Artem's friends would have found tragic but quite believable. The acquaintance had found Artem's address book in the apartment and thought it right to notify those in it with e-mail addresses.

During the first years, Artem didn't do anything in America. He didn't work. He had brought enough money to live, eat and rent a room. All this time, he learned about America. He wanted to find something that would allow him to live a rich and interesting life. Soon enough, he began to work with the same kind of criminals as before, except these were immigrants from Moscow. They did small-time scam jobs together. They provoked car accidents and collected money from insurance companies. Artem became an American citizen, but grew homesick and decided to visit Russia. But he was still looking for the perfect hustle. He wanted to earn money easily and he still had a sense of adventure.

Thus, it was that one day he visited the Black Sea where I lived and studied. We met on the beach. I was twenty-one years old. He was thirty-six, but looked much younger. He was tall, well-built, with the muscles of an athlete. He had chestnut hair without a touch of gray, a clean shaven face, a charming smile and bright-brown eyes that sparkled like the stars. I liked him at first sight.

Sochi is a vacation spot where short-lived affairs are a way of life. Young women looked on their vacation affairs as magazine love stories. They started passionately, developed rapidly, and finished in a few weeks. They allowed young women to experience lots of different emotions, learn new things about men, and make conclusions about the future. These affairs helped smart women create their own ideas about how to win over their men. Also, each new love taught her something new and enriched her sexual experience.

I don't think I was a prostitute. I just had my flings without any responsibilities. They were based on feelings of interest and attraction for each other. After a man finished his vacation, I would automatically place him on a list of ex-boyfriends who usually never appeared again.

Yet, to tell the truth, some women had long-term relationships that lasted for years. These women became mistresses. Her man would come every year on vacation. He came without his family precisely to be able to experience a romantic adventure. That type of relationship could be long-lasting because the couple didn't have enough time together to get bored with each other. One more year would pass and each of them would, to some degree, change the way they looked and acted. It made them feel like every year they were having an affair with a new person. Also, it didn't create any difficulties for the man. He could come on vacation to get rest and have a good time. He shared his joy and fantasies with the woman.

Affairs with single men visiting the Black Sea also ended upon his departure, sometimes with different results. Jealousy could appear. Hopes and promises might not come true as promised. Both sides would feel disappointed. But it could happen in other ways. Such relations could turn into serious situations. An ex-tourist might come back to propose to his summer woman. She would move to his city and marry him. And this is how a new family would be created.

Of course, there were still other affairs that ended extremely unhappily. But mostly these happened among silly Turgenev girls. They read romance novels and had only an imaginary understanding based on fiction about relations between a man and a woman. They lived with the idea that love would conquer everything and nothing could stop it. They wholly believed all the promises made by their vacationing men. And, accidentally, they became pregnant because they forgot about contraception when consumed with passion. At the end of the day, they became single mothers who couldn't give their children normal lives.

At first, they believed that the father of their child would come back and, after he saw their baby, would remain with her and the child forever. But, as a Russian saying goes, you can't keep a man by having his baby. I knew this from my personal experience. When a period of hopes and dreams ends, women become angry and calculating. In order to feed their children, many of them went on the road to sin. They offered sex for money without any more delusions.

When I met Artem-Ivan, I took him on as yet one more possible adventure in love. In my twenty-one years, I was already well-experienced. I had no doubts in my mind about my plan and how to get him for a while. I made myself seem very attracted to him, shall we say. Artem took to me as well. Together, we looked like a perfect couple. I had sun-faded, ash-blond hair and large blue playful eyes with long eyelashes. I looked older than I was. I was a skinny girl with long legs, which appeared to be growing all the way from my ears. I had a little butt and big breasts.

I went up to him. I asked if he had once been an athlete. We began to talk. He said that he came from America. I understood why he looked at me with such wild eyes. In America, he was hungry for beautiful native Russian girls. I could read his eyes. They screamed, "I want to fuck you badly, baby." I felt funny about this at first. Still, I flirted with him. I asked lots of inviting questions. But I was just testing my methods on him like any other guinea pig. He joined my game very quickly. We walked all day long around Sochi. We played on the beach, and went to restaurants or just kissed. He was a little mysterious. I didn't understand what he did for a living. But I was pretty sure that he wasn't married. I didn't tell him about myself either.

My life was very simple and dull, or so it seemed to me. I told him that I studied at a college. I told him that I lived with my father who was a car mechanic. I said that I wanted to start my own business. He became interested. I told Artem about an idea that I had about opening a sex tourism agency. This, I said, was very possible in Sochi and would be very profitable.

Artem liked my idea. He liked it a lot and was surprised at how smart I was. I quickly understood that this was right up his alley, which was all for lies, schemes, and hustling. It gave him a reason to live, to feel an adrenaline rush. I soon knew that I didn't want to lose him. I tried my best to make him fall in love with me. In some way, I wanted to be half of his soul, in spite of all I had told myself after Vitalik.

The day of Artem's departure to California came and my plan seemed to have worked. Artem, I believed, had fallen in love with me. He had even begun talking about having children with me. Suddenly, he proposed to me. It all happened very fast. I stayed with him at the airport because I wanted to say goodbye to him. For his part, he was worried and was shaking at the thought of loneliness in America.

Several times, he went outside and had a cigarette. When the boarding announcement was made, he kissed me passionately and hugged me tightly. He reached into his pocket, pulled out a jewelry box and asked me to become his wife. At that moment, it seemed very beautiful and touching. People who stood around applauded. Honestly, they sat on their suitcases and waited for my reply. I didn't want to lose Artem, not just as a sexual partner and nice supportive man. He was also my opportunity to leave Sochi and build my future. So, I agreed. He put the ring on my finger. He kissed me one more time before he left.

When I paused to think of it, I didn't know if it was real love and a genuine offer or if he just wanted to end our affair beautifully. After all, when any passionate relationship ends, each person wants to remain in the memory of the partner as forever special. Everyone wants to feel irreplaceable and wanted.

Artem called me three times a day, every day from America. He checked to see if I was already in bed or about to be in bed. He became very jealous. Of course, it was not without grounds. He knew that I had a lot of vacation affairs before. He just wanted to make sure he was my last one.

One day, he called and said that he had begun the process for my fiancée visa. I told him how glad I was. I wanted to leave Sochi. Nothing good could happen to me there except those vacation affairs and I was tired of them. It was only possible to become successful in Sochi if your parents had important connections, a business or worked for the government. In my case, I had a poor father who worked very hard as a mechanic. He always took care that I was nicely dressed and had everything middle-class girls had. My father worried his whole life that I might feel inferior because I didn't have a mother.

But honestly, I just wished that my father would relax and be happy. I wanted him to live the rest of his life in peace with himself and without always thinking about tomorrow. I graduated from college while my visa was being processed. I diligently kept on studying English. I wanted to arrive in the USA equipped to fight for my happiness and my rights.

All this while, I knew that as soon as Artem had left that day at the airport, my love for him had vanished. This was probably because, due to my past, I had got used to the idea that when a man leaves, it means that he is no longer an escape ticket for me. All that

I was left with was a memory of him. There was no reality about him. Nevertheless I did like Artem very much as a person and as a friend. I felt he was reliable and I knew I needed to have a strong, smart partner for my ideas.

I started to speak English well. People say that if you want something badly enough and try hard enough, you will definitely succeed. I planned everything very seriously and I expected a lot of surprises and difficulties in America. But I knew that Artem would be near. It wasn't important to me that I didn't love him. The most important thing was that I had a goal and went for it. I was sorry to leave my father alone. I was afraid that he would start drinking vodka from loneliness and would turn into an alcoholic. He had nobody in the world but me.

I remember when I was eighteen or nineteen, I took a walk and stayed out until four or six o'clock in the morning. My father almost always waited for me on the bench in front of our house. And sometimes he would sit at the kitchen table drinking tea and looking through my childhood photo album. I felt very sad about making him wait. He felt hurt. I was the only tree he could plant and grow in his life. I was the dearest person in the world to him.

When I told him about my plans to go to America, he was happy for me. He talked to Artem over the phone and, after a few conversations, he came to a conclusion. My father was sure that Artem was the man in whose hands he could entrust me. This was also an opportunity for my father, now fifty-two, to live his own life for once without any guilt and concern for me. When I was a little girl, he told me that no woman would ever come into his life and take the slightest bit of love away from me. For a long time, our single neighbor Galya offered my father a chance for them to live together. My father simply refused. He didn't want to hurt my feelings or disrupt my life. Despite this, Galya was always nice to me. She waited patiently and believed that the day would come when they could be together. Finally, she got what she wanted.

For my trip to America, my father gave me all of his savings, which equaled to one hundred dollars. Artem covered all the expenses regarding the visa and airfare.

During the flight, I became acquainted with a forty-year-old American. His name was Rudy. He told me that he went to Moscow three times a year to meet Russian women. He wanted a Russian wife. But something always went wrong and it didn't work out the way he wanted. Rudy believed that he would eventually find the one and only for him; that a Russian woman would bear him children and would create a comfortable home for him. He told me that he had already spent thousands of dollars for all the trips he had made. He was prepared to spend even more in order to find the right one.

When I walked out of the plane at the Burbank airport, Artem met me with a bouquet of flowers. He drove a 2003 model Mercedes. I liked this kind of chic from the first minute. Artem greeted me warmly. It felt like I was his longtime girlfriend or a fiancée for whom he had been waiting for a very long time. I knew I had to play the part of a woman in love. I needed to become his wife and to open a road to my future life. I tried not to show that I was afraid that he wouldn't marry me as he had promised.

He took me to his apartment in Beverly Hills. I fell in love with America. But it wasn't because there were palm trees, sky-scrapers and money everywhere. I felt that this country would give me everything I wanted and that I would have a prosperous life; I would make my dreams a reality. I knew most important thing was for me to be patient. I must be ready for everything and anything.

Artem took me to Las Vegas so that we could marry sooner. I remember lights everywhere. I remember gambling tables with Russian roulette and gamblers exhausted to the point of death. Some of them put all of their money and all their life into the roulette wheel. I thought at that moment that all of America was my casino. It was my game and I had to win my millions by playing. My whole life was daring and risky enough as it was.

We stayed at the Bellagio hotel. In the casino, I played a three-card game. I started to talk with the guy next to me. He was also an American who wanted a Russian wife. I was amazed by the extreme stereotype that American men had about Russian women.

They thought that she would be a perfect housewife who would be consistently kind, caring and unspoiled. But, in reality, those ideals are long gone! There are no more Russian women like this. Of course, there are exceptions for everything. But it's a lot like winning the lottery.

In Russia, the old-fashioned women were that way because of economic necessity. If in the past we had enough money in Russia, do you think that Russian women wouldn't have hired maids or cooks? In America, Russian women don't give a damn about the housework. Instead, they start a new life here which completely changes their old ways and they quickly develop an attitude. But my dear casino acquaintance still held on to the fantasy that he would get the wife he wanted in Odessa. He used to go there on business trips and every single time he went, he made a casting call for Russian women. I finally concluded that he just liked the process, but, in reality, he didn't want to make a decision or find a wife. It was just fun for him. He needed to feel liked by beautiful, and sometimes not so beautiful, Russian women. But, they didn't like him! They only liked the opportunity to come to America and he recognized that.

After we finished talking, a very interesting idea came to mind. I realized how I could make money without investing a cent. But I remembered my father's advice from childhood that decisions made in the morning are better than decisions made at night. So, I took some time to think everything through before I was ready to share my idea with Artem.

We married in one hour and later came back from Las Vegas to California. We applied for my papers. Slowly—sad to say—all the romantic things Artem used to do before our marriage disappeared. He turned into a nasty, aggressive, cheeky, and greedy bastard. He was never pleased with the way I looked. He said he didn't like the food I cooked even though he ate it with great pleasure. He said he didn't accept the way I cleaned the apartment, and asked me to redo it in front of him.

Although I looked much better than when we met in Sochi, he had numerous complaints. A woman from her twenties until about thirty-five opens up and blossoms like a tea rose. But I tolerated his criticisms. I knew I didn't want to leave everything my manipulations had gained and go back to Russia without pennies. Yet I realized that this relationship was like a prison. And a prisoner has to wait out the time set by the judge until he is free. I had to be a prisoner for two years in order to go through my interview and be granted a green card. During those two years, I couldn't go to Russia to visit my dad. Artem was against it. I could only talk to my father over the phone. Father lived with Galya in order not to die from loneliness. He rented out our little apartment. It was extra income.

Artem never told me that he didn't love me anymore or ask for a separation. He just wanted to be the master of our household, to be a real man and turn me into his slave. But he couldn't win in that department. I was stronger emotionally and I intentionally turned myself into a slave to bide myself some time. Convincingly, I declared my strong love for him. I fell down at his feet and asked him not to leave me or I would die. Such a performance lifted his mood and made him feel more secure and manly.

At such moments, I didn't care what I did. I had a goal. I felt like I was running in a long marathon. I saw the finish line. I just needed to be sure that I had enough strength and endurance. I decided that I wanted to go to work. Artem didn't object. But he said that my job could not interfere with the housework and the cooking. I promised it wouldn't and it didn't.

Intentionally, I got a job at a local dating/marriage agency specializing in Russian women. It helped me personally to learn about requests of American men and what they wanted in Russian women. I was paid $300 per week, but this was enough to save some money and to send a hundred dollars a month to my dad.

By now, Artem and I barely had a sex life. Actually, he just punished me by making me sexually hungry. He loved it when I asked him to fuck me. I understood his wish to appear like some kind of Casanova in my eyes. But I just did that in order to make him feel like I was hot for him. There were no more flowers, presents, or breakfasts in bed like before the wedding. But it didn't bother me because I didn't give a damn. I realized that before the wedding, he was afraid that he would lose me. He never wanted me to be alone. After the wedding, he knew that he had me on a leash and that I wouldn't run away. At least for the first two years.

The interview date arrived. We did wonderfully well. Before the interview, Artem said to me, "Marishka, today you graduated from my testing school. I realize that you really love me and accept me regardless of how I behave. I am now sure that you love me. This is everything I dreamt about my entire life."

That was the dream he had developed from his relationship with his mother. He never knew his father, but his mother used to make up different fascinating stories about real women, love, and all that a woman could do for her man.

After he said all that to me, I smiled secretly to myself. I knew it was a first victory. I got my green card. Artem began to love me even more than he did before the wedding. But it was probably out of fear. Now that I had my papers, I could leave him. I didn't plan to do that yet. I still needed him.

At the same time, Artem met me in Sochi, he met Misha. Misha was from the same criminal world as Artem. He had the same ambitions, but wasn't as clever. Misha was an intelligent-looking man in his thirties. He was always dressed in a conservative suit and tie. He had red hair and funny freckles all over his face. It made him look kind and not in the least bit dangerous. But looks can be deceiving. Misha and Artem wanted to start a business together. However, they didn't know what kind of business.

After two years with Artem, I was sure that he was a man that I could trust—up to a point. I wanted to work with Artem and create a partnership. I liked the fact that he was cunning, but not anymore than I was. People say that the wife is the neck and the husband is the head. The neck turns the head. The most difficult mission of any wife is to make her husband think that all her ideas and offers are actually his own. I should state that I believe being a good wife is a tough profession.

At last, I decided to share my idea with Artem. He shook with excitement. At the same moment, he was very proud of himself because I made it sound like it was all his idea! We decided that Artem would look for rich Americans in different states. He would introduce himself as a marriage broker who represented Russian women living in Russia. He would find Americans looking for the perfect Russian wife.

I wasn't a bad candidate. I already had a green card. I had experience in America. I had good language skills and a college degree. In addition to all that, I was a good looking woman. So, I possessed the full package that American men desired from their fantasy wives. They would like the fact that I already knew what life in America was like. It would make them confident that I wouldn't experience any culture shock, lack of language skills, or depression from being in a totally foreign environment.

We made up a simple story: I came to America on a work visa three years ago. We could show proof that I fell in love with an American man who, after our marriage, turned into an abusive monster and abused me verbally and physically.

I would say that after I got my documents, I went with him to Italy. I hoped that he would change his behavior and we could save our marriage. But he didn't. When we returned, I divorced him.

Artem and I needed to be divorced in order to start our business venture. I might have to show the proof.

We did it quickly. My story to the rich American would be that I had decided to go back to Russia because I wanted very much to have a family. I thought that maybe in Russia, I would meet a real man. I wanted to give children to my loving future husband and to cook different food for him every day.

The American, Artem and I were sure, would bite the bait. When he saw my pictures, he would be eager to jump on the next flight to Russia. The fish would eat the worm.

I went back to Russia. It was my first effort in our new business venture. Meanwhile, my father and Galya decided to get married. I couldn't miss the occasion. Artem said that even though we were divorced, we were still husband and wife in spirit; two people who loved each other. Thus, married in spirit, he would think he still had control over me! But he would be the only one who thought so. I had another plan. It wasn't exactly revenge; it was just my way to get rich and to achieve my goals.

So I went to Russia. Right after Father's small wedding celebration, Artem called me. He found a candidate for me. Artem had searched all possible elite parties, exhibitions and other events all over America to find the right person. He located our first victim in Florida. His name was Brian. He was a rich American Jew who owned a chain of jewelry stores in New York, Boston, and Chicago. In every one of these states, he had a three-story house. He owned a Lexus, Mercedes, BMW, and a Hummer. According to these facts, one could come to the conclusion that Brian was in need of a fiancée. But Brian wasn't lucky in love.

He went to a music festival in Florida with a certain girlfriend. She broke up with him because she met another man who, according to her, was better looking and had more money than Brian. Artem saw Brian at the bar of a Marriott hotel, drinking Captain Morgan rum and suffering from his certain failure. Artem had appeared at the right moment. He had witnessed the fight between Brian and his rival. The rival was handsome and sufficiently charming to have taken away Brian's girlfriend.

As Artem helped Brian lick his wounds, he showed him my picture. Artem played the marriage broker who could sell Brian hope. He told Brian all the best things about me and showed him more alluring pictures. To make his story as realistic as possible, he said that he knew me from America and secretly loved me. He told him that he'd marry me in a heartbeat if he didn't have such a lovely wife and child. It was an Academy Award-winning performance.

Artem often changed his appearance. He would wear a fake mustache and beard. He wore different colored contact lenses. He colored his hair and even placed a small pillow around his stomach to look fat. His objective was not to be recognized and to find good candidates. When Brian saw my picture, he forgot all about his bad luck with women. In a drunken conversation, he told Artem all about his career and financial worth and gave him his business card.

The next day, they set up a meeting at high noon in the same bar. Overnight, Artem investigated Brian. He knew this was a lucky opportunity which could supply us with the money we needed to launch our operations. That night, Artem also contacted Misha and told him what to do. Misha played the role of a Russian representative and an agent of the American marriage brokering agency called "Russian Beauty." Everything was set to go according to the plan. My mission was to look perfect, demonstrate my love for Brian, and be ready for anything for a chance to be with him.

All three of us opened exclusive e-mail addresses and, most of the time, we communicated by Internet. We made every effort to be very careful, especially as this was our first venture. We went online only in Internet cafes in different parts of the city. This was for purposes of anonymity so we would never be tracked down.

The following day, Artem and Brian met again. Brian told him that he had already called his travel agent and started the visa process for his trip to Russia. Artem called me right in front of Brian. He spoke English with me. He introduced himself as a marriage broker and asked me if I wanted to speak to one of my potential husband candidates over the phone. Brian sounded shy and could hardly breathe. He was nervous. Politely, he complemented me for my extraordinary beauty, my lovely voice and flawless English.

I spoke to him very politely and told him that I would be glad to meet him in Sochi. I promised we'd have an excursion around the most romantic places. I added that the phone number they called me at would be out of service because I had sold my old apartment and bought a new one, which didn't have a phone line yet. It was a good excuse so that we would only communicate by e-mail. I explained that there was a chance that we would be able to speak by phone if a miracle happened and they gave me a phone line without having to wait for the long line of applicants ahead of me. Otherwise, it could take up to a year. This provided me with an opportunity to complain about the misery of living in Russia.

Brian was very nice and he reacted as I expected. He said that he would e-mail me often before we met. Artem gave him my e-mail address. He introduced himself as Victor Shipko. He even gave Brian his fake business card. The card had a phone number that, when dialed, would always be busy. So, the only way they too could communicate was via the Internet.

Victor Shipko's name and the Russian Beauty Agency name were real. It was just a different company and a different man. Of course, at the beginning, Brian didn't seem a fool. He asked his people to call and check to see if the company existed and if it employed a Victor Shipko. Upon being informed that the information was real, he asked Victor/Artem where to send his six-thousand-dollar check. This was Artem's price for meeting me, for the hotel, and for Misha's services.

The price was high because the agency Artem pretended to work for, in reality, worked only with exclusive girls and guaranteed good service and top quality. For such assurance and guarantee, people usually didn't grudge the money. As the old saying goes, a greedy person always pays double. For Brian, the price meant nothing. After all, you cannot put a price on happiness. For the sake of being happy, loved, and desired, sometimes we are prepared to give all the money that we have, because that happiness is a condition of the soul, and money is a condition of your bank account.

Artem got the necessary amount from Brian and gave him my e-mail address. We began the correspondence. In the beginning, we were very shy. Later, we became gentle and warm.

Finally, Brian arrived and presented me with a wedding ring and a strong wish for us never to separate. Before he came, he sent me his picture. But, after seeing him in person, I wanted to burst into tears. I couldn't believe that I would have to be seen with him holding hands, kissing, and God-help-me maybe more.

Brian was short and fat with bald patches on his head. As the old saying goes, for such man, I wouldn't make love even for a plate of pancakes during the famine. But here was a deal worth hundreds of thousands of dollars. I couldn't fail.

As previously arranged, Brian was met at the airport by Misha, a representative of the agency. Brian walked and looked around. He wore thick glasses on his nose and looked like Austin Powers. He looked worried. But when he spotted his name on the card that Misha held up, he immediately came up to us. My fiancée was so short that he almost sucked in my belly button with his heavy breathing. He nimbly jumped up and kissed my cheek. According to our plan, I told him that instead of going to the hotel, Misha would drive us around Sochi, and later we would stay in a little cozy house on the bank of the Black Sea. The whole way, I touched his hand and looked at his eyes while Misha explained to Brian something about the Sochi climate.

Brian placed a diamond ring on my finger. He was amazed that in real life, I looked even better than in the pictures. He kept saying that he was looking for a woman like me his whole life. I told him that from the first moment when I talked to him over the phone, I felt that I had found the man of my dreams.

We stopped at an Armenian restaurant. We ate shashlik with fresh tomatoes—delicious. The shashlik was cooked on coals; it is little pieces of meat that are marinated in vinegar. One thing I noticed about Brian was that his nose always itched and he had gigantic eyes that reminded me of a dragonfly.

In the evening, Misha took us to the little house on the bank of the sea. I wore beautiful underwear and brought a silk robe just in case. I was scared. I didn't want to go to bed with a stranger who repulsed me. We lay down. Misha had left us a bottle of wine. We talked. At first, he offered to buy me some presents; he said we'd shop in the finest boutiques. I declined. He was surprised. Then he said that he wanted to put my name on the deeds of his cars and houses. I told him that I didn't need the money he earned without me definitely being part of his life. He was even more surprised. Later on, he said that he didn't want me to work anywhere. I said that I wanted to work and to help him pay our bills. I told him that the only condition I had was that we must get married in Sochi. I said that my best and only friend was pregnant and she couldn't attempt any flights in her condition; I wanted her to be my maid of honor.

I even cried and complained that the Russian bureaucracy was everywhere and we had to wait in line for a month in order to get married. Brian hugged me and said that tomorrow he would give Misha the money for a bribe, and that we would marry a few days later. I called Misha. He came and took two thousand dollars for the bribe as well as Brian's and my passports and driver's licenses in order to fill out the necessary paper work.

Brian couldn't believe his happiness. I was looking into his eyes and wondering just how much money my dear Brian would give me. Misha came back and offered to give Brian a bachelor party for just the two of them, since he was the only man Brian knew in Sochi. I kissed Brian before he left and said that I would wait up for him all night until he came back.

Artem called me right after Misha and Brian left. He said that he found out that Brian was a cocaine dealer and was documented by the authorities in Thailand where he frequented pedophilia clubs, a place where young children had sex with adults. That information, according to Artem's calculations, cost a lot of money.

Our wedding day came. Misha was the bearer of bad news. He told me not to marry Brian because he was under surveillance for a crime. Brian was shocked and frightened. He demanded to know, who told you? But he shut his mouth quickly. Misha explained to him that for such an omission of disclosure and putting my life and the life of my future children in danger, Brian had to pay one million dollars in cash. Otherwise, all information about him would be made available to the American press and police. Artem even sent Misha a criminal record printout with all of Brian's drug deals, and pictures of him with small children fulfilling his erotic fantasies.

Brian was screaming and saying he would go to the police in Russia. He wanted a lawyer who would defend him from all those lies. Maybe you can get a lawyer in all other countries, but not in Russia, Misha replied. Russian police would never deal with him because it was very complicated, and the record damned him. Brian had to take a train to the nearest American Embassy. But he couldn't. He didn't have any ID so he couldn't buy a railway ticket. He also didn't have any choice. Besides, if the truth was discovered, it meant a criminal record in the USA, financial ruin, a destroyed reputation and years of prison. If Brian gave in and paid up, his life would not be over.

So Misha, Brian and I went to the nearest international bank and, under the threatened barrel of a gun, Brian requested the necessary amount from his business account. He couldn't run away. He didn't have any place or know anyone. He couldn't complain to anybody in Sochi; no one would understand him.

And so Artem, Misha and I split the one million. We took Brian back to the airport and gave him the key to the locker where we had hidden his documents. All the e-mails had vanished. All pieces of evidence were turned over to him. Everybody was happy—even Brian. Upon leaving, he said: "You Russian smart asses. I hate you all but I thank you for not killing me."

Of course, we were all very happy that everything turned out so well. I flew back to America for a few weeks after Brian left. I didn't tell Artem, but I bought a two-bedroom apartment in Miami with an ocean view. I found a real estate agency that helped me with all the paperwork and agreed to manage it for me as a rental property.

I met Artem again in California and played the role of a loving wife. He just looked at me feeling so proud of himself, and repeatedly said that he knew how much I loved him and that I would die without him. We drank a bottle of champagne as we celebrated our first big victory.

Soon, I flew back to Sochi. I had much to do. My next American fiancé would soon be arriving and I had to be ready to welcome him with open and loving arms. Artem and Misha did their job brilliantly. I was a partner in the firm for nearly a year and a half. When I left, I owned three apartment buildings and two luxury houses in different cities in America.

The time came when I had to go and visit Artem. It was right after the last victory over a poor victim named Tim. He was a Massachusetts banker who took part in the murder of his partner. But I didn't show up. Artem didn't know where I was.

I felt that it was time to quit playing this dangerous game. I left quietly. I didn't say a word to anyone. At first, I moved in with my father and Galya in Rublevka. Rublevka is a rich suburb of Moscow filled with country houses. I bought them a two-story house and a Jeep. My father thought that I got all that money from Artem, whom he took to be the perfect husband for his precious daughter.

He didn't know that for eighteen months, I had lived in Sochi, a stone's throw from him. During that time, my ideal husband saw me twice. I was busy with my potential husbands. However, I repaid my dear father by providing for him and making sure that he was comfortable in his old age.

In America, the real estate market was booming. I sold all my property, which had appreciated a good deal. I only kept the apartment in Miami because I loved to vacation there a few times a year. I secured the rest of the money in the Cayman Islands. I bought a penthouse in Saint Petersburg. I have a new best friend, a dog named Artie. I want to live in Russia and in America. But now I have a new plan in my mind as to how to make money. I'll tell you about it when I see you. I learned just one thing: if you want to live a good life, you have to be on the move. Artem was too overconfident. He thought that I was his property, but I turned into a rented adventure. It's a crime when you don't have money. You have to be ashamed of yourself when you're poor. But you never have to be ashamed of how you go about earning money. I am twenty-six years old and my life just started.

ACKNOWLEDGMENTS

I wish to acknowledge the significant contributions made by so many generous and talented people that helped to turn this book into a reality.

I interviewed, and, for a short time shared the lives of hundreds of women from the former USSR in order to create the twenty-three stories that are told in this book. I would like to thank Natasha Shilaphikoff, Oxana Faradsheva, Valeriya Gortchkova, and Anna Darbinian for sharing their stories. The person I am most indebted to is Anna Parakhina, whose insight and talent proved to be invaluable. She colored in many verbal line drawings and turned them into portraits.

I also am thankful for the editing and typing contributions of Lalie Katavazi, Ariana Martinez, Julie McCarron, Henrietta Tiefenthaler and particularly the editor grace and skills of Les Whitten helped shape this vision into a reality. I also want to thank Sonia Fiore for her artistic eye in cover design and layout. It has been honor to work with and to know all of these people.